iAPX 88 BOOK

WITH AN INTRODUCTION TO THE iAPX 188

1983

Published for Intel
by
Reston Publishing Company, Inc.
(A Prentice-Hall Company)
Reston, Virginia 22090

Additional copies of the iAPX 88 Book can be purchased through Reston Publishing Company, Inc. ATTN: Special Sales, 11480 Sunset Hills Road, Reston, Virginia 22090. Phone: (703) 437-8900.

Copies of all other Intel literature may be obtained from:

Intel Corporation
Literature Department
3065 Bowers Avenue
Santa Clara, CA 95051

ABOUT THIS BOOK

This book describes the unique Intel 8088 microprocessor, the outstanding choice for 8-bit microcomputer applications requiring both high performance and low cost.

The Intel 8088 is the most powerful 8-bit microprocessor available today, yet as easy to use as other 8-bit microprocessors designers have used for years.

Chapter 1 introduces the *8088 CPU* with its key features that give it high performance, with *overviews* on the following topics:

- Pipelined architecture
- Register resources
- Memory addressing
- Instruction set
- System interfacing
- Functional extensions

Also an iAPX 188 overview is given.

Chapter 2 provides a detailed discussion of the *programmer's architecture* including:

- Register set
- Addressing modes
- Instruction set
- Assembly language

At the end of Chapter 2 is a complete set of instruction set reference pages that describe each instruction fully, one at a time.

Chapter 3 provides necessary information for the *hardware designer* to incorporate the 8088 microprocessor into cost effective iAPX* 88 microcomputer systems. Included is a discussion of the following:

- Bus Timing and Status
- Bus Interface including interface to MUX bus devices
- Memory and Peripheral Interface
- Wait States

- Interrupts
- Direct Memory Access
- Reset
- Building Large Systems

Chapter 4 gives some specific *8088 system design examples* for the simple to complex systems:

- Multiplexed bus small systems
- Demultiplexed systems with standard memories and peripherals
- S100 Bus System
- iAPX 88 based CRT
- MULTIBUS™ System

The *Supplement* provides an introduction to microcomputer concepts and terminology including:

- What is a microcomputer?
- What's inside the CPU?
- What are machine cycles?
- What are addressing modes?

The *Appendix* contains the following data sheets and comparison benchmark reports:

Data Sheets
- iAPX 88/10 data sheet
- 8284A data sheet
- 8282/8283 data sheet
- 8286/8287 data sheet
- iAPX 188

Benchmark Reports
- iAPX 88 vs. 6809
- iAPX 88 vs. Z80

Related Documentation:
- *The iAPX 86,88 User's Manual*
  Contains complete design information on building iAPX 86 and iAPX 88 systems, including the use of 8089 I/O processor and 8087 numerics processor extension. Several Application Notes are included.

*iAPX stands for Intel Advanced Processor System

- *The Peripheral Design Handbook*
  Contains data sheets and application notes featuring Intel peripheral devices.
- *The Intel Component Data Catalog*
  Contains data sheets for all Intel semiconductor components, including memories and peripherals.

Additional copies of the iAPX 88 Book can be purchased by contacting:

Reston Publishing
Special Sales
11480 Sunset Hills Road
Reston, Virginia 22090

All other documentation is available from:

Literature Department
Intel Corporation
3065 Bowers Ave.
Santa Clara, CA 95051

The material in the Assembly Language section of Chapter 2 was edited and reprinted with permission of Hayden Book Company, from *The 8086 Primer,* by Stephen P. Morse. Copyright 1980.

Furthermore, selected material was extracted from the following articles:

1) S.P. Morse, W.B. Pohlman, B.W. Ravenel, "The Intel 8086 Microprocessor: A 16-Bit Evolution of the 8080," *Computer,* June 1978.
2) S.P. Morse, B.W. Ravenel, S. Mazor, W.B. Pohlman, "Intel Microprocessors — 8008 to 8086," *Computer,* October 1980.

Table of Contents

List of Figures

(continued)

List of Figures (cont.)

(continued)

List of Figures (cont.)

Introduction To
iAPX 88

1

CHAPTER 1
INTRODUCTION

WHAT IS THE 8088?

An iAPX 88* Microcomputer system has the three main elements typical to most computer systems: The central processor (8088 CPU), the input/output ports, and memory (Fig. 1-1).

The iAPX 88 is unique in many ways, however, and the remainder of this chapter describes the basics of the 8088 CPU and iAPX 88 Microcomputer systems.

One of the most unique aspects of the 8088 is shown in the simple block diagram (Fig. 1-2). The 8088 combines the powerful resources of a 16-bit microprocessor internal architecture with an easy-to-use 8-bit bus interface. The bus interface is easy for hardware designers because it is similar to other 8-bit microprocessors. In particular, most of the bus lines are identical in function to the popular 8085A. Those designers who have interfaced memories and I/O devices to 8085

*iAPX refers to the entire microsystem built around the 8088 CPU.

microprocessors will find it easy to incorporate the 8088 into new systems.

16-BIT POWER ON AN 8-BIT BUS

The 16-bit internal architecture provides 16-bit wide registers, data paths, a 16-bit ALU, and a set of powerful 16-bit instructions identical to the ones found in the popular 8086 microprocessor.

With this new internal architecture, the 8088 has features that were never before available with an 8-bit microprocessor. Among these features is a 20-bit memory address range and a 16-bit input/output port address range for I/O cycles. This gives the 8088 a full megabyte (1,000,000-plus bytes) of memory

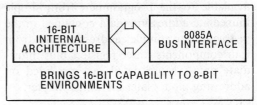

Figure 1-2. 8088 CPU

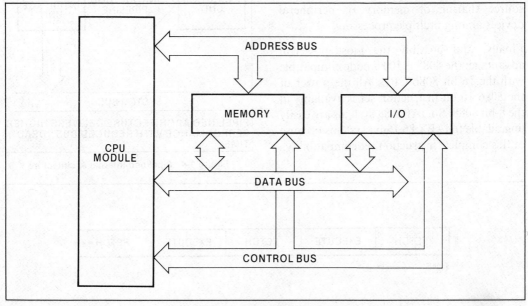

Figure 1-1. Microcomputer Block Diagram

addressability and 64,000 bytes of I/O addressability.

The iAPX 88 instruction set includes a full complement of arithmetic operations including addition, subtraction, multiplication, and division, on 8-bit or 16-bit quantities. This gives the 8088 the highest computational throughput of any 8-bit microprocessor for numerics intensive applications. The 8088 also has a complete set of string manipulation operations for performance and flexibility in applications where large amounts of data are involved.

To make efficient use of its megabyte of memory addressing, the 8088 provides the most powerful range of addressing modes available to the programmer; from simple immediate addressing (data contained in the instruction) to complex addressing built from four components (three registers plus immediate data). More details are provided on addressing modes later on in this chapter.

The 8088 has built-in hardware support for multi-processor systems to coordinate resource sharing of memory or peripheral devices among multiple processors.

Finally, and possibly the most powerful advantage: the 8088 is 100% code compatible with the 16-bit 8086 CPU. All the power of the 8086 16-bit instruction set is available in the 8-bit 8088. So, iAPX 88 systems are easily upgradable to iAPX 86 16-bit systems because of this complete instruction set compatibility.

HOW THE 8088 PIPELINED ARCHITECTURE INCREASES SYSTEM PERFORMANCE

Figure 1-3 shows how programs are executed over time in a standard microprocessor. First, the microprocessor must fetch the instruction to be performed, then it executes the instruction. Only after the execution is complete is the CPU ready to fetch in the next instruction, execute that instruction, etc. as the program proceeds from beginning to end.

The CPU hardware that executes instructions must obviously wait until the instruction is fetched and decoded before execution begins. Therefore, in standard microprocessors, the execution hardware (primarily the control circuitry and the arithmetic and logic unit) spends a lot of time waiting for instructions to be fetched. The 8088 eliminates this wasted time by dividing the internal CPU into *two* independent functional units (Fig. 1-4).

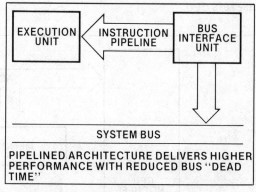

PIPELINED ARCHITECTURE DELIVERS HIGHER PERFORMANCE WITH REDUCED BUS "DEAD TIME"

Figure 1-4. Pipelined Internal Architecture

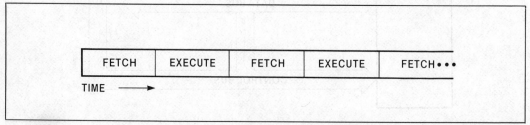

Figure 1-3. Program Execution in Standard Microprocessor

Bus Interface and Execution Units Work in Parallel

The 8088 has a separate bus interface unit called the BIU whose only job is to fetch instructions from memory and pass data to and from the execution hardware to the outside world over the bus interface. Since the execution unit and the bus interface unit are independent, the bus interface unit fetches additional instructions while the execution unit (sometimes called the EU) executes a previous instruction. This is made possible by the *instruction pipeline* (or queue) between the bus interface unit and the execution unit; the bus interface unit fills this pipeline with instructions awaiting execution. Thus, whenever the execution unit finishes executing a given instruction, the next instruction is usually ready for immediate execution without delays caused by instruction fetching. Figure 1-5 shows parallel fetching and executing in the 8088 CPU.

BENEFITS OF PIPELINING

Because the BIU is usually busy fetching instructions for the pipeline, the 8088 bus is more fully utilized making efficient use of the iAPX 88 system bus structure. Parallel fetching and executing also gives the 8088 almost as much performance as a microprocessor that moves data 16-bits at a time.

Another benefit of the parallel operation is that since the execution unit seldom needs to wait for the BIU to fetch the next instruction, there is less need for the BIU to fetch data quickly. Thus, the 8088 BIU allows maximum performance and processing power without high speed memory devices in the system.

The only time instruction fetch time is not totally transparent is when program execution transfers to a new, non-sequential address. When this happens, the bus interface unit is given the new address by the execution unit; it then begins fetching instructions sequentially from the new address. The execution unit must wait for the next instruction to be fetched the way most microprocessor units wait for *every* instruction to be fetched. After the first instruction is fetched from the new location the bus interface unit again continues to fill the pipeline with instructions and fetch-time becomes transparent.

HOW THE 8088 REGISTER RESOURCES PROVIDE EFFICIENT PROGRAM CODING

Figure 1-6 provides an overview of the registers available in the 8088 CPU. The 8088 provides the largest number of continuously available registers of any 8-bit microproces-

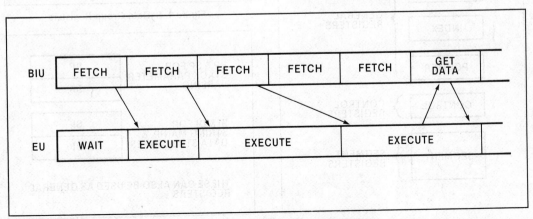

Figure 1-5. Parallel Operation in 8088 CPU

sor. Within the general register group there are eight 16-bit registers. Four of these can be referenced alternately as either 16-bit or as eight 8-bit registers. All of these registers are available to the programmer for general purpose activities.

In addition to the general registers, there are two 16-bit control registers and four 16-bit segment registers. The function of all 8088 registers is described in more detail in the following paragraphs.

Data Registers

The data group registers which, in their 16-bit form, are the AX, BX, CX and DX registers (Fig. 1-7). For 8-bit operations they are broken up into a high byte and low byte. AH is the high byte of the AX register, AL is the low byte of the AX register, and so on. As mentioned, these registers have general usage for simple arithmetic and logical operations.

Some registers have additional special functions which are performed in the execution of certain instructions. For example, the CX register is frequently used to contain a count value during repetitive instructions. The BX

register is used as a base register in some of the more powerful addressing modes.

Pointer and Index Registers

Figure 1-8 shows the pointer and index registers. The BP and SP registers both point to the 8088's stack, a linear array in the 8088's memory used for subroutine parameters, subroutine return addresses, or other data temporarily saved during execution of an 8088 program.

Most microprocessors have a single *stack pointer* register called the SP. The 8088 has an *additional* pointer into the stack called the BP or the *base pointer* register. While the SP is used similar to stack pointers in other machines (for pointing to subroutine and

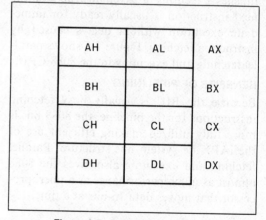

Figure 1-7. Data Group Registers

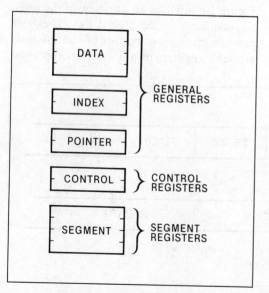

Figure 1-6. 8088 Register Set

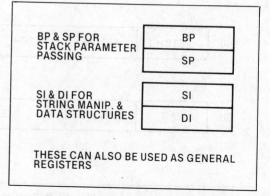

Figure 1-8. Base and Index Registers

interrupt return addresses), the BP register is available to the programmer for whatever use he desires. The BP register can contain an old stack pointer value, or it can mark a place in the subroutine stack independent of the SP register. Using the separate BP register to mark the stack saves the juggling of a single stack pointer to reference subroutine parameters and addresses.

The two *index registers* are the SI (source index) register and the DI (destination index) register (Fig. 1-8). These are both 16-bits wide and are used by string manipulation instructions and in building some of the more powerful 8088 data structures and addressing modes. Both the SI and DI registers have auto-incrementing and auto-decrementing capabilities. All base and index registers have general arithmetic and logical capabilities in addition to their special functions.

Control Registers

Figure 1-9 shows two 16-bit control registers. First is the IP or *instruction pointer* which points to the next instruction the bus interface unit will fetch. (The instruction pointer is similar to a Program Counter used in other microprocessors, except that the IP points to the next instruction being *fetched*, whereas the traditional program counter points to the next instruction to be *executed*). The second 16-bit control register (Fig. 1-9) contains *flags* or condition codes that reflect the results of arithmetic or logical operations as they are performed by the execution unit.

Segment Registers

The fourth group of registers, called the segment registers, are used by the 8088 in the formulation of memory addresses. Segment register usage is described in the following section on memory addressing.

THE iAPX 88 MEGABYTE MEMORY ADDRESSING MEANS QUICK ACCESS TO COMPLEX DATA STRUCTURES

As mentioned, the 8088 generates a 20-bit memory address during every memory reference operation, to address one million (1,048,576) bytes of memory. These bytes are stored sequentially starting from byte 0 to byte FFFFF in hexidecimal or base 16 notation. The 8088 has three uses for the memory it addresses: *programs, data* and *stack*. The 8088 may separate data into "local data" used by a particular program segment and "global data" accessible to all program segments. Alternately, you may have two data areas accessible to a given program at any point in time.

Every 20-bit memory address points either to program code, data, or stack area in memory (Fig. 1-10). For each of the four different memory spaces, the 8088 has a *segment base register*. Each segment register points to the *base* address of the corresponding area in

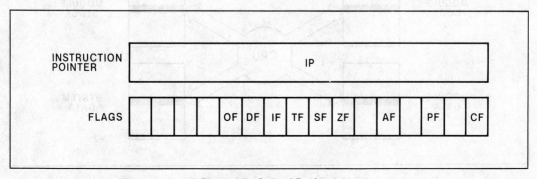

Figure 1-9. Control Registers

memory (Fig. 1-11). The *code segment register* points to the base of the program currently running. The *stack segment register* points to the base of the 8088's stack, the *data segment register* points to the base of one data area, and the *extra segment register* points to the base of another area where data can be stored. Each segment register is 16-bits wide, and one of the four is used in the computation of every memory address that the 8088 generates.

How are Addresses Generated?

Every time the 8088 needs to generate a memory address, one of the segment registers is automatically chosen and added to a *logical address* (Fig. 1-12).

For an instruction fetch, the code segment register is automatically added to the logical address (in this case the contents of the instruction pointer) to compute the value of the instruction address.

For an operation referencing the 8088's stack, the stack segment register is automatically added to the logical address (the SP register contents) to compute the value of the stack address.

For data reference operation, where either the data or extra segment registers are chosen

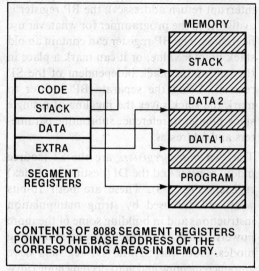

CONTENTS OF 8088 SEGMENT REGISTERS POINT TO THE BASE ADDRESS OF THE CORRESPONDING AREAS IN MEMORY.

Figure 1-11. Segment Registers

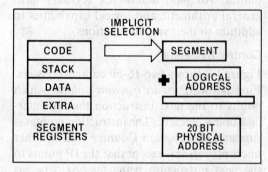

Figure 1-12. How an Address is Built

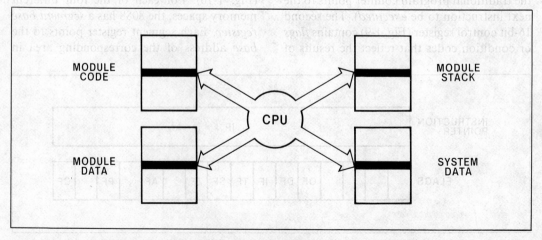

Figure 1-10. iAPX 88 Architecture Quick Access to Four Segment Types

as the base, the logical address can be made up of many different types of values: it can be just the immediate data value contained in the instruction, or, it can be the sum of an immediate data value, plus a base register, plus an index register.

For the sum of the addition to be 20-bits wide, the segment register value is automatically shifted left by four binary bits before it is added to the 16-bit logical address. The *result is always 20-bits of physical address.*

Note that since logical addresses are always 16-bits wide, you can address up to 64K bytes in a given segment without changing the value of the segment base register. In systems that do not have more than 64K bytes of program plus 64K bytes of stack, plus 64K bytes in each of two different data areas, it is possible to set the segment registers at the beginning of the program and then forget them. In a system where the *total* amount of memory is 64K bytes or less, it is possible to set all segment registers equal and have fully overlapping segments.

On the other hand, segment registers are very useful when you have a large programming task and you want isolation between your program code and the data area or isolation between module data and the stack information, etc. Segmentation also makes it easy to build relocatable and/or reentrant programs.

RELOCATABLE AND REENTRANT PROGRAMS

In many cases, the task of relocating an 8088 program (relocation means having the ability to run the same program in several different areas of memory without changing the program itself) simply requires moving the program code and then adjusting of the code segment register to point to the base of the new code area. Since programs can be written for the 8088 where branches or jumps in program flow may occur using new locations

relative only to the instruction pointer, the program does not care what value is kept in the code segment register. Figure 1-13 shows how an entire *process*, consisting of code, stack and data areas, can be relocated.

Likewise in a *reentrant* program, a single program uses multiple data areas. Before the reentrant code is entered the second time, the data segment register value is changed so that a different data area is made available to the program.

ADDRESSING MODES

Now, let's continue our discussion of addressing modes, providing more detail about how addresses are formed.

The 8088 has 24 different addressing modes to generate logical addresses. Figure 1-14 shows the different logical address combinations, from the simplest immediate data mode to the register addressing mode, where a selected register contains the data being used by the instruction. In the direct addressing mode, the instruction itself contains the *address* of the data. In the register indirect mode, the instruction points to a register containing the memory address of the desired data. There are both indexed and based addressing modes where the contents of an index or based register is added to an immediate data value contained in the instruction to form the memory address.

Exactly how the 8088 selects an addressing mode for a given instruction is encoded within the bits of the instruction code. This is discussed in more detail in Chapter 2.

If we examine the most complex and powerful of the addressing modes, which includes base register, index register, and displacement in the logical address, it can be seen that some fairly complex data structures can be easily addressed in a single instruction by the 8088.

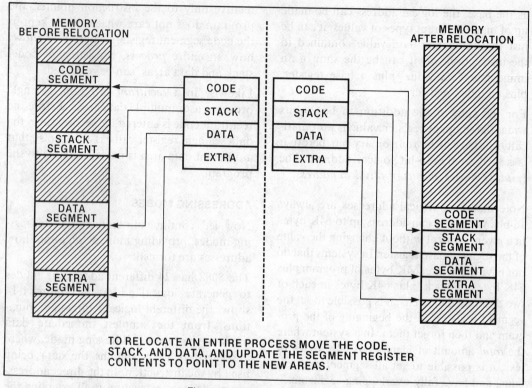

Figure 1-13. Process Relocation

MODE	LOCATION OF DATA
IMMEDIATE	WITHIN INSTRUCTION
REGISTER	IN REGISTER
DIRECT	AT MEMORY LOCATION POINTED TO BY ADDRESS CONTAINED IN INSTRUCTION.
REGISTER INDIRECT	AT MEMORY LOCATION POINTED TO BY ADDRESS CONTAINED IN REGISTER.
INDEXED OR BASED	AT MEMORY LOCATION POINTED TO BY SUM OF INDEX REGISTER OR BASE REGISTER CONTENTS AND IMMEDIATE DATA CONTAINED IN INSTRUCTION.
BASED AND INDEXED WITH DISPLACEMENT	MEMORY ADDRESS IS SUM OF BASE REGISTER CONTENTS AND INDEX REGISTER CONTENTS AND IMMEDIATE DATA.

THE LOCATION OF DATA IS REALLY THE LOGICAL ADDRESS, WHICH IS ADDED TO THE SEGMENT REGISTER VALUE TO FORM THE PHYSICAL MEMORY ADDRESS.

Figure 1-14. iAPX 88 Addressing Modes

FOUR-COMPONENT ADDRESSING

An example of four-component addressing (three-component logical address plus segment base) is shown in Figure 1-15, and is described as follows:

Suppose you're writing a program to compute the payroll for a large corporation. This corporation has several groups of employees. Within each group there are multiple employees, and for each employee certain data is kept in a record of information. Included in this data are the employee's address, social security number, and a wage code indicating how much that employee is being paid.

The task at hand is to select the wage code for a particular employee from the entire complex array of employee data. The 8088 can do it with a single instruction after the registers are set up. Here's how: First, set the data segment register to the base of the employee data, set a base register such as BX to contain the offset number of bytes between the employee data base address and the start of the data that applies only to the desired group of employees. Next we set an index register such as SI to index to the desired employee's information within the given group of employees. Finally, we use an absolute displacement value to point to the given employee's wage code within the employee's data record.

The single instruction MOV AX, [BX + SI + 12] then, will select the appropriate employee's wage code. To implement the same function with any other 8-bit microprocessor would require multiple instructions to build the address.

Symmetric Use of Memory

Another way these powerful addressing modes work is that memory locations can be used as either source or destination operand of most instructions. A single 8088 instruction can perform a logical AND between the contents of a given memory address and an immediate data value, and store the results back in the same memory address. The equivalent function would take multiple instructions on an 8-bit processor such as an 8080. It is as though you can treat any memory location as a CPU register for simple arithmetic and logic operations. Following are several operations which can be performed directly on memory locations.

AND [memory address], 7FH
OR [BX + SI + 12], 1F80H
ADD [memory address], 2500

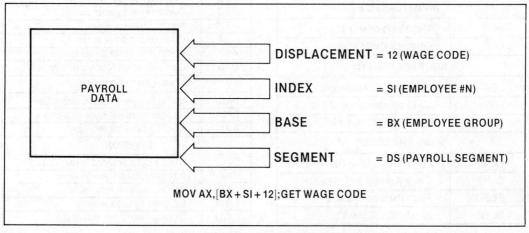

DISPLACEMENT = 12 (WAGE CODE)

INDEX = SI (EMPLOYEE #N)

BASE = BX (EMPLOYEE GROUP)

SEGMENT = DS (PAYROLL SEGMENT)

MOV AX, [BX + SI + 12]; GET WAGE CODE

Figure 1-15. Four-Component Addressing Example

THE 8088's POWERFUL 16-BIT INSTRUCTION SET

The 8088 has the most powerful instructions of any 8-bit microprocessor. In addition to the standard instruction types you would find on other 8-bit machines, the 8088 offers powerful 16-bit instructions that perform the function of multiple instructions on older 8-bit architectures. Figure 1-16 through 1-21 show the various groupings and the instruction names.

The 14 data transfer instructions (Fig. 1-16) move single bytes and words between memory and registers as well as between registers AL or AX and I/O ports. The stack manipulation instructions are included in this group as are instructions for transferring flag contents and for loading segment registers.

8088 arithmetic operations (Fig. 1-17) may be performed on four types of numbers: unsigned binary, signed binary integers, unsigned packed decimal and unsigned unpacked decimal numbers. Binary numbers may be 8-bits or 16-bits long, decimal numbers are stored in bytes, two digits per byte for packed decimal, and one digit per byte for unpacked decimal.

The 8088 provides three groups of bit manipulation instructions (Fig. 1-18) for manipulating bits within bytes and words and for performing logical shifts and rotates. The logical instructions include the Boolean operators NOT, inclusive OR, exclusive OR, plus a TEST instruction that sets the flags but does not alter either of its operands.

The bits in bytes or words may be shifted arithmetically or logically by the shift instructions. Up to 255 shifts may be performed according to the value of the count operand coded in the instruction. The count may be specified as the constant "1" or as the contents of register CL, allowing the shift count to be a variable supplied during program

GENERAL PURPOSE	
MOV	Move byte or word
PUSH	Push word onto stack
POP	Pop word off stack
XCHG	Exchange byte or word
XLAT	Translate byte
INPUT/OUTPUT	
IN	Input byte or word
OUT	Output byte or word
ADDRESS OBJECT	
LEA	Load effective address
LDS	Load pointer using DS
LES	Load pointer using ES
FLAG TRANSFER	
LAHF	Load AH register from flags
SAHF	Store AH register in flags
PUSHF	Push flags onto stack
POPF	Pop flags off stack

Figure 1-16. Data Transfer Instructions

ADDITION	
ADD	Add byte or word
ADC	Add byte or word with carry
INC	Increment byte or word by 1
AAA	ASCII adjust for addition
DAA	Decimal adjust for addition
SUBTRACTION	
SUB	Subtract byte or word
SBB	Subtract byte or word with borrow
DEC	Decrement byte or word by 1
NEG	Negate byte or word
CMP	Compare byte or word
AAS	ASCII adjust for subtraction
DAS	Decimal adjust for subtraction
MULTIPLICATION	
MUL	Multiply byte or word unsigned
IMUL	Integer multiply byte or word
AAM	ASCII adjust for multiply
DIVISION	
DIV	Divide byte or word unsigned
IDIV	Integer divide byte or word
AAD	ASCII adjust for division
CBW	Convert byte to word
CWD	Convert word to doubleword

Figure 1-17. Arithmetic Instructions

execution. Bytes and words also may be rotated. Bits rotated out of an operand are not lost as in a shift but are circled back into the other end of the operand.

POWERFUL STRING PROCESSING

Five basic string instructions called *primitives* allow a string of bytes or words to be operated on, one byte or word at a time. Strings of up to 64K bytes may be manipulated with these instructions. Instructions are available to move data from a source string to a destination string, or to compare two strings, or to scan one string for a given value. In addition, string instructions are provided to move string elements to and from the AX register in the 8088 (Fig. 1-19).

The specified operation is performed only once when the string primitive is encountered in the program. If the programmer desires the operation to be performed repetitively,

such as in a block or string manipulation operation, the basic string primitive may be proceeded by a special one byte "prefix" that causes the instruction to be repeated by the hardware. This prefix is called REPEAT. The use of the REPEAT prefix allows long strings to be processed much faster than would be possible with a software loop. The repetitions can be terminated by a variety of conditions and a repeated operation may be interrupted and resumed. The CX register counts the number of times the string operation is performed.

When the 8088 moves a 16-bit quantity, it does so 8 bits at a time automatically in the hardware. Because of the variety of string operations and the fact the 8088 can move both 8-bit and 16-bit quantities using its string instructions, the 8088 has the most powerful string processing capabilities of any 8-bit microprocessor.

The program transfer instructions are shown in Figure 1-20. These instructions redirect the flow of instruction execution to other locations in memory and many of them are equivalent to instructions found in other 8-bit microprocessors. The 8088, however, offers much more flexibility in how an instruction is performed. The unconditional transfer instructions may transfer control to a target

LOGICALS	
NOT	"Not" byte or word
AND	"And" byte or word
OR	"Inclusive or" byte or word
XOR	"Exclusive or" byte or word
TEST	"Test" byte or word
SHIFTS	
SHL/SAL	Shift logical/arithmetic left byte or word
SHR	Shift logical right byte or word
SAR	Shift arithmetic right byte or word
ROTATES	
ROL	Rotate left byte or word
ROR	Rotate right byte or word
RCL	Rotate through carry left byte or word
RCR	Rotate through carry right byte or word

Figure 1-18. Bit Manipulation Instructions

MOVS	Move byte or word string
CMPS	Compare byte or word string
SCAS	Scan byte or word string
LODS	Load byte or word string
STOS	Store byte or word string
REP	Repeat
REPE/REPZ	Repeat while equal/zero
REPNE/REPNZ	Repeat while not equal/not zero

Figure 1-19. String Instructions

instruction within the current code segment for an intrasegment transfer, or to a different code segment with an intersegment transfer. The transfer is made unconditionally any time the instruction is executed. An intrasegment transfer is always made relative to the current value of the instruction pointer. Program segments which only use intrasegment transfers are, therefore, relocatable in memory. The conditional transfer instructions may or may not transfer control, depending on the state of the CPU flags at the time the instruction is executed.

The 18 instructions (Fig. 1-20), each test a different combination of flags for a condition. If the condition is true, control is transferred to the target address specified for the instruction. If the condition is false, then control passes to the instruction that follows the conditional jump.

The iteration control instructions regulate the repetition of software loops. These instructions use the CX register as a counter. The LOOPNE instruction for instance decrements a count, checks to see if the count is zero, and branches back to the beginning of the program loop. The equivalent function would require multiple instructions in an older 8-bit instruction set, such as the 8080's.

The interrupt instructions allow interrupt service routines to be activated by both programs and external hardware devices. The effect of software initiated interrupts is similar to hardware initiated interrupts.

The processor control instructions (Fig. 1-21) allow programs to control various CPU functions to update flags and to synchronize the 8088 with external events. Finally, the NOP instruction causes the 8088 CPU to do nothing.

CONDITIONAL TRANSFERS		UNCONDITIONAL TRANSFERS	
JA/JNBE	Jump if above/not below nor equal	CALL	Call procedure
JAE/JNB	Jump if above or equal/not below	RET	Return from procedure
JB/JNAE	Jump if below/not above nor equal	JMP	Jump
JBE/JNA	Jump if below or equal/not above		
JC	Jump if carry	ITERATION CONTROLS	
JE/JZ	Jump if equal/zero		
JG/JNLE	Jump if greater/not less nor equal	LOOP	Loop
JGE/JNL	Jump if greater or equal/not less	LOOPE/LOOPZ	Loop if equal/zero
JL/JNGE	Jump if less/not greater nor equal	LOOPNE/LOOPNZ	Loop if not equal/not zero
JLE/JNG	Jump if less or equal/not greater	JCXZ	Jump if register CX = 0
JNC	Jump if not carry		
JNE/JNZ	Jump if not equal/not zero	INTERRUPTS	
JNO	Jump if not overflow		
JNP/JPO	Jump if not parity/parity odd	INT	Interrupt
JNS	Jump if not sign	INTO	Interrupt if overflow
JO	Jump if overflow	IRET	Interrupt return
JP/JPE	Jump if parity/parity even		
JS	Jump if sign		

NOTE:
"Above" and "below" refer to the relationship of two unsigned values. "Greater" and "less" refer to the relationship of two signed values.

Figure 1-20. Program Transfer Instructions

Well-Planned Instructions

The 8088 instructions can be from one byte to seven bytes in length, depending on the number of operands and immediate data fields included in the instruction. Great care has been taken in the design of the instruction set to allow for efficient programs to be written. The 8088 instructions need not be word aligned (starting at even addresses) contrary to many other 16-bit instruction sets, therefore saving bytes otherwise wasted. It is also possible to use one-byte constants, one-byte displacements, and jump offsets, saving code when compared with other machines that always require 16-bit quantities be used.

The 8088 instruction set also has been designed such that some registers are always used for certain functions. The CX register, for example, is used for a count value by some repetitive instructions. This implied use of registers allows shorter programs because the register address need not be contained in those instructions.

Because of the symmetric use of memory and the ability to build sophisticated data structures using the 8088 addressing modes, the 8088's instruction set is ideal for the implementation of higher level languages. And because the instruction set is bit-efficient, the higher level language programs consume less memory. Benchmarks have shown that the 8088 can generate both assembly language and higher level language programs with 30% less source and object code than other 8- and 16-bit microprocessors. This code savings results in both higher performance and lower memory cost. The instruction set of the 8088 is discussed in more detail in Chapter 2.

INTERFACING THE 8088 IS EASY, FLEXIBLE

We have talked at some length about what goes on inside the 8088, what its instruction set is and the resources available for the programmer. Following is a brief overview of how the 8088 interfaces with other components in an iAPX 88 system.

Figure 1-22 is a simple diagram showing some of the bus interface lines that are provided on the 8088 CPU chip. The 8088 is shown here opposite the 8085A, another popular 8-bit microprocessor, to emphasize the similarity between the two interfaces. Both the 8088 and the 8085A time-multiplex the low order 8 bits of the address bus with the 8- bits of the data bus. This means that during part of an 8088 machine cycle, the 8 bits of the multiplexed bus (AD_0-AD_7) contain address information, and during the remainder of the machine cycle the same 8 lines contain data being transferred to/from the 8088. On both the 8088 and the 8085A there is a control line, called ALE, which signals when the multiplexed address and data lines contain address information. ALE can be used to enable an external latch to latch up the address for the remainder of the machine cycle.

FLAG OPERATIONS	
STC	Set carry flag
CLC	Clear carry flag
CMC	Complement carry flag
STD	Set direction flag
CLD	Clear direction flag
STI	Set interrupt enable flag
CLI	Clear interrupt enable flag
EXTERNAL SYNCHRONIZATION	
HLT	Halt until interrupt or reset
WAIT	Wait for $\overline{\text{TEST}}$ pin active
ESC	Escape to external processor
LOCK	Lock bus during next instruction
NO OPERATION	
NOP	No operation

Figure 1-21. Processor Control Instructions

The next higher order address lines, A_8 through A_{15}, are present throughout the machine cycle on both the 8088 and the 8085A. Note that the 8088 has four other address lines, A_{16} through A_{19} not present on the 8085A and which the 8088 time-multiplexes with status information during the machine cycle.

The three control lines $\overline{RD}$, $\overline{WR}$, and $IO/\overline{M}$ signal the actual data transfer during a machine cycle, whether the 8088 is reading or writing, and whether that transfer is taking place with respect to I/O devices or memory

devices. Also, the 8088, like the 8085A, has other lines containing cycle status information available at the beginning of the machine cycle to inform other devices in the system what type of machine cycle is being performed.

There are several other control lines used with the 8088 such as interrupts, HOLD, READY. See Chapter 3 for details.

Using Special Multiplexed Bus Parts

Because the 8088 is so much like the 8085A, you may connect the 8088 directly to a whole family of multiplexed bus components de-

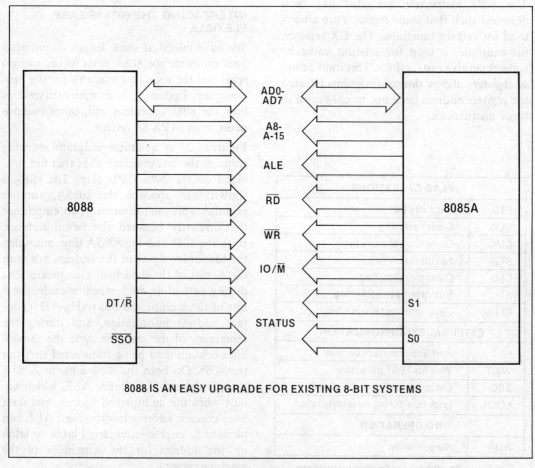

8088 IS AN EASY UPGRADE FOR EXISTING 8-BIT SYSTEMS

Figure 1-22. 8088 Bus Interface is Similar to 8085

signed for the 8085A, without additional interface logic. Figure 1-23 shows just a small system. The multiplexed bus components are the 8155, the 8355, 8755A, and the 8185. Each of these contains an internal address latch that demultiplexes internally the 8088's bus. The multiplexed bus devices are highly integrated as they combine multiple functions to provide a low cost, high-functionality system in a very small number of components. The 8155 contains 256 bytes of static RAM, 22 parallel I/O lines, and a 14-bit timer/counter. The 8355 and 8755A contain 2K (2048) bytes of either ROM or EPROM, and 16 parallel I/O lines. The 8185 is a 1K byte static RAM in a narrow 18-pin package. Note also in Figure 1-23 that the 8088 uses an external clock generator chip called the 8284A.There is another multiplexed-bus memory called the 21821, brand new, that adds 4K bytes of RAM memory to an iAPX 88 system.

BUILDING A STANDARD INTERFACE

Most applications, of course, require more memory or I/O capacity than provided by a multiplexed bus system like the one just described. In the average system, the designer would like to use some commonly available non-multiplexed RAM chips for data storage, some standard EPROM or ROM chips for program storage and some special peripheral devices. To build a standard non-multiplexed bus structure, a whole family of support components are provided for use with the 8088. These support devices are shown in Figure 1-24.

The 8088's bus can be demultiplexed very easily using an 8282 or 8283 latch as shown in Figure 1-24. The 8282 is a non-inverting 8-bit latch in a narrow 20-pin package. The 8283 provides inverted outputs over the bus ("1" inputs become "0" outputs and vice versa).

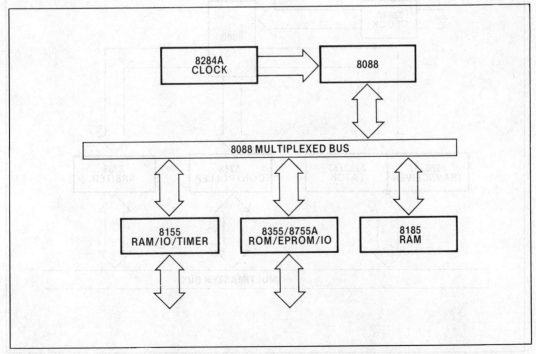

Figure 1-23. Multiplexed Bus Components for Low Chip-Count Applications

To provide extra drive capability for the data lines, the 8286 and 8287 8-bit transceivers are available; the 8287 being the inverting version of the 8286. Also shown in Figure 1-24 is the 8288 bus controller. This optional system device decodes some status information coming from the 8088 CPU to provide special control signals for the bus. The 8288 provides separate memory read, memory write, I/O read, and I/O write control signals. Without the 8288, the 8085A-compatible $\overline{RD}$, $\overline{WR}$, and IO/$\overline{M}$ signals would be used.

Also shown in Figure 1-24 is the 8289 bus arbiter. It is also an optional component used in multi-master iAPX 88 systems. A multi-master system could be one where multiple 8088's share control of the multi-master bus. At any one point in time, only one of the several 8088's would be allowed to take control of the bus to access a shared resource such as a memory. Each 8088 would have its own 8289 bus arbiter. Handshaking signals between the 8289's ensure that only one of the possible masters takes control of the bus at a time, thus preventing conflicts between them.

Once the standard bus structure is created, the 8088 interfaces easily with standard memory and peripheral devices. In fact, the performance requirement on memory devices and peripherals imposed by an 8088 is much lighter than any other high-performance 8-bit microprocessor.

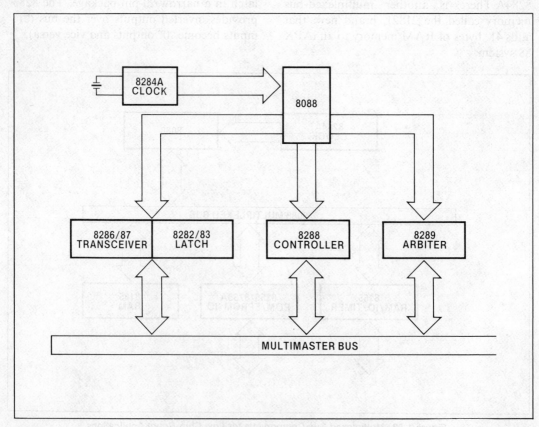

Figure 1-24. iAPX 88 Bipolar Support Components

iAPX 88 PERFORMANCE IS COST EFFECTIVE

Figure 1-25 shows the 8088's memory speed requirements compared to other 8-bit microprocessors. The memory access times listed refer to the time available from when the address first comes out of the CPU during a memory read machine cycle until the data must be available coming back from the memory into the CPU.

The 8088 running at 5MHz allows 460ns for memory devices to receive the address and return the data. The fastest Z80 and the fastest 6809 allow only 140ns and 320ns respectively for the same activity to take place. This means that the 8088 can offer its full performance while using slower and presumably cheaper memories than any other high-performance 8-bit microprocessor.

Note that according to the benchmark reports in the Appendix, the 5MHz 8088 use slower memories while offering an average of 30% more performance than either the 2MHz 6809 or the 6MHz Z80B.

How does the 8088 offer higher performance yet use slower memory devices? The main reason is that parallel instruction fetch and execute using the instruction pipeline allows the bus interface to be much more relaxed while execution takes place at the full speed. The 8088 can run at full speed using readily available 450ns EPROM devices whereas its counterparts, the 68B09 and Z80B require wait states in their machine cycles to do the same.

PROCESSOR EXTENSIONS FOR FLOATING POINT ARITHMETIC AND HIGH SPEED I/O

Up to now, we have justified that the 8088 CPU itself offers a lot of performance, and many systems will be built around the 8088 as the only central processing unit. Note that there are other ways to expand on the 8088 architecture to add additional processing power to the basic CPU. These additional processing modules are called processor extensions. There are two processor extension chips that can be added to the iAPX 88 system (Fig. 1-26).

Numerics Processor Extension

The iAPX 88/20 is an optional numerics processor extension (NPX) added alongside the 8088 CPU. This configuration has the effect of adding the additional set of numerics instructions to the 8088 instruction set. The NPX picks its own instructions out of the

CPU	8088 5MHz	68B09 2MHz	Z80A 4MHz	Z80B 6MHz
MEMORY ACCESS TIME	460 NS	320 NS	250 NS	140 NS

LONGER ACCESS TIME MEANS SLOWER (AND CHEAPER) MEMORIES CAN BE USED WITH iAPX 88

Figure 1-25. iAPX 88 Longer Memory Access Time

8088 instruction stream. The instructions that the NPX interprets as special purpose numerics instructions are regarded almost like "no-operations" for the 8088. The NPX contains an additional register set of eight 80-bit floating point registers which are manipulated with by the additional numerics instructions. Together, the 8088 with the NPX have approximately 100 times the performance of a standalone iAPX 88 system for numerics-intensive applications.

I/O Processor

The 8088 IOP, on the other hand, does not receive instructions from the 8088 instruction stream. It is a separate microprocessor with its own instruction set. The IOP is an input/output channel processor and off-loads I/O interfacing from the 8088 general purpose CPU. The IOP's instruction set, different from the 8088, is specifically tailored for peripheral control and high speed data transfer. With the IOP, it is

possible to configure a dual-bus system, where the 8089 interfaces with peripheral devices on a separate "local" bus while the 8088 runs its application programs in parallel, interfacing with memories over the system bus.

The IOP has a high-speed direct memory access (DMA) mode that transfers data between memory and peripherals or between memory and memory at 1.25 megabytes per second. The IOP is also capable of on-the-fly processing activities such as masked comparison operations or data translations. If you have an application that requires very high performance floating point numerics capabilities, numerous peripheral devices, or very high performance peripheral devices, the NPX and IOP should be considered for inclusion in your system. More information on these devices is contained in other manuals from Intel. This book will focus on single CPU-systems build around the 8088 alone.

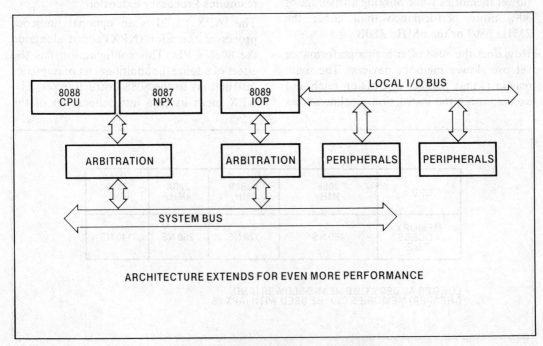

Figure 1-26. iAPX 88 Processor Extensions

REVIEW

This chapter has provided a basic introduction to the 8088 CPU and iAPX 88 systems.

The 8088's pipelined architecture efficiently uses the available bus time to maximize CPU performance and make it possible to get increased performance, even with slower memory devices.

The 8088's register set makes a large number of 16-bit registers available and some registers have special functions allowing more efficient instruction encoding for compact programs.

The 8088's addressing modes provide quick access to complex data structures.

The 8088's instruction set includes powerful 16-bit instructions that lead to smaller programs because many 8088 instructions replace multiple instruction sequences in other 8-bit machines.

The smaller 8088 programs run faster.

With the 8088, it is possible to build lower-cost systems than with other 8-bit microprocessors because the 8088 requires less code memory and runs at high performance with less expensive memories than other 8-bit machines.

Interfacing the 8088 to 8-bit systems is easy with processor extension chips that further increase the 8088's performance through parallel processing using specialized I/O and numeric instructions and registers.

The 8088 is a unique CPU with optimal combination of performance, ease of use, and system economy that meets the needs of system designers in the 1980's.

The following chapters describe iAPX 88 software, hardware, and system design in more detail.

THE iAPX 188 CPU

The iAPX 188 is a highly integrated CPU board-on-a-chip. Most previous highly integrated microprocessors were optimized for real-time control applications and supported relatively small programs in their integrated memory. Examples of this type of chip are Intel's 8048 and 8051 and Zilog's Z8. The iAPX 188, however, is optimized for computing applications. It retains all the bus interface capabilities of multi-chip microprocessors, yet it integrates common peripheral functions used in computer applications. As shown in Figure 1, the integrated functions on the iAPX 188 include the CPU, clock generator, timers, DMA channels, interrupt controller, I/O and memory chip selects, ready generation, and added internal registers to control these devices (Figure 2). The iAPX 188 can replace 15–20 of the most common chips found in a typical microcomputer system.

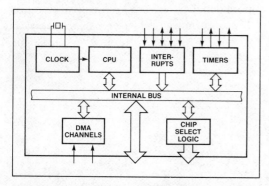

Figure 1. iAPX 188 CPU (80188) Block Diagram

Clock Generator
The 80188 provides an internal clock oscillator, which requires a single external crystal or TTL-level frequency source. The system clock output is a standard 8 MHz, 50% duty cycle clock at half the 16 MHz crystal frequency. This output can be used to drive the clock inputs of other system components and hence makes additional clock generation devices unnecessary. Synchronous and asynchronous ready inputs are supplied for flexible peripheral-device synchronization.

Timers
Two independent 16-bit programmable timer/counters are provided to count or time external events and generate nonrepetitive waveforms. A third 16-bit programmable timer, not connected externally, is useful for implementing time delays and as a prescaler for the two externally connected timers. The iAPX 188 integrated timers are very flexible and can be configured to time/count a variety of distributed I/O activities.

Each of the three timers is equipped with a 16-bit timer register that contains the current value of the timer. It can be read or written at any time, independent of whether the timer is running. Each timer is also equipped with a 16-bit count register containing the maximum value the timer will reach. In addition, the two externally connected timers each have a second 16-bit count register which enables the timers to alternate their count between two different max count values as programmed by the user. When a terminal count is reached, an interrupt may be generated, and the timer value is reset to zero.

The timers have several flexible programmable modes of operation. All three timers can be set to halt or continue on a terminal count value, so no external event or device need wait for a timer reset. The two externally connected timers can select between internal and external clocks, alternate between max count registers or use only one, and be set to retrigger on external events.

DMA Channels
The on-chip DMA controller unit in the iAPX 188 contains two independent high-speed DMA channels. DMA transfers can occur between memory and I/O spaces (i.e., M–I/O) or within the same space (i.e., M–M, I/O–I/O). The latter feature allows I/O devices and memory buffers to be freely located anywhere in the distributed system. For example, memory-mapped I/O can be handled without

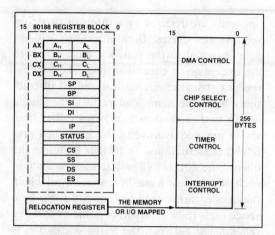

Figure 2. iAPX 188 Register Architecture

any external decode logic to select the required I/O space or device. Each DMA channel maintains two 20-bit source and destination pointers that can be incremented, decremented, or left unchanged after each transfer. Data transfers occur a byte at a time and can be anywhere in the 1 megabyte of directly addressable memory space. This allows a maximum transfer rate of 1 megabyte per second. The user can specify several different modes of DMA operation via the on-chip 16-bit DMA channel control word.

By using the 80188 DMA facilities, data can be input onto local system memory, processed, passed on to the host computer (if needed), and output to another I/O device, all by the use of the two independent, high-speed, on-chip DMA channels.

Interrupt Controller

The 80188 interrupt controller resolves priority among interrupt requests that arrive simultaneously. It can accept interrupts from up to five external hardware sources (NMI + 4) and internal sources as well (timers, DMA channels). Each interrupt source has a programmable priority level and a preassigned interrupt vector type, used to derive an address to a table in memory where interrupt

service routine addresses are located. This enhancement of predefined vector types makes the interrupt response time about 50% faster than the typical iAPX 88 response time. The 8259A programmable interrupt controller (PIC) interrupt modes, such as fully nested and specially fully nested, are provided by the 80188 as well. In addition, multiple 8259As can be cascaded to provide the system with up to 128 external interrupts.

Chip Select/Ready Generation

The iAPX 188 contains programmable chip select logic to provide chip select signals for memory components, peripheral components, and programmable ready (wait state) generation logic. The result of this integrated logic is a lower system part count, since as many as 11 TTL packs will be saved. In addition to a lower system cost, the performance of the system will improve as a result of the elimination of external propagation delays. Another advantage involves flexibility in the choice of memory component size and speed. Three memory ranges (lower, middle, upper) can be programmed to variable lengths (1K, 2K, 4K, . . . 256K) so that a variety of memory chip sizes can be used. Further, anywhere from zero to three wait states can be programmed so either high-speed or low-cost, slower memories can be used. With respect to the peripheral chip selects, as many as seven different peripheral components can be addressed via I/O or memory space. Again, programmable wait states may be injected to synchronize slower peripherals with the 80188 itself or memory.

The chip select/ready logic contributes to making the iAPX 188 an optimum, low-cost choice for a distributed processing node. In the past, this necessary logic had to be designed, debugged, and programmed. Now, with the 80188, the design, debug, and programming are done by initializing the associated 16-bit on-chip control registers.

CPU Internal Registers

The added functionality of the iAPX 188 (i.e., timers, DMA, interrupt controller, and chip selects) uses on-chip 16-bit control registers for each integrated device. They are contained in a 256-byte control block (see Figure 2) included in the 80188 CPU register architecture. The control register block may be either I/O or memory-mapped, based on initialization for a new control block pointer in the CPU. Except for these additions, the register architecture of the iAPX 188 is identical to the iAPX 88.

The iAPX 188 is similar to the recently announced iAPX 186. The major difference is in the data bus width (8 vs. 16 bits). Sixteen-bit operands are fetched or written in two consecutive bus cycles. Both processors will appear identical to the software engineer, with the exception of execution time. The internal register structure is identical and all instructions have the same end result. The queue length is shortened to four bytes rather than six to prevent overuse of the bus when prefetching instructions. To further optimize the queue, the 80188 will prefetch an instruction each time there is a one-byte space available in the queue, rather than waiting for a two-byte space for a 16-bit instruction in the 80186. The relationship between the 80188 and 80186 is similar to the relationship between the 8088 and 8086.

iAPX 88 Architecture
And Instructions

CHAPTER 2
THE iAPX 88 ARCHITECTURE AND INSTRUCTIONS

INTRODUCTION

This chapter describes the programmer's architecture of the 8088 CPU. The programming model is presented first, including the memory and I/O port organizations and the CPU registers. The addressing modes are described next, followed by an introduction to the instruction set and the iAPX 88 assembly language. The iAPX 88 instruction set reference pages that describe each instruction in detail conclude the chapter.

iAPX 88 ARCHITECTURE

The iAPX 88 processor architecture comprises a memory structure, a register structure, an instruction set, and a set of addressing modes. The 8088 CPU can access up to one million bytes of memory and up to 64K input/output ports.

The 8088 has three register files:

1) *data registers* to hold intermediate results;
2) *pointer and index registers* to reference within specified portions of memory;
3) *segment registers* used to specify these portions of memory.

The 8088 has nine flags that are used to record the state of the processor and to control its operations.

The 8088 instruction set and addressing modes are richer and more symmetric than the 8080. And the 8088 external interface, providing such things as interrupts, multiprocessor synchronization, and resource sharing, exceeds the facilities provided in the 8080, the 8085, or the Z80®.

Memory Structure

The 8088 input/output space and memory space are treated in parallel and are collectively called the memory structure. Code and data reside in the memory space while (non-memory-mapped) peripheral devices reside in the I/O space.

Z80 is a registered trademark of Zilog Corp.

Memory Space

The memory in an iAPX 88 system is a sequence of up to one million bytes (a 64-fold increase over the 8080). An 8088 *word* is any two consecutive bytes in memory. Like the 8080, *words are stored in memory with the most significant byte at the higher memory address.*

The one-megabyte memory can be conceived of as an arbitrary number of *segments*, each containing at most 64K bytes. The starting address of each segment is evenly divisible by 16 (the four least significant address bits are 0). At any moment, the program can immediately access the contents of four such segments:

1) Current code segment
2) Current data segment
3) Current stack segment
4) Current extra segment

Each of these segments can be identified by placing the 16 most significant bits of the segment starting address into one of the four 16-bit segment registers. By contrast, the 8080 memory structure is simply the 8088 memory structure with all four of the current segments starting at 0.

An 8088 instruction can refer to bytes or words within a segment by using a 16-bit offset address. The processor constructs the 20-bit byte or word address automatically by adding the 16-bit offset address (also called the *logical address*) to the contents of a 16-bit segment register, with four low-order zeros appended (Fig. 2-1).

Input/Output Space

The 8088 I/O space consists of 64K ports (a 256-fold increase over the 8080). Ports are addressed the same way as memory except there are no port segment registers. That is, all ports are considered to be in one segment. Like memory, ports may be 8- or 16-bits in size.

The first 256 ports are directly addressable (address in the instruction) by some input/output instructions, other instructions let you address the total 64K ports indirectly (address in a register).

REGISTER STRUCTURE

The 8088 processor contains the thirteen 16-bit registers and nine 1-bit flags shown in Figure 2-2. Notice that the thirteen registers are divided into three files of four registers each plus the thirteenth register, namely the instruction pointer (IP) (called the program counter in earlier processors). The IP is not directly accessible to the programmer; it is manipulated with control-transfer instructions.

Data Register File

The data registers (top file Fig. 2-2) can be addressed as either 8- or 16-bit registers. (Note vertical line showing byte divisions).

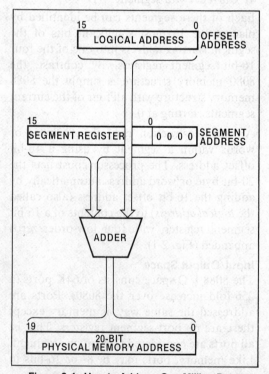

Figure 2-1. How to Address One Million Bytes

The data registers handle both byte and word quantities with equal ease. Figure 2-2 shows that the 16-bit registers are named AX, BX, CX, and DX; and the 8-bit registers are named AL, AH, BL, BH, CL, CH, DL, and DH (the L or H suffix designates high-order or low-order byte).

Generally, the data registers participate interchangeably in both arithmetic and logical operations of the 8088. However, some instructions (e.g. string instructions) require certain general registers for specific uses. Figure 2-3 shows which registers are implicitly used for special operations. Notice how Figure 2-3 relates to Figure 2-2.

To review, data registers may be addressed as either 8-bit or 16-bit registers as shown in Figure 2-2. The registers in the next 2 files are addressed *only* as 16-bit registers.

Pointer and Index Register File

The pointer and index registers of the 8088 consist of the 16-bit registers SP, BP, SI, and DI as shown in Figure 2-2. These registers usually contain offset addresses for addressing within a segment. They reduce program size by eliminating the need for each instruction to specify frequently used addresses. These registers serve another (and perhaps more important) function; they provide for dynamic logical address computation as described in the section on operand addressing below. To accomplish this, the pointer and index registers participate in arithmetic and logical operations along with the 16-bit data registers described above.

Figure 2-2 shows this file divided into the pointer subfile (SP and BP) and the *index* subfile (SI and DI). The pointer registers provide convenient access to the current stack segment (as opposed to the data segment). Unless otherwise specified in the instruction, pointer registers refer to the current stack segment while index registers refer to the current data segment.

In certain instances, specific uses of these four registers are indicated by the mnemonic phrases "stack pointer," "base pointer," "source index," and "destination index." (Fig. 2-2).

Segment Register File

The segment registers of the 8088 are 16-bit registers. These registers specifically identify the four currently addressable memory segments: CS (code segment), DS (data segment), SS (stack segment), and ES (extra segment).

All instructions are fetched from the current code segment offset by the instruction pointer (IP) register. The segment for operand fetches can usually be designated by appending a special one-byte prefix to the instruction. This prefix, and other prefixes described later, has unique encoding that distinguishes it from the opcodes. In the absence of such a prefix (the usual case), the operand is usually fetched from the current data segment or current stack segment, depending on whether the offset address was calculated from the contents of a pointer register.

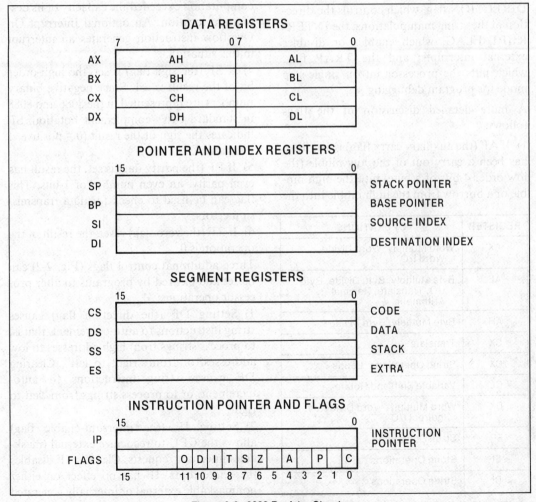

Figure 2-2. 8088 Register Structure

Programs can be dynamically relocated by changing the segment registers, provided the program itself does not load or manipulate the segment registers.

Flag Register File

Six flags provide processor status information (Fig. 2-2). Five are the 8080/8085 flags and usually reflect the status of the latest arithmetic or logical operation. The sixth, an OVERFLOW flag, reflects a signed overflow condition.

The 8088 also contains three flags that control processor operations. These are the DIRECTION flag, which controls the direction of the string manipulations; the INTERRUPT FLAG, which enables or disables external interrupts; and the TRAP flag, which puts the processor into a single-step mode for program debugging.

A more detailed discussion of the flags follows:

1) If AF (the auxiliary carry flag) is set, there has been a carry out of the low nibble (the low order 4-bits of a byte) into the high nibble or a borrow from the high nibble into the low nibble of an 8-bit quantity (low-order byte of a 16-bit quantity). This flag is used by decimal arithmetic instructions.

2) If CF (the carry flag) is set, there has been a carry out of, or a borrow into, the high-order bit of the result (8- or 16-bit). The flag is used by instructions that add and subtract multibyte numbers. Rotate instructions can also isolate a bit in memory or a register by placing it in the carry flag.

3) If OF (the overflow flag) is set, an arithmetic overflow has occurred; that is, a significant digit has been lost because the size of the computation exceeded the capacity of its destination location. An optional Interrupt On Overflow instruction generates an interrupt in this situation.

4) If SF (the sign flag) is set, the high-order bit of the result is a 1. Since negative binary numbers are represented in the 8086 and 8088 in standard two's complement notation, SF indicates the sign of the result (0 = positive, 1 = negative).

5) If PF (the parity flag) is set, the result has even parity, an even number of 1-bits. This flag can be used to check for data transmission errors.

6) If ZF (the zero flag) is set, the result of the operation is 0.

Three additional control flags (Fig. 2-2) can be set and cleared by programs to alter processor operations:

1) Setting DF (the direction flag) causes string instructions to auto-decrement, that is, to process strings from high addresses to low addresses, or from "right to left". Clearing DF causes string instructions to auto-increment, or to process strings from "left to right."

2) Setting IF (the interrupt-enable flag) allows the CPU to recognize external (maskable) interrupt requests. Clearing IF disables these interrupts. IF has no effect on either nonmaskable external or internally generated interrupts.

REGISTER	OPERATIONS
AX	Word Multiply, Word Divide, Word I/O
AL	Byte Multiply, Byte Divide, Byte I/O, Translate, Decimal Arithmetic
AH	Byte Multiply, Byte Divide
BX	Translate
CX	String Operations, Loops
CL	Variable Shift and Rotate
DX	Word Multiply, Word Divide, Indirect I/O
SP	Stack Operations
SI	String Operations
DI	String Operations

Figure 2-3. Implicit Use of General Registers

3) Setting TF (the trap flag) puts the processor into single-step mode for debugging. In this mode, the CPU automatically generates an internal interrupt after each instruction, allowing a program to be inspected as it executes instruction by instruction.

Instruction Pointer

The 16-bit instruction pointer (IP), as shown in Figure 2-2, is analogous to the program counter (PC) in the 8080/8085 CPUs and points to the next instruction. The instruction pointer contains the offset (distance in bytes) of the next instruction from the beginning of the current code segment. During normal execution, IP contains the offset of the next instruction to be fetched. Whenever IP is saved on the stack, however, it first is automatically adjusted to point to the next instruction to be executed. Programs do not have direct access to the instruction pointer, but instructions cause it to change and to be saved on and restored from the stack.

Stack Implementation

The 8088's stack is implemented in memory and is located by the stack segment register (SS) and the stack pointer register (SP). A system may have an unlimited number of stacks, and a stack may be up to 64K bytes long, the maximum length of a segment. (An attempt to expand a stack beyond 64K bytes overwrites the beginning of the stack). One stack is directly addressable at a time; this is the current stack often referred to simply as "the" stack. SS contains the base address of the current stack and SP points to the top of the stack (TOS). In other words, SP contains the offset of the top of the stack from the stack segment's base address. Note, however, that the stack's base address (contained in SS) is not the "bottom" of the stack.

Instructions that operate on a stack add or remove one word (2 bytes) at a time. An item is *pushed onto* the stack by decrementing SP by 2 and writing the item at the new TOS. An item is *popped off* the stack by copying it from TOS and incrementing SP by 2. In other words, the stack grows down in memory toward its base address. Stack operations never move items on the stack, nor do they erase them. The top of the stack changes only as a result of updating the stack pointer.

ADDRESSING MODES

Instructions in the 8088 usually perform operations on one or two source operands, with the result overwriting one of the operands. The first operand of a two-operand instruction can be usually either a register or a memory location; the second operand can be either a register or a constant within the instruction. (The terms first and second operand are used to distinguish the operands only — their use does not imply directionality for data transfers). Typical formats for two-operand instructions are shown in Figure 2-4.

Single-operand instructions generally allow either a register or a memory location to serve as the operand. Figure 2-4 also shows a typical one-operand format. Virtually all 8088 operators may specify 8- or 16-bit operands.

Memory Operands

An instruction may address an operand residing in memory in one of the following ways, as determined by the "mod" and "r/m" field in the instruction (Fig. 2-5):

DIRECT ADDRESSING — 16-bit offset address contained in the instruction.

INDIRECT ADDRESSING — optionally with an 8- or 16-bit displacement contained in the instruction:

1) through a base register (BP or BX)
2) through an index register (SI or DI)
3) through the sum of a base register and an index register

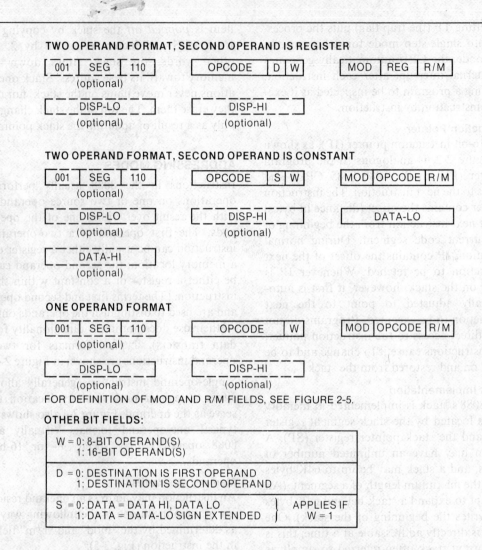

TWO OPERAND FORMAT, SECOND OPERAND IS REGISTER

001	SEG	110
(optional)

| OPCODE | D | W |

| MOD | REG | R/M |

| DISP-LO |
(optional)

| DISP-HI |
(optional)

TWO OPERAND FORMAT, SECOND OPERAND IS CONSTANT

| 001 | SEG | 110 |
(optional)

| OPCODE | S | W |

| MOD | OPCODE | R/M |

| DISP-LO |
(optional)

| DISP-HI |
(optional)

| DATA-LO |

| DATA-HI |
(optional)

ONE OPERAND FORMAT

| 001 | SEG | 110 |
(optional)

| OPCODE | W |

| MOD | OPCODE | R/M |

| DISP-LO |
(optional)

| DISP-HI |
(optional)

FOR DEFINITION OF MOD AND R/M FIELDS, SEE FIGURE 2-5.

OTHER BIT FIELDS:

| W = 0: 8-BIT OPERAND(S) |
| 1: 16-BIT OPERAND(S) |

| D = 0: DESTINATION IS FIRST OPERAND |
| 1: DESTINATION IS SECOND OPERAND |

| S = 0: DATA = DATA HI, DATA LO | APPLIES IF |
| 1: DATA = DATA-LO SIGN EXTENDED | W = 1 |

SEG:	SEGMENT REG
00	ES
01	CS
10	SS
11	DS

	REGISTER	
REG:	8-BIT (W = 0)	16-BIT (W = 1)
000	AL	AX
001	CL	CX
010	DL	DX
011	BL	BX
100	AH	SP
101	CH	BP
110	DH	SI
111	BH	DI

Figure 2-4. Defining Bits in Instructions with One and Two Operands

FIRST OPERAND CHOICE DEPENDS ON ADDRESSING MODE:

FIRST OPERAND IN MEMORY		FIRST OPERAND IN REGISTER		
INDIRECT ADDRESSING	DIRECT ADDRESSING			
00* : DISP = 0 MOD = 01 : DISP = DISP-LO SIGN EXTENDED 10 : DISP = DISP-HI, DISP-LO	MOD = 00 AND R/M = 110	MOD = 11		
	OPERAND EFFECTIVE ADDRESS = DISP-HI, DISP-LO		REGISTER	
R/M: OPERAND EFFECTIVE ADDRESS		R/M:	8-BIT (W = 0)	16-BIT (W = 1)
000 (BX) + (SI) + DISP		000	AL	AX
001 (BX) + (DI) + DISP		001	CL	CX
010 (BP) + (SI) + DISP		010	DL	DX
011 (BP) + (DI) + DISP		011	BL	BX
100 (SI) + DISP		100	AH	SP
101 (DI) + DISP		101	CH	BP
110 (BP) + DISP		110	DH	SI
111 (BX) + DISP		111	BH	DI

Where ( ) means "contents of"
*Exception—direct addressing mode

Figure 2-5. Determining First Operand

DATA STRUCTURE	DATA MEMORY		STACK
	WITHOUT BASE	WITH BASE	
SIMPLE VARIABLE	DIRECT	BX + OFFSET	BP + OFFSET
ARRAYS	SI DI	BX + SI BX + DI	BP + SI BP + DI
ARRAYS OF RECORDS	SI + OFFSET DI + OFFSET	BX + SI + OFFSET BX + DI + OFFSET	BP + SI + OFFSET BP + DI + OFFSET

Figure 2-6. Effective Addresses Used with Different Data Structures

TYPE OF MEMORY REFERENCE	DEFAULT SEGMENT BASE	ALTERNATE SEGMENT BASE	LOGICAL ADDRESS
Instruction Fetch	CS	NONE	IP
Stack Operation	SS	NONE	SP
String Source	DS	CS,ES,SS	SI
String Destination	ES	NONE	DI
BP Used As Base Register	SS	CS,DS,ES	Effective Address
General Data Read/Write	DS	CS,ES,SS	Effective Address

Figure 2-7. 8088 Address Components

Register Operands

An instruction may address an operand residing in one of the general registers or in one of the pointer or index registers. Fig. 2-5 shows the register selection as determined by the "r/m" field (first operand) or the "reg" field (second operand) in the instruction.

Immediate Operands

In general, one of the two operands of a two-operand instruction can be "immediate" data contained within the instruction. These operands are represented in 2's-complement form and may be 8-bits or 16-bits in length.

Addressing Mode Usage

The addressing modes were designed to permit efficient implementation of high-level language features. For example, a simple variable is accessed with the direct mode, whereas an array element in a based record (at a memory address pointed to by some other base variable) may be accessed within the indirect-through-BX-plus-SI-plus-offset mode (where BX points to start-of-record, offset points to the start of the array within the record, and index register SI contains the index into the array).

The addressing modes involving the BP base register allow accessing data in the stack segment instead of in the data segment. Recursive procedures and block-structured languages frequently store data in the stack. Address modes for accessing data elements use effective addresses shown in Fig. 2-6.

Addressing Summary

Fig. 2-7 summarizes the address components that are combined to generate memory addresses. The Default segment base is the segment register automatically chosen by the 8088 for the corresponding type of memory reference. The Alternate segment base may replace the Default segment if a special "segment override" prefix precedes the instruction. The Logical address is automatically added to the chosen segment register to form the memory address. The 8088 Assembly language simplifies the task of selecting the desired addressing modes for use with basic 8088 instruction types.

Dedicated and Reserved Memory Locations

Two areas in extreme low and high memory are dedicated to specific processor functions or are reserved by Intel Corporation for use by Intel hardware and software products. As shown in Figure 2-8, the locations are: 0H through 7FH (128 bytes) and FFFF0H through FFFFFH (16 bytes). These areas are used for interrupt and system reset processing. iAPX 88 systems should not use these areas for any other purpose. Doing so may make these systems incompatible with future Intel products.

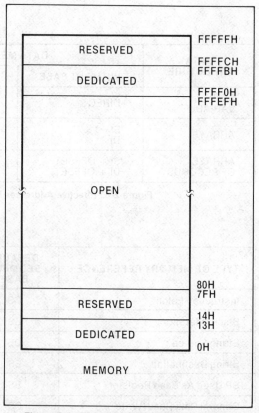

Figure 2-8. Reserved and Dedicated Memory Locations

The interrupt pointer (or interrupt vector) table (Fig. 2-9) is the link between an interrupt type code and the procedure designated to service interrupts associated with that code. The interrupt pointer table occupies up to 1K bytes of low memory. There may be up

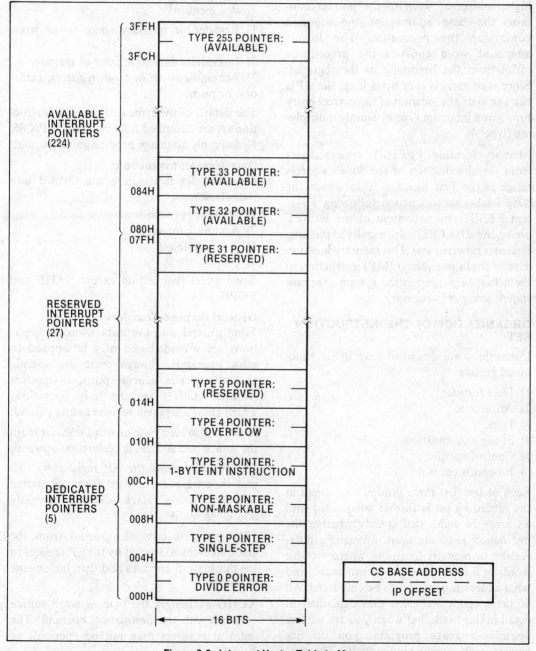

Figure 2-9. Interrupt Vector Table in Memory

to 256 4-byte entries in the table, one for each interrupt type that can occur in the system. Each entry is a doubleword pointer (4 bytes) containing the address of the procedure. The higher-addressed word of the pointer contains the base address of the segment containing the procedure. The lower-addressed word contains the procedure's offset from the beginning of the segment. Since each entry is four bytes long, the CPU can calculate the location of the correct entry for a given interrupt type by simply multiplying (type*4).

Memory location FFFF0H, sixteen bytes from the absolute top of the 8088's address range is the first location from which the 8088 fetches an instruction following a system RESET (the activation of the RESET pin on the 8088 CPU chip, usually at the time system is powered up). This memory location usually contains a jump (JMP) instruction to the actual beginning of the system program somewhere else in memory.

ORGANIZATION OF THE INSTRUCTION SET

Instructions are described here in six functional groups:

1) Data transfer
2) Arithmetic
3) Logic
4) String manipulation
5) Control transfer
6) Processor control

Each of the first three groups mentioned in the preceding list is further subdivided into an array of codes that specify whether the instruction is to act upon immediate data, register or memory locations, whether 16-bit words or 8-bit bytes are to be processed, and what addressing mode is to be employed. All of these codes are listed and explained in detail in this book, but when you are writing assembly-language programs you do not have to code each one individually. The con-

text of your program automatically causes the assembler to generate the correct code.

There are three general categories of instructions within each of the three functional groups mentioned:

1) Register or memory space to or from register
2) Immediate data to register or memory
3) Accumulator to or from registers, memory, or ports

The details of the syntax of the 8088 instruction set are described fully in Intel's iAPX 86, 88 assembly language programming manual.

Data Transfer Instructions

Data transfer instructions are divided into four classes:

1) General purpose
2) Accumulator-specific
3) Address-object
4) Flag

None affect flag setting except SAHF and POPF.

General Purpose Transfers

Four general purpose data transfer operations are provided and may be applied to most operands, though there are specific exceptions. The general purpose transfers (except XCHG) are the only operations which allow a segment register as an operand.

MOV performs a byte or word transfer from the source operand to the destination operand.

PUSH decrements the SP register by two and then transfers a word from the source operand to the stack element currently addressed by SP.

POP transfers a word operand from the stack element addressed by the SP register to the destination operand and then increments SP by 2.

XCHG exchanges the byte or word source operand with the destination operand. The segment registers may not be operands of XCHG.

Accumulator-Specific Transfers

Three accumulator-specific transfer operations are provided:

IN transfers a byte (or word) from an input port to the AL register (or AX register for a word). The port is specified either with an inline data byte, allowing fixed access to ports 0 through 255, or with a port number in the DX register, allowing variable access to 64K input ports.

OUT is similar to IN except that the transfer is from the accumulator to the output port.

XLAT performs a table lookup byte translation. The AL register is used as an index into a 256-byte table whose base is addressed by the BX register. The byte operand so selected is transferred to AL.

Address-Object Transfers

Three address-object transfer operations are provided:

LEA (load effective address) transfers the offset address of (rather than its value) to the destination operand. The source operand must be a memory operand and the destination operand must be a 16-bit general, pointer, or index register.

LDS (load pointer into DS) transfers a "pointer-object" (i.e., a 32-bit object containing an offset address and a segment address) from the source operand (which must be a memory operand) to a pair of destination registers. The segment address is transferred to the DS segment register. The offset address must be transferred to a 16-bit general, pointer, or index register.

LES (load pointer into ES) is similar to LDS except that the segment address is transferred to the ES segment register.

Flag Register Transfers

Four flag register transfer operations are provided:

LAHF (load AH with flags) transfer the flag registers SF, ZF, AF, PF, and CF (the 8080 flags) into specific bits of the AH register.

SAHF (store AH into flags) transfers specific bits of the AH register to the flag register, SF, ZF, AF, PF, and CF.

PUSHF (push flags) decrements the SP register by two and transfers all of the flag registers into specific bits of the stack element addressed by SP.

POPF (pop flags) transfers specific bits of the stack element addressed by the SP register to the flag registers and then increments SP by two.

Arithmetic Instructions

The 8088 provides the four basic mathematical operations in a variety of instructions. Both 8- and 16-bit operations and both signed and unsigned arithmetic are provided. Standard twos complement representation of signed values is used. The addition and subtraction operations serve as both signed and unsigned operations to be made (see Conditional Transfer). Correction operations allow arithmetic to be performed directly on packed or unpacked decimal numbers.

Flag Register Settings

Six flag registers are set or cleared by arithmetic operations to reflect results of the operation. They generally follow these rules:

CF is set if the operation results in a carry out of (from addition) or a borrow into (from subtraction) the high-order bit of the result; otherwise CF is cleared.

AF is set if the operation results in a carry out of (from addition) or a borrow into (from subtraction) the low-order four bits of the result; otherwise AF is cleared.

ZF is set if the result of the operation is zero; otherwise ZF is cleared.

SF is set if the high-order bit of the result of the operation is set; otherwise SF is cleared.

PF is set if the modulo 2 sum of the low-order eight bits of the operation is 0 (even parity); otherwise PF is cleared (odd parity).

OF is set if the operation results in a carry into the high-order bit of the result but not a carry out of the high-order bit, or vice versa; otherwise OF is cleared.

Addition

Five addition operations are provided:

ADD performs an addition of the two source operands and returns the result to one of the operands.

ADC (add with carry) performs an addition of the two source operands, adds one if the CF flag is found previously set, and returns the result to one of the operands.

INC (increment) performs an addition of the source operand and returns the result to the operand.

AAA (unpacked BCD [ASCII] adjust for addition) performs a correction of the result in AL of adding two unpacked decimal operands, yielding an unpacked decimal sum.

DAA (decimal adjust for addition) performs a correction of the result in AL of adding two packed decimal operands, yielding a packed decimal sum.

Subtraction

Seven subtraction operations are provided:

SUB performs a subtraction of the two source operands and returns the result to one of the operands.

SBB (subtract with borrow) performs a subtraction of the two source operands, subtracts one if the CF flag is found previously set, and returns the result to one of the operands.

DEC (decrement) performs a subtraction of one from the source operand and returns the result to the operand.

NEG (negate) performs a subtraction of the source operand from zero and returns the result to the operand.

CMP (compare) performs a subtraction of the two source operands causing the flags to be affected but does not return the result.

AAS (unpacked BCD [ASCII] adjust for subtraction) performs a correction of the result in AL of subtracting two unpacked decimal operands, yielding an unpacked decimal difference.

DAS (decimal adjust for subtraction) performs a correction of the result in AL of subtracting two packed decimal operands, yielding a packed decimal difference.

Multiplication

Three multiplication operations are provided:

MUL performs an unsigned multiplication of the accumulator (AL or AX) and the source operand, returning a double length result to the accumulator and its extension (AL and AH for 8-bit operation, AX and DX for 16-bit operation). CF and OF are set if the top half of the result is non-zero.

IMUL (integer multiply) is similar to MUL except that it performs a signed multiplication. CF and OF are set if the top half of the result is not the sign-extension of the low half of the result.

AAM (unpacked BCD [ASCII] adjust for multiply) performs a correction of the result in AX of multiplying two unpacked decimal operands, yielding an unpacked decimal product.

Division

Three division operations are provided and two sign-extension operations to support signed division:

DIV performs an unsigned division of the accumulator and its extension (AL and AH for 8-bit operation, AX and DX for 16-bit operation) by the source operand and returns the single length quotient to the accumulator (AL or AX), and returns the single length remainder to the accumulator extension (AH or DX). The flags are undefined. Division by zero generates an interrupt of type 0.

IDIV (integer division) is similar to DIV except that it performs a signed division.

AAD (unpacked BCD [ASCII] adjust for division) performs a correction of the dividend in AL before dividing two unpacked decimal operands, so that the result will yield an unpacked decimal quotient.

CBW (convert byte to word) performs a sign extension of AL into AH.

CWD (convert word to double word) performs a sign extension of AX into DX.

LOGIC INSTRUCTIONS

The 8088 provides the basic logic operation for both 8- and 16-bit operands.

Single-Operand Operations

Three single-operand logical operations are provided:

NOT forms the ones complement of the source operand and returns the result to the operand. Flags are not affected.

Shift operations of four varieties are provided for memory and register operands, **SHL** (shift logic left), **SHR** (shift logic right), **SAL** (shift arithmetic left), and **SAR** (shift arithmetic right). Single bit shifts, and variable bit shifts with the shift count taken from the CL register are available. The CF flag becomes the last bit shifted out; OF is defined only for shifts with count of 1, and set if the final sign bit value differs from the previous value of the sign bit; and PF, SF, and ZF are set to reflect the result value.

Rotate operations of four varieties are provided for memory and register operands, **ROL** (rotate left), **ROR** (rotate right), **RCL** (rotate through CF left), and **RCR** (rotate through CF right). Single bit rotates, and variable bit rotates with the rotate count taken from the CL register are available. The CF flag becomes the last bit rotated out; OF is defined only for shifts with count of 1, and is

set if the final sign bit value differs from the previous value of the sign bit.

Two-Operand Operations

Four two-operand logical operations are provided. The CF and OF flags are cleared on all operations; SF, PF, and ZF reflect the result.

AND performs the bitwise logical conjunction of the two source operands and returns the result to one of the operands.

TEST performs the same operations as AND causing the flags to be affected but does not return the result.

OR performs the bitwise logical inclusive disjunction of the two source operands and returns the result to one of the operands.

XOR performs the bitwise logical exclusive disjunction of the two source operands and returns the result to one of the operands.

STRING MANIPULATION INSTRUCTIONS

One-byte instructions perform various primitive operations for the manipulation of byte and word strings (sequences of bytes or words). Any primitive operation can be performed repeatedly in hardware by preceding its instruction with a repeat prefix. The single-operation forms may be combined to form complex string operations with repetition provided by iteration operations.

Hardware Operation Control

All primitive string operations use the SI register to address the source operands, which are assumed to be in the current data segment. The DI register addresses the destination operands, which reside in the current *extra* segment. If the DF flag is cleared, the operand pointers are incremented after each operation (once for byte operations and twice for word operations). If the DF flag is set, the operand pointers are decremented after each operation. See Processor Control for setting and clearing DF.

Any of the primitive string instructions may be preceded with a one-byte prefix indicating that the operation is to be repeated until the operation count in CX is satisfied. The test for completion is made prior to each repetition of the operation. Thus, an initial operation count of zero will cause zero executions of the primitive operation.

The repeat prefix byte also designates a value to compare with ZF flag. If the primitive operation is one which affects the ZF flag, and the ZF flag is unequal to the designated value after any execution of the primitive operation, the repetition is terminated. This permits the scan operation to serve as a scan-while or a scan-until.

During the execution of a repeated primitive operation the operand pointer registers (SI and DI) and the operation count register (CX) are updated after each repetition, whereas the instruction pointer will retain the offset address of the repeat prefix byte (assuming it immediately precedes the string operation instruction). Thus, an interrupted repeated operation will be correctly resumed when control returns from the interrupted task.

You should avoid using the two other prefix bytes with a repeat-prefixed string instruction. One overrides the default segment addressing for the SI operand and one locks the bus to prohibit access by other bus masters. Execution of the repeated string operation will not resume properly following an interrupt if more than one prefix is present preceding the string primitive. Execution will resume one byte before the primitive (presumably where the repeat prefix resides), thus ignoring the additional prefixes.

Primitive String Operations

Five primitive string operations are provided:

MOVS transfers a byte or word operand from the source operand to the destination operand. As a repeated operation this moves a string from one location in memory to another.

CMPS subtracts the destination byte or word operand from the source operand and affects the flags but does not return the result. As a repeated operation this compares two strings. With the appropriate repeat prefix it is possible to determine after which string element the two strings become unequal, thereby establishing an ordering between the strings.

SCAS subtracts the destination byte or word operand from AL (or AX) and affects the flags but does not return the result. As a repeated operation this scans for the occurrence of, or departure from a given value in the string.

LODS transfers a byte or word operand from the source operand to AL (or AX). This operation ordinarily would not be repeated.

STOS transfers a byte or word operand from AL (or AX) to the destination operand. As a repeated operation this fills a string with a given value.

In all cases above, the source operand is addressed by SI and the destination operand is addressed by DI.

Software Operation Control

The repeat prefix provides for rapid iteration in a hardware-repeated string operation. The iteration control operations provide this same control for implementing software loops to perform complex string operations. These iteration operations provide the same operation count update, operation completion test, and ZF flag tests that the repeat prefix provides.

By combining the primitive string operations and iteration control operations with other operations, it is possible to build sophisticated yet efficient string manipulation routines. One instruction that is particularly useful in this context is XLAT; it permits a byte fetched from one string to be translated before being stored in a second string, or before being operated upon in some other fashion. The translation is performed by using the value in the AL register as an index into a table pointed at by the BX register. The translated value obtained from the table then replaces the value initially in the AL register.

Here is an example problem solved by use of primitive string operations and iteration control operations to implement a complex string operation: An input driver must translate a buffer of EBCDIC characters into ASCII, and transfer characters until one of several EBCDIC control characters is encountered. The transferred ASCII string is to be terminated with an EOT character.

To initialize the translation sequence, SI points to the beginning of the EBCDIC buffer, DI points to the beginning of the receiving ASCII buffer, BX points to an EBCDIC-to-ASCII translation table, and CX contains the length of the EBCDIC buffer (possibly empty). The translation table contains the ASCII equivalent for each EBCDIC character, perhaps with ASCII NULs for illegal characters. The EOT code is placed into the table corresponding to EBCDIC stop characters. The 8088 instruction sequence to implement this example is the following:

```
Next:

JCXZ      Empty      ;skip if input buffer empty
LODS      Ebcbuf     ;fetch next EBCDIC character
XLAT      Table      ;translate it to ASCII
CMP       AL, EOT    ;test for the EOT
STOS      Ascbuf     ;transfer ASCII character
LOOPNE    Next       ;continue if not EOT
.
.
.
Empty:
```

The body of this loop requires seven bytes of code.

CONTROL TRANSFER INSTRUCTIONS

Four classes of control transfer operations

may be distinguished:

1) calls, jumps, and returns;
2) conditional transfers;
3) iteration control; and
4) interrupts.

All control transfer operations cause the program execution to continue at some new location in memory, possibly in a new code segment.

Calls, Jumps, and Returns

Two basic varieties of call jumps, and returns are provided — those which transfer control within the current code segment, and those which transfer control to an arbitrary code segment, which then becomes the current code segment. Both direct and indirect transfers are supported; indirect transfers make use of the standard addressing modes.

The three transfer operations are described below:

CALL pushes the offset address of the next instruction onto the stack (in the case of an inter-segment transfer the CS segment register is pushed first) and then transfers control to the target operand.

JMP transfers control to the target operand.

RET transfers control to the return address saved by a previous CALL operation, and optionally may adjust the SP register to discard stacked parameters.

Intra-segment direct calls and jumps specify a self-relative direct replacement, thus allowing **position independent code**. A short jump instruction (optional use) transfers −128 to +127 bytes from the current instruction for code compaction.

Conditional Jumps

The conditional transfers of control perform a jump continuing upon various Boolean functions of the flag registers. The destination must be within −128 to +127 bytes from the instruction.

Iteration Control

The iteration control transfer operations perform leading- and trailing-decision loop control. The destination of iteration control transfers must be within −128 to +127 bytes from the instruction. These operations are particularly useful with string manipulation operations.

There are four iteration control transfer operations provided:

LOOP decrements the CX ("count") register by one and transfers if CX is not zero.

LOOPZ (also called LOOPE) decrements the CX register by one and transfers if CX is not zero and the ZF flag is set (loop while zero or loop while equal).

LOOPNZ (also called LOOPNE) decrements the CX register by one and transfers if CX is not zero and the ZF flag is cleared (loop while not zero or loop while not equal).

JCXZ transfers if the CX register is zero.

Interrupts

Program execution control may be transferred by means of operations similar in effect to that of external interrupts. All interrupts transfer by pushing the flag registers onto the stack (as in PUSHF), and perform an indirect call (of the inter-segment variety) through an interrupt vector table located at absolute locations 0 through 3FFH. This vector contains a four-byte element for each of up to 256 different interrupt types.

There are three interrupt transfer operations provided:

INT pushes the flag registers (as in PUSHF), clears the TF and IF flags, and transfers control with an indirect call through any one of the 256 vector elements. A one-byte form of this instruction is available for interrupt type 3.

INTO pushes the flag registers (as in PUSHF), clears the TF and IF flags, and transfers control with an indirect call through vector element 4 if the OF flag is set (trap on overflow). If the OF flag is cleared no operation takes place.

IRET transfers control to the return address saved by a previous interrupt operation and restores the saved flag register (as in POPF).

See Chapter 3 for further details on interrupt operations.

PROCESSOR CONTROL INSTRUCTIONS

Various instructions and mechanisms control the processor and its interaction with its environment.

Flag Operations

Seven operations provided operate directly on individual flag registers:

CLC clears the CF flag.

CMC complements the CF flag.

STC sets the CF flag.

CLD clears the DF flag, causing the string operations to auto-increment the operand pointer.

CLI clears the IF flag, disabling external interrupts (except for the non-maskable external interrupt.

STI sets the IF flag, enabling external interrupts after the execution of the next instruction.

Processor Halt

The **HLT** instruction causes the 8088 processor halt. The halt state is cleared by RESET, or an enabled external interrupt, or NMI.

Processor Wait

The **WAIT** instruction causes the processor to enter a wait state if the signal on its TEST pin is not asserted. The wait state may be interrupted by an enabled external interrupt. When this occurs the saved code location is that of the WAIT instruction, so that upon return from the interrupting task the wait state is reentered. The wait state is asserted. Execution resumes without allowing external interrupts until after the execution of the next instruction. This instruction allows the processor to synchronize itself with external hardware.

Processor Escape

The **ESC** instruction provides a mechanism by which other processors (such as the Numeric Processor Extension) may receive their instructions from the 8088 instruction stream and make use of the 8088 addressing modes. The 8088 processor does no operation for the ESC instruction other than to access a memory operand.

Bus Lock

A special one-byte lock prefix may precede any instruction to cause the processor to assert its bus-lock signal for the duration of the operation caused by that instruction. This has use in multiprocessing applications.

Single Step

When the TF flag register is set, the processor generates a type 1 interrupt after execution of each instruction. During interrupt transfer sequences caused by any type of interrupt, the TF flag is cleared after the pushflags step of the interrupt sequence. No instructions are provided for setting or clearing TF directly. Rather, the flag register image saved on the stack by a previous interrupt operation must be modified, so the subsequent interrupt return operation (IRET) restores TF set. This allows a diagnostic task to single-step through a task under test, while still executing normally itself.

If the single-stepped instruction itself clears the TF flag, the type 1 interrupt will still occur upon completion of the single-stepped instruction. If the single-stepped instruction generates an interrupt or if an enabled external interrupt occurs prior to the completion of the single-stepped instruction, the type 1 interrupt sequence will occur after the interrupt sequence of the generated or external interrupt, but before the first instruction of the interrupt service routine is executed.

INSTRUCTION TIMINGS

Instruction timings are included with the detailed instruction set pages at the back of this chapter. They are provided as the number of clock periods required to execute a particular form (register-to-register, immediate-to-memory, etc.) of the instruction. If a system is running with a 5 MHz maximum clock, the maximum clock period is 200 ns. Where memory operands are used, "+EA" denotes a variable number of additional clock periods needed to calculate the operand's effective address. Fig. 2-10 lists all effective address calculation times.

For control transfer instructions, the timings given include any additional clocks required to reinitialize the instruction queue as well as the time required to fetch the target instruction.

Note that four clocks are required for each memory reference. Therefore, the execution time of memory reference instructions will depend on the number of byte transfers.

Several additional factors can increase actual execution time over the figures shown in the instruction set reference pages. The time provided assumes that the instruction has already

EA COMPONENTS		CLOCKS*
Displacement Only		6
Base or Index Only (BX,BP,SI,DI)		5
Displacement + Base or Index	(BX,BP,SI,DI)	9
Base + Index	BP + DI, BX + SI	7
	BP + SI, BX + DI	8
Displacement + Base + Index	BP + DI + DISP BX + SI + DISP	11
	BP + SI + DISP BX + DI + DISP	12

*Add 2 clocks for segment override

Figure 2-10. Effective Address Calculation Time

been prefetched and that it is waiting in the instruction queue, an assumption that is valid under most, but not all operating conditions. A series of fast executing (fewer than two clocks per opcode byte) instructions can drain the queue and increase execution time.

Execution time also is slightly impacted by the interaction of the CPU's internal instruction execution unit (EU) and BU's interface unit (BIU) when memory operands must be read or written. If the EU needs access to memory, it may have to wait for up to one clock if the BIU has already started an instruction fetch bus cycle. The EU can detect the need for a memory operand and post a bus request far enough in advance of its need for this operand to avoid waiting a full 4-clock bus cycle. Of course, the EU does not have to wait if the instruction queue between the BIU and EU is full, because the BIU is idle. (Note: 8088 queue contains 4 bytes.)

With typical instruction mixes, the time actually required to execute a sequence of instructions will typically be within 5-10% of the sum of the individual timings given in the instruction set sequence. Cases can be constructed, however, in which execution time may be much higher than the sum of the figures provided. The execution time for a given sequence of instructions, however, is always repeatable, assuming comparable external conditions (interrupts, coprocessor activity, etc.) If the execution time for a given series of instructions must be determined exactly, the instructions should be run on an actual system hardware implementation.

ASSEMBLY LANGUAGE PROGRAMMING[1]

This section, while not meant to be a compendium of all features and rules of ASM-86 (the Intel assembler for 8088 instructions) covered in detail by the Intel iAPX 86,88 Assembly Language Reference Manual, presents most of the ASM-86 features in a form

[1] Edited and reprinted with permission of Hayden Book Co. from *The 8086 Primer*, by Stephen P. Morse. Copyright 1980.

to enable you to write meaningful programs. Not covered are many advanced ASM-86 features; attention is focused on underlying concepts of the language.

Object Code

Let's first consider a simple program that reads in word values from input port 5, increments each value read, and writes the results to output port 2. The program is as follows:

Memory Address (Hexadecimal)	Memory Contents (Binary)	Comments
00000	11100101	read word into AX...
00001	00000101	...from input port 5
00002	01000000	increment AX
00003	11100111	write word from AX...
00004	00000010	...to output port 2
00005	11101011	repeat by jumping...
00006	11111001	...back seven bytes
00007	...	

The first two columns specify the address and contents of each relevant memory location and, as such, constitute the only form of the program comprehensible to the processor. This is called *object code*, and the language of 1's and 0's in which the object code is written is called *machine language*. Once we have the program in object code form, we can store it in memory and then have the 8088 execute it.

Source Code

Writing a program in 1's and 0's is tedious and repetitive, a task that computers do well. So, instead of writing the program in machine language, we write the program in a language more familiar to us and then use a computer to translate it into the 8088's language. A program written in this more familiar language is called *source code*, and the computer program that translates source code into object code is called a *translator*. (Fig. 2-11)

There are two kinds of translator languages for writing source code: *assembly languages* and *high-level languages* described below and illustrated in Fig. 2-12

The process of translation might involve performing some additional activities before the output is truly machine code. These activities, like *relocation* and *linkage,* are part of the translation process. Throughout this text, references to translation (assembling, compiling) imply all necessary activities to produce object code.

A program written in assembly language is a symbolic representation of the machine-language program.

The relation between the assembly-language program statements and the resulting object code is usually obvious while the relation between high-level language statements and the resulting object code is often not obvious. Assembly language gives you complete control over the resulting object code and thereby allows you to generate very efficient object code (providing you're a very efficient programmer).

A high-level language compiler frees you from thinking about the object code and lets

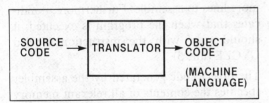

Figure 2-11. Translation Process

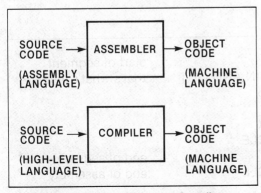

Figure 2-12. Assemblers and Compilers

you concentrate on the task you are programming. The compiler may generate less efficient object code, but good compilers can sometimes generate more efficient object code than you could have written in assembly language.

SYMBOLIC NAMES

The primary advantage of using assembly language instead of machine language is the ability to use symbolic names. Let's illustrate this point using assembly-language source code:

```
CYCLE:
IN      AX,5      ;read word from port 5 into AX
INC     AX        ;increment AX
OUT     2,AX      ;write result to port 2
JMP     CYCLE     ;keep repeating
```

The above program is simpler to read and understand because it uses symbolic names instead of numbers as much as possible. The opcodes of the four instructions are 1110010-, 01000---, 1110011-, and 11101011 in the object code. They are IN, INC, OUT, and JMP in the assembly-language source code. Symbolic names for opcodes are called *instruction mnemonics*. The symbolic opcode names used throughout this book are the instruction mnemonics of ASM-86 that generate corresponding bit patterns for object code.

Register Names

Besides the opcode fields, there are other fields in the object code (see above example). The contents of these fields must be specified in the assembly-language source code, so the assembler can generate the appropriate bit patterns in the object code.

For example, the INC instruction has a 3-bit *reg* field, indicating which register is to be incremented when the instruction is executed. The contents of this *reg* field are specified in the source code by indicating the symbolic name of the register, as in "INC AX."

The symbolic register names used in ASM-86 are the names that are used for the registers throughout this book —

AX	BL	CH	DI
BX	CL	DH	CS
CX	DL	BP	DS
DX	AH	SP	ES
AL	BH	SI	SS

Input/Output

Both the IN and OUT instructions have a 1-bit w field and an 8-bit port number field. The port numbers are simply specified in the source code by "IN AX,5" and "OUT 2,AX". The w field is specified more subtly by the presence of the AX in "IN AX,5" and "OUT 2,AX". Input/output always uses AX when words are involved and AL when bytes are involved. So the appearance of AX instead of AL in the IN and OUT instructions indicates that the w field is a 1. (The AMS-86 convention is to place the destination before the source; hence AX precedes port number on the IN instruction and follows it on the OUT instruction).

Jump Cycle

Another example of a symbolic name in the above program is the label CYCLE on the IN instruction. This permits the JMP instruction to refer to the location of the IN instruction by name as in "JUMP CYCLE." The assembler now has enough information to

determine that this is a jump backwards of seven bytes and can generate a -7 in the appropriate field of the JMP instruction.

A Complete Program

In the previous section, we used a fragment of an ASM-86 program. To make that fragment into a complete program, we need some additional statements (see below).

This entire program will reside in a single segment in the 8088 memory. During the assembly process, we don't know (nor do we care) where that segment will be located; that decision will be made prior to loading the segment into memory.

During the assembly process, we refer to the starting address of the segment by the symbolic name IN_AND_OUT. Lines 1 and 7 delimit the extent of the segment; line 1 introduces the segment name IN_AND_OUT, and line 7 marks the *end* of the segment (ENDS).

Line 8 flags the end of the source program, thereby telling the assembler that there are no more lines to assemble. Furthermore, it indicates that when the program is executed, it should start with the instruction labeled CYCLE (line 3).

The object code generated by the assembler specifies the contents of all relevant memory locations plus this starting address.

```
1.  IN_AND_OUT    SEGMENT                       ;start of segment
2.                ASSUME     CS: IN_AND_OUT     ;that's what's in CS
3.  CYCLE:        IN         AX,5
4.                INC        AX
5.                OUT        2,AX
6.                JMP        CYCLE
7.  IN_AND_OUT    ENDS                          ;end of segment
8.                END        CYCLE              ;end of assembly
```

The ASSUME statement on line 2 complies with the following rule:

at the very beginning of any segment containing code, we must tell the assembler what to assume is in the CS register when that code is executed. This will always be the starting address, without the last four "0" bits of the segment, so we must include the statement:

ASSUME   CS: Name_of_segment

ASM-86 Program Structure

Now consider a more detailed ASM-86 program (shown below) to understand the structure of such programs in general. This program will be referred to as the "sample program" throughout this chapter.

Line 1 introduces a segment somewhere in the 8088 memory (we don't care where) and gives it the name MY_DATA.

Line 3 ends the segment. The only thing in

the segment is SUM, defined to be a byte (DB) of data.

The question mark on line 2 indicates that the generated object code needs to reserve a place in memory for SUM, but it need not specify any particular initial contents for that location. MY_DATA is apparently going to be used as a data segment.

Lines 4-18 define another segment with the name MY_CODE. An examination of lines 7 to 17 reveals that the segment contains instructions for use as a code segment.

Line 19 flags the end of the source program and indicates that when the program is executed, execution should start with the instruction labeled GO (line 7).

Assumption About DS
The ASSUME statement on line 5 tells the assembler what it should assume will be in the CS and DS register when the segment of code is executed.

1.	MY_DATA	SEGMENT		;data segment
2.	SUM	DB	?	;reserve a byte for SUM
3.	MY_DATA	ENDS		
4.	MY_CODE	SEGMENT		;code segment
5.		ASSUME	CS:MY_CODE, DS:MY_DATA	
				;contents of CS and DS
6.	PORT_VAL	EQU	3	;symbolic name for port number
7.	GO:	MOV	AX,MY_DATA	;initialize DS to MY_DATA
8.		MOV	DS,AX	
9.		MOV	SUM,0	;clear sum
10.	CYCLE:	CMP	SUM,100	;if SUM exceeds 100
11.		JNA	NOT_DONE	
12.		MOV	AL,SUM	;...then output SUM to port 3
13.		OUT	PORT_VAL,AL	
14.		HLT		;...and stop execution
15.	NOT_DONE:	IN	AL,PORT_VAL	;otherwise add next input
16.		ADD	SUM,AL	
17.		JMP	CYCLE	;and repeat the test
18.	MY_CODE	ENDS		
19.		END	GO	;this is the end of the assembly

The need for an assumption about DS is that some assembly-language instructions in the code segment access data directly, particularly, the byte SUM. The assembler must generate machine-language instructions that address SUM using the direct addressing mode. These generated instructions specify the offset of SUM and some segment register, typically DS, containing the starting address of the segment (namely MY_DATA) containing SUM.

The assembler needs to know which segment registers (if any) will contain MY_DATA's starting address, at the time these instructions are executed. With this information, the assembler can determine if a segment-overriding prefix is required on these instructions, and if so, which segment register should be specified by the prefix. It would be the case if, for example, MY_DATA's starting address were contained only in ES. Furthermore, if none of the registers will contain MY_DATA's starting address at instruction-execution time, the assembler knows that it cannot generate any instructions capable of accessing SUM and will be able to report this error at instruction-assembly time.

SUMMARY

So, why assume some segment register would contain MY_DATA's starting address at instruction-execution time? So that SUM can be accessed. Why is DS used? Because no segment-overriding prefix is necessary. Make sure this assumption is satisfied by executing certain instructions (lines 7 and 8) prior to the first access to SUM.

PORTS 3 AND 4

Line 6 specifies that PORT_VAL is equivalent to the constant 3. This permits PORT_VAL to be used in place of 3 on succeeding lines. This makes PORT_VAL a symbolic name for port 3 and refers to PORT_VAL whenever port 3 is wanted. Now if we decide

to rewrite the program to use port 4 instead, we need make only one change: line 6 is changed to:

PORT_VAL EQU 4

The instructions on lines 7 through 17 will keep adding inputs from port 3 until the sum exceeds 100, output that sum to port 3, then halt. This is accomplished as follows: The instruction on line 7 puts — the 16 most-significant bits of — the starting address of segment MY_DATA into register AX; on line 8 this value is moved from AX to DS. This makes SUM accessible in succeeding instructions.

The instruction on line 9 initializes SUM to 0. Observe that on lines 7, 8, and 9, the destinations, such as SUM on line 9, are *always written before the sources,* as 0 on line 9.

Line 10 compares (CMP) the value in SUM to 100 and sets processor flags, indicating comparison results.

Line 11 tests the flags and jumps, if SUM was not above 100 (JNA). The target of the jump is the instruction labeled NOT_DONE (line 15). If the jump on line 11 is *not* taken (SUM > 100), the SUM is moved into AL (line 12); the contents of AL is sent to output port 3 (line 13), and the processor halts (line 14).

If the jump on line 11 *is* taken (SUM < 100), the value on input port 3 is sent to AL (line 15), added to SUM (line 16), and the jump on line 17 transfers control back to line 10.

General Conclusions

Now, from the above example, what can be noticed about the structure of an ASM-86 program? It consists of one or more segment blocks followed by an END statement. Each segment block starts with a SEGMENT statement and ends with an ENDS (end-of-segment) statement. Between the SEGMENT and ENDS statements is a sequence of other statements. Each statement normally occupies one line. If succeeding lines are needed, they start with "&". The structure of an ASM-86 program is:

```
NAME1       SEGMENT
            statement
               .
               .
            statement
NAME1       ENDS
NAME2       SEGMENT
            statement
               .
               .
            statement
NAME2       ENDS
               .
               .
               .
            END
```

The programs presented here all display a consistent tabular pattern.

Such tabulation is not part of the program structure; it is optional to the assembler, but highly recommended to make programs easier to read and understand.

In the untabulated version of the IN_AND_

OUT program below, the assembler would assemble faster, but the program would be much less-comprehensible to us.

Tokens

Before examining the kinds of statements from which ASM-86 programs are built, we must become familiar with the building blocks of statements. Statements are composed of such things as *identifiers, reserved words, delimiters, constants,* and *comments.* These building blocks, sometimes called *tokens,* are described below.

IDENTIFIERS

Identifiers are names that you, the programmer, are free to make up. Identifiers in the sample program are SUM, CYCLE, and PORT_VAL. An identifier is a sequence of letters, numbers, and underscore characters (_), but may not start with a number. An identifier may be up to 31 characters long, which means the length is practically unlimited. Examples of identifiers are:

```
X
GAMMA
JACK5
THIS_NODE
THISNODE
```

The last two examples are indeed different identifiers.

```
IN_AND_OUT SEGMENT          ;start of segment
ASSUME CS:IN_AND_OUT        ;that's what's in CS
CYCLE:IN AX,5
INC AX
OUT2,AX
JUMP CYCLE
IN_AND_OUT ENDS             ;end of segment
END CYCLE                   ;end of assembly
```

RESERVED WORDS

Reserved words, look like identifiers, but they have a special meaning in the language, and you must not use them as identifier names (Fig. 2-14). The sample program uses reserved words like SEGMENT, MOV, EQU, and AL. Thus, it would be perfectly acceptable for us to make up a name like EQUAL as in:

        EQUAL   DB   ?

but it would be improper for us to write:

        EQU   DB   ?

Refer to pg. 2-43, Fig. 2-14 for complete list of ASM-86 Reserved Words.

DELIMITERS

Delimiters are non-alphanumeric characters that have special meaning in the 8088 assembly language. In the sample program, we saw such delimiters as : and ;. In this chapter we will use many of the delimiters. For a complete list of delimiters in ASM-86, see Fig. 2-13.

CONSTANTS

Constants are fixed values appearing in ASM-86 programs. In the sample program there are constants 0, 3, and 100. These are whole-number constants. The assembly language also allows for string constants.

A whole-number constant is any non-fractional number between 0 and 65535 (2^{16} — 1). It is normally written as a decimal number, but can also be written in binary, ending with a B, octal, ending with a Q, or hexadecimal, ending with an H.

To avoid confusion with identifiers, a hexadecimal constant must start with a numeric digit; a leading zero would suffice. Examples of whole-number constants are 15, 1010B, 27Q, 3A0H, and 0BFA3H.

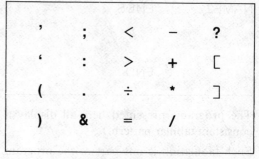

Figure 2-13. Delimiters in ASM-86

String Constant

A string constant is one or two characters enclosed with apostrophes. Strings of more than two characters are permitted in restricted cases, but are not discussed here. An apostrophe itself may be included in a string constant by writing it as two consecutive apostrophes. Examples of string constants are 'A', 'AB', and ''''. The last example is the string consisting of the apostrophe character.

The value of a string constant is the ASCII code of the character(s) in the string. For example, the value of 'A' is 41H and the value of 'AB' is 4142H. Thus, string constants and whole-number constants can be used interchangeably.

COMMENTS

Any sequence of characters following a semicolon (;) up to the end of the line are comments. They are ignored by the assembler and should be used generously in your program to document what you are doing. While comments like

```
INC     CX          ;increment CX
```

convey little information, comments like

```
INC     CX          ;increment outer
                     loop counter
```

make a program more readable.

Expressions

One more building block, namely expressions, must be introduced before we can build statements. Expressions are built up from some of the tokens just described.

Loosely speaking, an expression is a sequence of operands and operators combined to produce a value at program assembly time. How are operands and operators combined to produce the value of an expression?

OPERANDS

An operand is something that has either a *numeric* value or a *memory address* value.

Operands with numeric values are constants, or identifiers that represent constants. Some numeric-valued operands, appearing in our sample program are 100 and PORT_VAL. The permissible range of values for such operands is from -65,535 to +65,535.

Note that the value of an operand may be negative, but a *constant is never negative*. A minus sign can be written in front of a constant, but is never considered a part of the constant; it is an arithmetic operator.

Memory-address operands are frequently identifiers, such as SUM and CYCLE in the sample program. The value of a memory address is not simply a number; it is a set of components, each component generally being a number. One component is the 16 most-significant bits of the segment starting address where the memory address is contained. The four least-significant bits of a segment starting address are always zeros.

Another component is the offset address within the segment. These two components are referred to as the *segment* and *offset* of the memory-address operand.

Another operand is an expression itself, enclosed in parentheses, and used in some bigger expression, as in 3*(PORT_VAL+5).

OPERATORS

An operator takes the value of one or more operands and produces a new value. There are five kinds of operators in ASM-86

1) arithmetic operators
2) logical operators
3) relational operators
4) analytic operators
5) synthetic operators

Arithmetic Operators

Arithmetic operators are the familiar addition operator (+), subtraction operator (—), multiplication operator (*), and division operator (/). Another arithmetic operator, MOD, produces the remainder after doing a division. Thus 19/7 is 2, whereas 19 MOD 7 is 5.

Arithmetic operators may always be applied to a pair of numeric operands, and the result will be numeric. The rules for applying arithmetic operators on memory-addressing operands are more restrictive: such operations are valid *only if the result has a meaningful physical interpretation.*

For example, the product of two memory addresses has no meaningful interpretation. What segment would it be in? What offset would it have? Hence, it is a prohibited operation.

The difference of two memory addresses in the same segment is the numeric distance between them — the difference in their offsets.

The only other meaningful arithmetic operation on a memory address is adding or subtracting a numeric value. Thus SUM+2, CYCLE-5, and NOT_DONE-GO would all be valid expressions in the sample program. SUM −CYCLE would not be a valid expression because they are in different segments.

NOTE: The value of SUM+2 is a memory address two bytes beyond SUM in the MY _DATA segment; it is *not* the numeric value that is 2 plus-the-contents-of-location-SUM. Such contents are not known until program execution, whereas *expressions are evaluated at assembly time.*

Logical Operators
The logical operators are bit-by-bit AND, OR, XOR (exclusive-or), and NOT.

The operands of logical operators must be numeric only — memory-address operands are *not* allowed — and the result will be numeric. This is shown by:

```
1010101010101010B AND 1100110011001100B
    is 1000100010001000B;
1100110011001100B OR 1110000111110000B
    is 1111110011111100B
NOT 1111111111111111B is 0000000000000000B
    and
1111000111110000B XOR SUM is invalid.
```

As an example of logical operators, consider:

```
IN     AL,PORT_VAL
OUT    PORT_VAL AND 0FEH,AL
```

The IN instruction gets input from PORT _VAL, wherever that is.

Execution of the OUT instruction sends output to port PORT_VAL AND 0FEH, which is either the same port, if PORT_VAL is even, or the next lower-numbered port, if PORT _VAL is odd. The actual port value of the OUT instruction is determined when the instruction is assembled, not when it is executed.

Observe that AND, OR, XOR, and NOT are instruction mnemonics as well as ASM-86 operators. As ASM-86 operators, they cause a value to be computed when the program is being assembled. As instruction mnemonics, they perform their roles when the program is being executed:

```
AND    DX,PORT_VAL AND 0FEH
```

will cause the assembler to compute the value of PORT_VAL AND 0FEH and then generate an AND-immediate instruction containing that value in its data field. When this instruction is later executed, it will cause the contents of the DX register to be ANDed with that value and the result placed in the DX register.

Relational Operators
1) Equal (EQ)
2) not-equal (NE)
3) less-than (LT)
4) greater-than (GT)
5) less-than-or-equal (LE)
6) greater-than-or-equal (GE)

PORT_VAL LT 5 is a relational operator. The two operands must both be numeric or must both be memory addresses in the same segment. The result is always a numeric value. It will be 0 if the relationship is false, and 0FFFFH (16 bits of 1's) if the relationship is true.

Using a relational operator:

MOV   BX,PORT_VAL LT 5

The assembler will assemble

MOV   BX,0FFFFH

if the value of PORT_VAL is < 5;

otherwise the assembler will assemble

MOV   BX,0

At first it may appear that relational operators are not useful. It's not often that you want to generate an instruction with a field that contains either 0 or 0FFFFH, and no other choices. However, by combining relational operators with logical operators, the two relational results of 0 and 0FFFFH can be molded into any numeric values you desire:

MOV   BX,((PORT_VAL LT 5)AND 20)
& OR ((PORT_VAL GE5) AND 30)

---

will assemble

MOV   BX,20

if PORT_VAL is less than 5, and

MOV   BX,30

otherwise.

Note the generous use of parentheses to force the order that operators are applied. If you always use parentheses to make the ordering explicit, you won't have to memorize the rules about which operators get evaluated first.

Analytic and Synthetic Operators

The analytic operators decompose memory-address operands into their components, while synthetic operators build memory-address operands from their components. A discussion of these operators is presented after we learn more about memory-address operands. (see page 2-30)

Statements

There are two kinds of ASM-86 program statements: instruction statements (MOV, ADD, JMP, etc.) and *directive statements* (DB, SEGMENT, EQU, etc.)

Each instruction statement causes the assembler to generate an instruction in the object code. Directive statements tell the assembler what kind of code to generate for succeeding instruction statements. The directive statement

MY_PLACE   DB   ?

tells the assembler that MY_ PLACE is defined as a byte. The assembler allocates a memory address for MY_PLACE. Later, when the assembler encounters the instruction statement

INC   MY_PLACE

it will generate an object code instruction to increment the contents of MY_ PLACE. Because of the previously-encountered directive statement, the assembler will know to place a '0' (to indicate a byte) in the **w** field of the increment instruction.

The formats of the two kinds of statement are similar. The instruction statements are of the form

label: mnemonic argument,...,argument ;comment

The directive statements are of the form

name directive argument,...,argument ;comment

The label in an instruction statement is followed by a colon, whereas the name in a directive statement is not. This highlights the difference between the two kinds of statements.

A label associates a symbolic name with the location of an instruction. A label can be used as an operand in a jump or call instruction.

The name in a directive statement has no relation to an instruction location and can *never* be jumped to.

Labels in instruction statements are always optional; names in directive statements can be mandatory, optional, or prohibited, depending on the particular directive.

Mnemonics in instruction statements specify the purpose of the statement. Directives, in directive statements, specify the purpose of the statement. The instruction mnemonics correspond to the set of approximately 100 opcodes available in the 8088. The directives correspond to the set of some 20 *functions* provided by the ASM-86 assembler (Fig. 2-14).

The mnemonic or directive may require additional information to define its purpose completely. This information is provided by a sequence of arguments.

Optional comments make the program more readable; when present they must be preceded by a semicolon.

Directive Statements

The various directive statements in ASM-86 are:

1) symbol-definition
2) data-definition
3) segmentation-definition
4) procedure-definition
5) termination

Symbol-Definition Statements

The EQU statement provides a means for defining symbolic names to represent values or other symbolic names. The two forms of the EQU statement are illustrated:

| name | EQU | expression |
| new name | EQU | old_name |

Some examples are:

BOILING_POINT	EQU	212
BUFFER_SIZE	EQU	32
NEW_PORT	EQU	PORT_VAL+1
COUNT	EQU	CS

The last example differs from the other three in that COUNT does not represent a value; it is a synonym for the CX register.

A symbolic name can be "undefined" by a PURGE statement so it may later represent something entirely different:

PURGE   BUFFER_SIZE

Data-Definition Statements

Data-definition allocates memory for a data item, associates a symbolic name with that memory address, and optionally supplies an initial value for the data. Symbolic names associated with data items are called variables. Examples of data-definition statements are: (see below)

In the example below, THING is a symbolic name associated with a byte in memory, BIGGER_THING with two consecutive bytes in memory, and BIGGEST_THING with four consecutive bytes in memory.

Initial Values

Before we can discuss the question marks (?), we need to introduce the concept of initial values of data items.

The object code produced by the assembler contains the 1's and 0's that make up each instruction and the memory address at which each instruction should reside. After the object code is produced, the instructions are

THING	DB	?	;defines a byte
BIGGER_THING	DW	?	;defines a word (2 bytes)
BIGGEST_THING	DD	?	;defines a doubleword (4 bytes)

loaded into memory at the indicated addresses and then executed.

At the time the instructions are loaded, initial values for data items could also be loaded into memory. This means that the object code, besides containing instructions and their addresses, may also contain initial values for data items and their addresses. These initial values are specified to the assembler in the data definition statements.

The following statement will cause the assembler to produce object code that, when loaded into memory, will result in a 25 being placed in the memory address allocated to THING;

THING DB 25 :byte initially contains 25

A question mark in place of an initial value means that we do not choose to specify an initial value for that data item; we will be satisfied with whatever initially appears in the corresponding memory location.

When the assembler sees the question mark, it still allocates memory for the data item, but does not produce object code to initialize the memory location (although it could).

In general, the initial value could be specified by an expression, since expressions are evaluated at assembly time. So we can write statements like:

```
IN_PORT     DB     PORT_VAL
OUT_PORT    DB     PORT_VAL+1
```

Recall that expressions come in two varieties — numeric and memory address. It is meaningful to initialize either a byte, or a word, or a double-word with a numeric value. But,

what about a memory-address value? It won't fit into a byte, but the offset component fits into a word; and, both the segment and address components fit into a double word. So we can write initialization statements like those shown at the bottom of this page.

The initialization of LITTLE_CYCLE permits an indirect intrasegment jump or call to use the date item named LITTLE_CYCLE to transfer control to the label named CYCLE.

Similarly, an intersegment jump or call transfers control to CYCLE by using the data item named BIG_CYCLE.

Tables

So far we have used data-definition statements to define one byte, word, or double-word at a time. Often, we deal with tables of bytes, words, or double words. For example, the 8088 XLAT instruction uses a table of bytes to translate an encoded value into the same value under a different encoding. The 8088 interrupt mechanism uses a table of double-words, starting at memory location 0 to point to the starting addresses of the interrupt service routines. And, the 8088 string instructions operate on tables of bytes or words containing the string elements.

A table is defined by placing several initial values on a data-definition statement. The following statement defines a table of bytes containing powers of 2:

```
POWERS_2    DB     1,2,4,8,16
```

The byte at the memory address corresponding to POWERS_2 will be initialized to 1 (when the object code is loaded into memory).

```
LITTLE_CYCLE        DW   CYCLE      ;offset of CYCLE
BIG_CYCLE           DD   CYCLE      ;offset and segment of CYCLE
   .
   .
   .
CYCLE                    MOV BX,AX
```

The next four bytes will be initialized to 2,4,8, and 16, respectively. A table of bytes, all initialized to zero, can be defined by

```
ALL_ZERO    DB    0,0,0,0,0,0
```

or by the shorthand notation

```
ALL_ZERO    DB    6 DUP (0)
```

And, finally, an un-initialized table can be defined by either of the following equivalent statements:

```
DONT_CARE   DB    ?,?,?,?,?,?,?,?
DONT_CARE   DB    8 DUP (?)
```

TYPES OF MEMORY LOCATIONS

ASM-86 associates a *type* with every memory location referred to in the program so it can generate the correct code for instructions that accesses memory. For example, the data-definition statement

```
SUM    DB    ?
```

informs the assembler that the memory location SUM is of type BYTE. Later, when the assembler encounters an instruction statement such as

```
INC    SUM
```

the assembler will know to generate a byte-increment instruction, rather than a word-increment instruction.

A memory location can be one of the following types:

1) **BYTE** of data, as in:

```
SUM   DB   ?   ;defining a byte
```

2) **WORD** of data (two consecutive bytes), as in:

```
BIGGER_SUM   DW   ?   ;defining a word
```

3) **DWORD** of data (four consecutive bytes), as in:

```
BIGGEST_SUM   DD   ?   ;defining a doubleword
```

4) **NEAR** instruction location, as in:

```
CYCLE:   CMP   SUM,100
```

5) **FAR** instruction location:

(means of defining such locations will be discussed shortly)

An instruction location can appear in a jump or call instruction statement. The assembler will generate an intrasegment jump or call if the location type is NEAR, and an intersegment jump or call if it is FAR. For example, the labeled instruction statement

```
CYCLE:   CMP   SUM,100
```

informs the assembler that the memory location CYCLE is of type NEAR. (We will see shortly how the synthetic operators PTR and THIS are used to define a memory location of type FAR). Later, when the assembler encounters an instruction such as

```
JMP    CYCLE
```

the assembler will know to generate an intrasegment jump instruction, rather than an intersegment jump instruction.

A memory address built by adding or subtracting a numeric value *to* or *from* some other memory address has the same type as the original memory address. For example, SUM+2 is a BYTE, BIGGER_SUM-3 is a WORD, and CYCLE+1 is a NEAR instruction location.

ANALYTIC AND SYNTHETIC OPERATORS

We now know enough about memory addresses to complete the discussion of operators.

The analytic operators decompose memory-address operands into their components. These operators are:

1) SEG
2) OFFSET
3) TYPE
4) SIZE
5) LENGTH

The SEG operator returns the segment component of the memory-address operand. The OFFSET operator returns the offset component. Both of these components are generally numeric values.

The TYPE operator returns a numeric value, which is the type component of the memory-address operand. The value of the type component for the various memory-address operands is:

Memory Address Operand	Type Component
BYTE of data	1
WORD of data	2
DWORD of data	4
NEAR instruction location	-1
FAR instruction location	-2

Notice that the type component for bytes, words, and double words corresponds to the number of bytes that each occupies. The value of the type component for instruction locations does not have a physical interpretation.

The LENGTH and SIZE operators apply only to data-memory-address operands (BYTE, WORD, or DWORD).

The LENGTH operator returns a numeric value for the number of units (bytes, words, or double words) associated with the memory-address operand.

The SIZE operator returns a numeric value for the number of bytes allocated for the memory-address operand. For example, if MULTI_WORDS is defined by

MULTI_WORDS   DW   50 DUP (0)

then LENGTH MULTI_WORDS is 50 and SIZE MULTI_WORDS is 100. Notice that SIZE X is equal to (LENGTH X)* (TYPE X).

PTR and THIS

The synthetic operators build memory-address operands from their components. These operators are PTR and THIS.

The PTR operator builds a memory-address operand that has the same segment and offset of some other memory-address operand, but has a different type. Unlike a data-definition statement, the PTR operator does not allocate memory; it merely gives another meaning to previously-allocated memory. For example, if TWO_BYTE were defined by,

TWO_BYTE   DW   ?

then we could name first the byte in the word as follows:

ONE_BYTE   EQU   BYTE PTR TWO_BYTE

In this example, the PTR operator creates a new memory-address operand having the same segment and offset components as TWO_BYTE, but having a type component of BYTE. We can name the second byte of TWO_BYTE either as

OTHER_BYTE   EQU   BYTE PTR   (TWO_BYTE+1)

or more simply as

OTHER_BYTE   EQU   ONE_BYTE+1

The PTR operator can also create words and double-words as illustrated below:

MANY_BYTES	DB	100 DUP (?)	;an array of 100 bytes
FIRST_WORD	EQU	WORD PTR MANY_BYTES	
SECOND_DOUBLE	EQU	DWORD PTR (MANY_BYTES +4)	

Further, the PTR operator can create locations of instructions:

INCHES:	CMP	SUM,100	;type of INCHES is NEAR
	JMP	INCHES	;intrasegment jump
MILES	EQU	FAR PTR INCHES	;type of MILES is FAR
	JMP	MILES	;intersegment jump

Notice that the above shows ways to build new memory-address operands from old ones by

1) using the PTR operator as in BYTE PTR TWO_BYTE
2) using expressions as in ONE_BYTE+1
3) using a combination of PTR and expressions as in BYTE PTR (TWO_BYTE+1)

Expressions are useful when we wish to change the offset component but leave the type component unchanged.

Neither expressions, nor PTR, changes the segment component. And the new memory-address operand, created by either expressions or PTR, will have a length component of 1 (providing it's not an instruction location).

The synthetic operator THIS, like PTR, builds a memory-address operand of a specified type, without allocating memory for it. The segment and offset component of the new memory-address operand is the segment and offset of the next memory location available for allocation. For example:

MY_BYTE	EQU	THIS BYTE
MY_WORD	DW	?

would create MY_BYTE with type component of BYTE, and with the same segment and offset components as MY_WORD. In this example, MY_BYTE could have been built with the PTR operator instead:

MY_BYTE EQU   BYTE PTR MY_WORD

The THIS operator is convenient for defining FAR instruction locations:

MILES	EQU	THIS FAR
	CMP	SUM,100
	.	
	.	
	JMP	MILES

Note that the use of the THIS operator in the example made it unnecessary to have a NEAR instruction location with the same segment and offset as MILES. If we used the PTR operator instead of the THIS operator, such a NEAR instruction would have been necessary.

Segmentation-Definition Statements
The segmentation-definition statements organize our program to use the 8088 memory segments. These directives are:

1) SEGMENT
2) ENDS
3) ASSUME
4) ORG

The SEGMENT and ENDS statement subdivide the assembly-language source program into segments. Such segments correspond to the memory segments where the resulting object code will eventually be loaded. The assembler is concerned with program segmentation for the following reasons.

First, intrasegment jump and call instructions require only the offset (16-bits) of the new location. Intersegment jump and call instructions require the segment (another 16-bits) in addition to the offset.

Second, data-accessing instructions that use the current data segment and current stack segment in the manner most optimal for the 8088 architecture contain only the offset (16-bits) of the data location. Any other instruction that accesses a data location within one of the four currently-addressable segments must contain a segment-overriding prefix (another 8-bits) in addition to the offset. Here, current refers to when the instruction is executed, not assembled.

Therefore, to assemble the correct object code, the assembler must know the segment structure of the program and which segments will be addressable — pointed at by segment registers — when various instructions are executed. This information is supplied by the ASSUME directive.

The following example shows how the SEGMENT, ENDS, and ASSUME directives can be used to define a code, data, extra, and stack segment:

```
MY_DATA     SEGMENT
X           DB          ?
Y           DW          ?
Z           DD          ?
MY_DATA     ENDS

MY_EXTRA    SEGMENT
ALPHA       DB          ?
BETA        DW          ?
GAMMA       DD          ?
MY_EXTRA    ENDS

MY_STACK    SEGMENT
            DW          100 DUP (?)             ;this is the stack
TOP         EQU         THIS WORD
MY_STACK    ENDS

MY_CODE     SEGMENT
            ASSUME      CS:MY_CODE,DS:MY_DATA
            ASSUME      ES:MY_EXTRA,SS:MY_STACK
START:      MOV         AX,MY_DATA              ;initializes DS
            MOV         DS,AX
            MOV         AX,MY_EXTRA             ;initializes ES
            MOV         ES,AX
            MOV         AX,MY_STACK             ;initializes SS
            MOV         SS,AX
            MOV         SP,OFFSET TOP           ;initializes SP
            .
            .
            .
MY_CODE     ENDS
            END         START
```

Observe that the code at the head of the MY_CODE segment will, at program execution, initialize the various segment registers to point to the appropriate segments, and the code will initialize the stack pointer to point to the end of the stack segment.

The ASSUME statement makes the assembler aware of segment register values when the code is executed.

To illustrate the purpose of the ASSUME statement, let's consider code (within SEGMENT MY_CODE) that moves the contents of byte X to byte ALPHA. To do this, we need an instruction that moves the contents of X into a register, say BL, and an instruction that moves the contents of the register into ALPHA. How about:

```
MOV    BL,X        ;from X to BL
MOV    ALPHA,BL    ;from BL to ALPHA
```

During execution of such MOV instructions, the 8088 processor would normally use the DS register to find the starting address of the segment where the specified item (X or ALPHA) is located. This will work fine when accessing X — the first instruction — because DS will indeed contain the starting address of segment MY_DATA where X is located.

But, this will not work when accessing ALPHA — the second instruction — because the starting address of segment MY_EXTRA, where ALPHA is located, will not be contained in DS.

The ASSUME statement has made the assembler aware that the first instruction will execute properly. The assembler is also aware (thanks to the ASSUME statement) that the starting address of MY_EXTRA, although not in DS, will be in one of the other segment registers — namely ES. The assembler, therefore, generates a segment-overriding prefix for the second instruction so that it too, will execute properly.

It's not always possible to know what will be in the segment registers when a particular instruction will be executed. Consider:

```
OLD_DATA    SEGMENT
OLD_BYTE    DB          ?
OLD_DATA    ENDS
NEW_DATA    SEGMENT
NEW_BYTE    DB          ?
NEW_DATA    ENDS
MORE_CODE   SEGMENT
            ASSUME      CS:MORE_CODE
            MOV         AX,OLD_DATA             ;put OLD_DATA into
            MOV         DS,AX                   ;...DS and
            MOV         ES,AX                   ;...ES
            ASSUME      DS:OLD_DATA,ES:OLD_DATA
            .
            .
CYCLE:      INC         OLD_BYTE                ;what's in DS now?
            .
            .
            MOV         AX,NEW_DATA             ;put NEW_DATA
            MOV         DS,AX                   ;...into DS
            JMP         CYCLE
            .
            .
MORE_CODE   ENDS
```

The first time the INC instruction is executed, DS will contain OLD_DATA and the indicated assumption on DS will be correct. But then DS will be changed to NEW _DATA, and the same INC instruction will be executed a second time. Therefore, it would be wrong for the assembler to make assumptions about the contents of DS when the INC instruction is executed. The assembler must generate a segment-override prefix — specifying the extra segment — on the INC instruction, even though this prefix would be unnecessary on the first execution of INC.

In order to tell the assembler not to make any assumptions about DS, we must place the following assumption just before the INC instruction:

```
          .
          .
          .
          ASSUME   DS:NOTHING
CYCLE:    INC      OLD_BYTE
          .
          .
          .
```

Prior to, or at the very beginning of any segment containing code, we must tell the assembler (via an ASSUME statement) what it should assume will be in the CS register when that segment of code is executed.

Instead of using an ASSUME statement, we could tell the assembler which segment register should be used for the execution of each instruction. For example, the move of X to ALPHA in the previous example could be written as:

```
MOV    BX, DS:X
MOV    ES:ALPHA,BX
```

This says that DS should be used when X is accessed, and ES should be used when ALPHA is accessed. Since the processor would normally use DS when executing these instructions, the assembler produces a segment-overriding prefix when generating object code for the second instruction, but not for the first instruction.

Efficient Programming

Now let's look at one of the shortcomings of memory segments to see how to get around it.

Memory segments *always* start on 16-byte boundaries. Remember that the last 4 bits of segment starting addresses are zero. A segment can be up to 2^{16} bytes long. If a segment does not use all of its approximately 65,000 bytes, some other segment can start just beyond the last byte used by the first segment. But the second segment must also start on a 16-byte boundary, and, therefore, may not start immediately after the last byte used by the first segment. This means there could be up to 15 bytes wasted between segments.

Suppose the first segment starts at address 10000 (hexadecimal) and uses only 6D (hexadecimal) bytes. So the last byte used is at address 1006C. The closest the second segment could start would be at address 10070, thereby wasting the bytes at 1006D, 1006E, and 1006F.

Now, instead of starting the second segment at the lowest 16-byte boundary beyond the last byte used by the first segment, start the second segment at the highest 16-byte boundary that does not cause any bytes to be wasted: thus, we could start the second segment at address 10060. This results in the last few bytes — 13 to be exact — used by the first segment to be also in the second segment.

But the second segment would then simply not use its first few bytes, which is efficient. So, if the second segment starts at 10060, the bytes in the second segment below offset 000D are simply not used by the second segment. Therefore, no bytes are wasted.

Ordinarily, it doesn't matter where in memory segments are located, so we let the translator make that choice. However, we might want to give the translator some constraints such as "don't overlap this segment with any other segment," "make sure the first byte used by this segment is at an even address" or "start this segment at the following address." We can write these constraints into the source program:

1) Don't overlap. First usable byte in segment is on a 16-byte boundary and has an offset of 0000.

```
MY_SEG   SEGMENT        ;this is the normal case
                .
                .
MY_SEG   ENDS
```

2) Overlap if you must, but first usable byte must be on a word boundary.

```
MY_SEG   SEGMENT  WORD      ;word aligned
                .
                .
MY_SEG   ENDS
```

3) Overlap if you must, and place first usable byte anywhere you like.

```
MY_SEG   SEGMENT  BYTE        ;byte aligned
                .
                .
MY_SEG   ENDS
```

4) Start segment at specified 16-byte boundary. First usable byte is at specified offset.

```
MY_SEG   SEGMENT   AT 1A2BH ;address 1A2B0
         ORG       0003H    ;address 1A2B3
                .
                .
MY_SEG   ENDS
```

The last example introduced another statement, ORG (for *origin*). It specifies the next offset to be used in the segment.

Procedure-Definition Statements

Procedures are sections of code that are called into execution from various places in the program. Each time a procedure is called upon, the instructions that make up the procedure are executed, then control is returned to the place from which the procedure was originally called.

The 8088 instructions to call and return from a procedure are CALL and RET. These instructions come in two flavors — intrasegment and intersegment.

The intersegment instructions push (CALL) and pop (RET) both the segment and the offset of the place where the procedure should return.

The intrasegment ones push and pop only the offset.

Near and Far

Procedures called with intrasegment CALLs must return with intrasegment RETurns. Such procedures are known as NEAR procedures. Similarly, procedures that are called with intersegment CALLs must return with intersegment RETurns and are known as FAR procedures.

The procedure-definition statements, PROC and ENDP (end procedure), delimit a procedure and indicate whether it is a NEAR or FAR procedure. This helps the assembler in two ways. First, when assembling CALLs to that procedure, the assembler will know which kind of CALL to assemble. Secondly, when assembling RETs from that procedure, the assembler will know which kind of RET to assemble: (see table on next page)

Since UP_COUNT is declared to be NEAR procedure, all CALLs to it are assembled as intrasegment CALLs, and all RETurns within it are assembled as intrasegment returns.

This example points out some similarities between the RET instructions and the HLT instruction. There may be more than one

```
MY_CODE    SEGMENT
UP_COUNT   PROC        NEAR
           ADD         CX,1
           RET
UP_COUNT   ENDP
START:     .
           .
           .
           CALL        UPCOUNT
           .
           .
           .
           CALL        UPCOUNT
           .
           .
           HLT
MY_CODE    ENDS
           END         START
```

RET in a procedure, just as there may be more than one HLT in a program.

The last instruction in a procedure (program) need not be a RET or (HLT); but, if it isn't, that instruction *should* be a jump back to somewhere within the procedure (program).

The ENDP (END) tells the assembler where the procedure (program) ends, but does not cause the assembler to generate a RET (HLT) instruction.

Termination Statements

With one exception, each terminating statement is paired up with some beginning statement. For example, SEGMENT and ENDS, PROC and ENDP. These terminating statements are described with their corresponding beginning statements.

The one exception is END, which flags the end of the source program. It tells the assembler that there are no more instructions to assemble. The form of the END statement is

END   expression

where the expression must yield a memory-address value. That address is the address of the first instruction to be executed when the program is executed.

The following example illustrates the use of the END statement:

START: .
           .
           .

```
           END         START
```

Instruction Statements

The instruction statements, for the most part, correspond to the instructions of the 8088 processor. Each instruction statement causes the assembler to generate one 8088 instruction. An 8088 instruction consists of an opcode field and fields specifying the operand-addressing mode (mod field, r/m field, reg. field).

So the instruction statements in ASM-86 must contain an instruction mnemonic as well as sufficient addressing information to permit the assembler to generate the instruction.

INSTRUCTION MNEMONICS

Most of the instruction mnemonics are the same as the symbolic opcode names for the 8088 instructions. Some additional instruction mnemonics, NIL and NOP, make the assembly language more versatile.

No-Operation

The instruction mnemonic NOP causes the assembler to generate the 1-byte instruction that exchanges the contents of the AX register with the contents of the AX register (hexadecimal opcode 90). Besides not doing anything, NOP doesn't waste any time not doing it, since it doesn't make any memory accesses. Does it seem strange to waste precious memory locations on instructions that do nothing? There are good reasons for doing so.

The NOPs might serve as placeholders for instructions to be filled in later, possibly when the program is executing — an old trick.

They might also be used to slow down a portion of the program where precise timing relationships are important.

Placeholder

NIL is the only instruction mnemonic that does not cause the assembler to generate any instructions. In contrast to NOP, which causes the assembler to generate an instruction that does nothing when executed, NIL doesn't even cause an instruction to be generated.

NIL serves as a convenient placeholder for labels in the assembly-language program:

```
CYCLE:      NIL
            INC     AX
```

Although this is equivalent to

```
CYCLE:      INC     AX
```

the NIL makes it much easier to insert instructions ahead of the INC instruction in the source program, if the need arises later.

INSTRUCTION PREFIXES

The 8088 instruction set permits instructions to start off with one or more prefix bytes. The three possible prefixes are:

1) segment-override
2) repeat
3) lock

ASM-86 permits the following prefixes to be included with the instruction mnemonic:

```
LOCK
REP         (repeat)
REPE        (repeat while equal)
REPNE       (repeat while not equal)
REPZ        (repeat while zero)
REPNZ       (repeat while non-zero)
```

A sample instruction statement using a prefix is:

```
CYCLE:      LOCK DEC     COUNT
```

The segment-overriding prefix is generated automatically by the assembler whenever the assembler realizes that a memory access requires such a prefix. The asembler makes this decision in two steps.

First, it selects a segment register that will make the instruction execute properly. The assembler selects the segment register based on information it received from previous ASSUME statements. However, we can force the assembler to select a particular segment register by including that register in the instruction as in:

```
MOV     BX,ES:SUM
```

Secondly, the assembler determines if a segment-overriding prefix is necessary to force execution of the instruction to use the selected segment register.

OPERAND-ADDRESSING MODES

The 8088 processor provides various operand-addressing modes. ASM-86 must therefore provide a means of expressing each mode when writing instruction statements: For example:

1) Immediate:

```
MOV   AX,15              ;15 is an immediate operand
```

2) Register:

```
MOV   AX,15              ;AX is a register operand
```

3) Direct:

```
SUM   DB    ?
          .
          .
      MOV   SUM,15   ;SUM is a direct memory
                      operand
```

4) Indirect through base register:

```
MOV        AX,(BX)
MOV        AX,(BP)
```

5) Indirect through index register:

```
MOV        AX,(SI)
MOV        AX,(DI)
```

6) Indirect through base register plus index register:

```
MOV     AX,(BX)     (SI)
MOV     AX,(BX)     (DI)
MOV     AX,(BP)     (SI)
MOV     AX,(BP)     (DI)
```

7) Indirect through base or index register plus offset:

```
MANY_BYTES  DB      100 DUP(?)
                .
                .
            MOV     AX,MANY_BYTES(BX)
            MOV     AX,MANY_BYTES(BP)
            MOV     AX,MANY_BYTES(SI)
            MOV     AX,MANY_BYTES(DI)
```

8) Indirect through base register plus index register plus offset:

```
MANY_BYTES  DB      100 DUP(?)
                .
                .
            MOV     AX,MANY_BYTES(BX) (SI)
            MOV     AX,MANY_BYTES(BX) (DI)
            MOV     AX,MANY_BYTES(BP) (SI)
            MOV     AX,MANY_BYTES(BP) (DI)
```

The assembler uses its knowledge about a memory location's type when generating instructions that reference that memory location. For example, the assembler generates a byte-increment when encountering the following:

```
SUM  DB     ?       ;type is BYTE
        .
        .
        .
     INC    SUM     ;a byte increment
```

However, with indirect operand-addressing modes, it is not always possible for the assembler to know the type of the memory location, as illustrated by:

```
MOV     AL,(BX)
```

Even though the assembler does not know the type of the source operand in the above instruction, it does know that the type of the destination operand, AL, is BYTE. So the assembler assumes that (BX) is also of type BYTE and generates a byte-move instruction.

But now consider the statement:

```
INC     (BX)
```

There is no second memory location here to help the assembler determine the type of (BX). So the assembler cannot decide whether to generate a byte-increment instruction or a word-increment instruction. The above statement *must* therefore be written as shown so the assembler can determine the type:

```
INC BYTE PTR (BX) ;a byte-increment
```

or

```
INC WORD PTR (BX) ;a word-increment
```

STRING INSTRUCTIONS

The assembler can usually discern the type of an operand from its declaration, and hence know what kind of code to generate for accessing that operand.

However, we have just seen that, when using an indirect-addressing mode, we might have to supply the assembler with additional information so it can determine the type.

String Primitives

String instructions also need such additional information. Consider the string instruction MOVS.

This instruction moves the contents of the memory address whose offset is in SI into the memory address whose offset is in DI. We should not need to specify any operands, since the instruction has no choice as to which items to move and where.

However, the instruction could move either a byte or a word. The assembler must know which is being moved, so it can generate the correct instruction. For this reason, the ASM-86 statement for the MOVS instruction *must* specify the items that have been moved into SI and DI.

For example:

```
ALPHA     DB        ?
BETA      DB        ?
          .
          .
          .
          MOV       SI,OFFSET ALPHA
          MOV       DI,OFFSET BETA
          MOVS      BETA,ALPHA
```

The presence of BETA and ALPHA in the MOVS statement tells the assembler to generate a MOVS instruction that moves bytes, because the TYPE components of both BETA and ALPHA are BYTE. Further, from the SEG components of BETA and ALPHA, the assembler determines if the operands of the MOVS instruction are inaccessible segments. The OFFSET components of ALPHA and BETA are ignored.

Like MOVS, the other four string primitives contain operands, MOVS and CMPS have two operands, while SCAS, LODS, and STOS have one. For example:

```
CMPS      BETA,ALPHA
SCAS      ALPHA
LODS      ALPHA
STOS      BETA
```

XLAT also requires an operand; the item that was moved into BX to serve as the translation table. The SEG component of this operand enables the assembler to determine if the translation table is in a currently accessible segment; the OFFSET component is ignored. An example of an XLAT statement is as follows:

```
MOV       BX,OFFSET TABLE
XLAT      TABLE
```

Details of ASM-86

Sample One:

Translate the values from input port 1 into a Gray code and send result to output port 1.

```
MY_DATA     SEGMENT
GRAY        DB          18H,34H,05H,06H,09H,0AH,0CH,11H,12H,14H
MY_DATA     ENDS

MY_CODE     SEGMENT
            ASSUME      CS:MY_CODE, DS:MY_DATA
GO:         MOV         AX,MY_DATA              ;establish data segment
            MOV         DS,AX
            MOV         BX,OFFSET GRAY          ;translation table into BX
CYCLE:      IN          AL,1                    ;read in next value
            XLAT        GRAY                    ;translate it
            OUT         1,AL                    ;output it
            JMP         CYCLE                   ;and repeat
MY_CODE     ENDS
            END         GO
```

Sample Two:

Add two unpacked BCD (ASCII) strings together.

```
MY_DATA     SEGMENT
STRING_1    DB          '1','7','5','2'             ;value is 2571
STRING_2    DB          '3','8','1','4'             ;value is 4183
MY_DATA     ENDS

MY_CODE     SEGMENT
            ASSUME      CS:MY_CODE, DS:MY_DATA
GO:         MOV         AX,MY_DATA                 ;establish data segment
            MOV         DS,AX
            MOV         ES,AX
            CLC                                    ;no carry initially
            CLD                                    ;forward strings
            MOV         SI,OFFSET STRING_1         ;establish string pointers
            MOV         DI,OFFSET STRING_2
            MOV         CX,LENGTH STRING_1
            JCXZ        FINISH
CYCLE:      LODS        STRING_1                   ;get STRING_1 element
            ADC         AL,[DI]                    ;add STRING_2 element
            AAA                                    ;correct for ASCII
            STOS        STRING_2                   ;result into STRING_2
            LOOP        CYCLE                      ;repeat for entire element
FINISH:     HLT
MY_CODE     ENDS
            END         GO
```

Sample Three:

Decimal multiplication algorithm.

```
MY_DATA     SEGMENT
A           DB          '3','7','5','4','9'
B           DB          '6'
C           DB          LENGTH (A) DUP (?)
MY_DATA     ENDS

MY_CODE     SEGMENT
            ASSUME      CS:MY_CODE,DS:MY_DATA
GO:         MOV         AX,MY_DATA                 ;establish data segment
            MOV         ES,AX
            CLD                                    ;forward strings
            MOV         SI,OFFSET A                ;establish pointers
            MOV         DI,OFFSET C
            MOV         CX,LENGTH A                ;establish count
            AND         B,0FH                      ;clear upper half of b
            MOV         BYTE PTR [SI],0            ;clear c[I]
            JCXZ        FINISH
CYCLE:      LODS        A                          ;get a[i]
            AND         AL,0FH                     ;clear its high-order bits
            MUL         AL,B                       ;multiply by b
            AAM                                    ;correct for ASCII
            ADD         AL,[DI]                    ;add to c[i]
            AAA                                    ;adjust for ASCII
            STOS        C                          ;store in c[i]
            MOV         [DI],AH                    ;...and c[I]
            LOOP        CYCLE                      ;repeat for entire string
FINISH:     HLT
MY_CODE     ENDS
            END         GO
```

Sample Four:

Move 50 bytes between two overlapping
strings.

```
MY _DATA      SEGMENT
STRING        DB            1000 DUP (?)
STRING _1     EQU           STRING+7
STRING _2     EQU           STRING+25
MY _DATA      ENDS

MY _CODE      SEGMENT
              ASSUME        CS:MY _CODE, DS:MY _DATA
STRING _ SIZE EQU           50                        ;number of bytes to move
GO:           MOV           AX,MY _DATA               ;establish data segment
              MOV           DS,AX
              MOV           ES,AX
              MOV           CX,STRING _ SIZE
              MOV           SI,OFFSET STRING _1       ;source string
              MOV           DI,OFFSET STRING _2       ;destination string
              CLD                                     ;assume a forward move
              CMP           SI,DI                     ;if source string comes first
              JLT           OK
              STD                                     ;...we need backwards move
              ADD           SI,STRING _ SIZE—1        ;set SI and DI to
              ADD           DI,STRING _ SIZE—1        ;...end of strings
OK:           REPEAT MOVS   STRING _ 2,STRING _1      ;move the string
              HLT
MY _ CODE     ENDS
              END           GO
```

DUAL FUNCTION KEYWORD

AND	NOT	OR	SHL	SHR	XOR

SYMBOLS

AAA	ES	FLD1	FSUBRP	JNGE	PUSH
AAD	ESC	FLDCW	FTST	JNL	**PUSHF**
AAM	F2XM1	FLDENV	FWAIT	JNLE	RCL
AAS	FABS	FLDL2E	FXAM	JNO	RCR
ADC	FAC	FLDL2T	FXCH	JNP	REP
ADD	FADD	FLDLN2	FXTRACT	JNS	REPE
AH	FADDP	FLDLG2	FYL2X	JNZ	**REPNE**
AL	FALC	FLDPI	FYL2XPI	JO	REPNZ
ARPL	FBLD	FLDZ	HLT	JP	REPZ
AX	FBSTP	FMUL	IDIV	JPE	RET
BH	FCHS	FMULP	IMUL	JPO	ROL
BL	FCLEX	FNCLEX	IN	JS	ROR
BOUND	FCOM	FNDISI	INC	JZ	SAHF
BP	FCOMP	FNENI	INT	LAHF	SAL
BX	FCOMPP	FNINIT	INTO	LDS	SAR
CALL	FDECSTP	FNOP	IRET	LEA	SBB
CBW	FDISI	FNSAVE	JA	LES	SCAS
CH	FDIV	FNSTCW	JAE	LOCK	**SCASB**
CL	FDIVP	FNSTENV	JB	LODS	**SCASW**
CLC	FDIVR	FNSTSW	JBCZ	LODSB	SI
CLD	FDIVRP	FPATAN	JBE	LODSW	SP
CLI	FENI	FPREM	JC	LOOP	SS
CLTS	FFREE	FPTAN	JCXE	LOOPE	ST
CMC	FIADD	FRNDINT	JE	LOOPNE	STC
CMP	FICOM	FRSTOR	JG	LOOPNZ	STD
CMPS	FICOMP	FSAVE	JGE	LOOPZ	STI
CMPSB	FIDIV	FSCALE	JL	MOV	STOS
CMPSW	FIDIVR	FSQRT	JLE	MOVS	STOSB
CS	FILD	FST	JMP	MOVSB	STOSW
CWD	FMUL	FSTCW	JNA	MOVSW	SUB
CX	FINCSTP	FSTENV	JNAE	MUL	TEST
DAA	FINIT	FSTP	JNB	NEG	WAIT
DAS	FIST	FSTSW	JNBE	NIL	XCHG
DEC	FISTP	FSUB	JNC	OUT	XLAT
DH	FISUB	FSUBP	JNE	POP	XLATB
DI	FISUBR	FSUBR	JNG	POPF	??SEG
DIV	FLD				
DL					
DS					
DX					

Figure 2-14. ASM-86 Reserved Words

NON-CONFLICTING KEYWORDS

DA	NOPR
DATE	NOPRINT
DEBUG	NOSB
EJ	NOSYMBOLS
EJECT	NOXR
EP	NOXREF
ERRORPRINT	OBJECT
GEN	OJ
GENONLY	PAGELENGTH
GO	PAGEWIDTH
IC	PAGING
INCLUDE	PI
LI	PL
LIST	PR
MACRO	PRINT
MEMORY	PW
MR	RESTORE
NODB	RS
NODEBUG	SA
NOEP	SAVE
NOERRORPRINT	SB
NOGE	STACK
NOGEN	SYMBOLS
NOLI	TITLE
NOLIST	TT
NOMACRO	WF
NOMR	WORKFILE
NOOBJECT	S
NOOJ	ES
NOPAGING	XR
NOPI	XREF

HANDS-OFF KEYWORDS

ABS	NE
ASSUME	NEAR
AT	NOSEGFLX
BYTE	NOTHING
COMMON	OFFSET
CODEMACRO	ORG
DB	PAGE
DD	PARA
DQ	PREFX
DT	PROC
DUP	PROCLEN
DW	PTR
DWORD	PUBLIC
END	PURGE
ENDM	QWORD
ENDP	RECORD
ENDS	RELB
EQ	RELW
EQU	RFIX
EVEN	RFIXM
EXTRN	FNFIX
FAR	FNFIXM
GE	RWFIX
GROUP	SEG
GT	SEGFIX
HIGH	SEGMENT
INPAGE	SHORT
LABEL	SIZE
LE	STRUC
LENGTH	TBYTE
LOW	THIS
LT	TYPE
MASK	WIDTH
MOD	WORD
MODRM	?
NAME	

Figure 2-14. ASM 86 Reserved Words (Continued)

REF

REFERENCES FOR INSTRUCTION SET

REF

Key to following Instruction Set Reference Pages

IDENTIFIER	USED IN	EXPLANATION
destination	data transfer, bit manipulation	A register or memory location that may contain data operated on by the instruction, and which receives (is replaced by) the result of the operation.
source	data transfer, arithmetic, bit manipulation	A register, memory location or immediate value that is used in the operation, but is not altered by the instruction.
source-table	XLAT	Name of memory translation table addressed by register BX.
target	JMP, CALL	A label to which control is to be transferred directly, or a register or memory location whose *content* is the address of the location to which control is to be transferred indirectly.
short-label	cond. transfer, iteration control	A label to which control is to be conditionally transferred; must lie within −128 to +127 bytes of the first byte of the next instruction.
accumulator	IN, OUT	Register AX for word transfers, AL for bytes.
port	IN, OUT	An I/O port number; specified as an immediate value of 0-255, or register DX (which contains port number in range 0-64k).
source-string	string ops.	Name of a string in memory that is addressed by register SI; used only to identify string as byte or word and specify segment override, if any. This string is used in the operation, but is not altered.
dest-string	string ops.	Name of string in memory that is addressed by register DI; used only to identify string as byte or word. This string receives (is replaced by) the result of the operation.
count	shifts, rotates	Specifies number of bits to shift or rotate; written as immediate value 1 or register CL (which contains the count in the range 0-255).
interrupt-type	INT	Immediate value of 0-255 identifying interrupt pointer number.
optional-pop-value	RET	Number of bytes (0-64k, ordinarily an even number) to discard from stack.
external-opcode	ESC	Immediate value (0-63) that is encoded in the instruction for use by an external processor.
above-below	conditional jumps	Above and below refer to the relationship of two unsigned values.
greater-less	conditional jumps	Greater and less refer to the relationship of two signed values.

Key to Operand Types

IDENTIFIER	EXPLANATION
(no operands)	No operands are written
register	An 8- or 16-bit general register
reg 16	An 16-bit general register
seg-reg	A segment register
accumulator	Register AX or AL
immediate	A constant in the range 0-FFFFH
immed8	A constant in the range 0-FFH
memory	An 8- or 16-bit memory location[1]
mem8	An 8-bit memory location[1]
mem16	A 16-bit memory location[1]
source-table	Name of 256-byte translate table
source-string	Name of string addressed by register SI
dest-string	Name of string, addressed by register DI
DX	Register DX
short-label	A label within −128 to +127 bytes of the end of the instruction
near-label	A label in current code segment
far-label	A label in another code segment
near-proc	A procedure in current code segment
far-proc	A procedure in another code segment
memptr16	A word containing the offset of the location in the current code segment to which control is to be transferred[1]
memptr32	A doubleword containing the offset and the segment base address of the location in another code segment to which control is to be transferred[1]
regptr16	A 16-bit general register containing the offset of the location in the current code segment to which control is to be transferred
repeat	A string instruction repeat prefix

[1] Any addressing mode—direct, register indirect, based, indexed, or based indexed—may be used (see section 2.8).

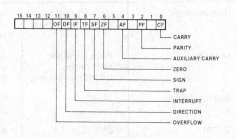

Effective Address Calculation Time

EA COMPONENTS		CLOCKS*
Displacement Only		6
Base or Index Only	(BX,BP,SI,DI)	5
Displacement + Base or Index	(BX,BP,SI,DI)	9
Base + Index	BP + DI, BX + SI	7
	BP + SI, BX + DI	8
Displacement + Base + Index	BP + DI + DISP	11
	BX + SI + DISP	
	BP + SI + DISP	12
	BX + DI + DISP	

*Add 2 clocks for segment override

Notation Key

+	Addition
−	Subtraction
*	Multiplication
/	Division
%	Modulo
:	Concatenation
&	And
←	Assignment

REFERENCES
FOR INSTRUCTION SET

"reg" Field Bit Assignments:

16-Bit (w = 1)		8-Bit (w = 0)		Segment	
000	AX	000	A L	00	ES
001	CX	001	C L	01	CS
010	DX	010	D L	10	SS
011	BX	011	B L	11	DS
100	S P	100	AH		
101	BP	101	CH		
110	S I	110	DH		
111	D I	111	BH		

"mod" Field Bit Assignments:

mod xxx r/m

mod	Displacement
00	DISP = 0*, disp-low and disp-high are absent
01	DISP = disp-low sign-extended to 16-bits, disp-high is absent
10	DISP = disp-high: disp-low
11	r/m is treated as a "reg" field

"r/m" Field Bit Assignments:

r/m	Operand Address
000	(BX) + (SI) + DISP
001	(BX) + (DI) + DISP
010	(BP) + (SI) + DISP
011	(BP) + (DI) + DISP
100	(SI) + DISP
101	(DI) + DISP
110	(BP) + DISP
111	(BX) + DISP

DISP follows 2nd byte of instruction (before data if required).

*except if mod = 00 and r/m = 110 then EA = disp-high: disp-low.

AAA ASCII ADJUST FOR ADDITION AAA

Operation:

if ((AL) & 0FH) >9 or (AF) = 1 then
   (AL) ← (AL) + 6
   (AH) ← (AH) + 1
   (AF) ← 1
(CF) ← (AF)
(AL) ← (AL) & 0FH

Flags Affected:

AF, CF.
OF, PF, XF, ZF undefined

Description:

AAA (ASCII Adjust for Addition) changes the contents of register AL to a valid unpacked decimal number; the high-order half-byte is zeroed. AAA updates AF and CF; the content of OF, PF, SF and ZF is undefined following execution of AAA.

Encoding:

| 00110111 |

AAA Operands	Clocks	Transfers	Bytes	AAA Coding Example
(no operands)	4	—	1	AAA

AAD

ASCII ADJUST FOR DIVISION

AAD

Operation:

(AL) ← (AH) * 0AH + (AL)
(AH) ← 0

Flags Affected:

PF, SF, ZF.
AF, CF, OF undefined

Description:

AAD (ASCII Adjust for Division) modifies the numerator in AL *before* dividing two valid unpacked decimal operands so that the quotient produced by the division will be a valid unpacked decimal number. AH must be zero for the subsequent DIV to produce the correct result. The quotient is returned in AL, and the remainder is returned in AH; both high-order half-bytes are zeroed. AAD updates PF, SF and ZF; the content of AF, CF and OF is undefined following execution of AAD.

Encoding:

11010101	00001010

AAD Operands	Clocks	Transfers	Bytes	AAD Coding Example
(no operands)	60	—	2	AAD

AAM

ASCII ADJUST FOR MULTIPLY

AAM

Operation:

(AH) ← (AL) / 0AH
(AL) ← (AL) % 0AH

Flags Affected:

PF, SF, ZF.
AF, CF, OF undefined

Description:

AAM (ASCII Adjust for Multiply) corrects the result of a previous multiplication of two valid unpacked decimal operands. A valid 2-digit unpacked decimal number is derived from the content of AH and AL and is returned to AH and AL. The high-order half-bytes of the multiplied operands must have been 0H for AAM to produce a correct result. AAM updates PF, SF and ZF; the content of AF, CF and OF is undefined following execution of AAM.

Encoding:

11010100	00001010

AAM Operands	Clocks	Transfers	Bytes	AAM Coding Example
(no operands)	83	—	2	AAM

AAS

ASCII ADJUST FOR SUBTRACTION

AAS

Operation:

if ((AL) & 0FH) >9 or (AF) = 1 then
  (AL) ← (AL) - 6
  (AH) ← (AH) - 1
  (AF) ← 1
(CF) ← (AF)
(AL) ← (AL) & 0FH

Flags Affected:

AF, CF.
OF, PF, SF, ZF undefined

Description:

AAS (ASCII Adjust for Subtraction) corrects the result of a previous subtraction of two valid unpacked decimal operands (the destination operand must have been specified as register AL). AAS changes the content of AL to a valid unpacked decimal number; the high-order half-byte is zeroed. AAS updates AF and CF; the content of OF, PF, SF and ZF is undefined following execution of AAS.

Encoding:

```
00111111
```

AAS Operands	Clocks	Transfers	Bytes	AAS Coding Example
(no operands)	4	—	1	AAS

ADC ADD WITH CARRY ADC

Operation:

if (CF) = 1 then (DEST) ← (LSRC)
  + (RSRC) + 1
else (DEST) ← (LSRC) + (RSRC)

Flags Affected:

AF, CF, OF, PF, SF, ZF

Description:

ADC destination,source

ADC (Add with Carry) sums the operands, which may be bytes or words, adds one if CF is set and replaces the destination operand with the result. Both operands may be signed or unsigned binary numbers (see AAA and DAA). ADC updates AF, CF, OF, PF, SF and ZF. Since ADC incorporates a carry from a previous operation, it can be used to write routines to add numbers longer than 16 bits.

Encoding:

Memory or Register Operand with Register Operand:

000100 d w	mod reg r/m

if d = 1 then LSRC = REG, RSRC = EA, DEST = REG
else LSRC = EA, RSRC = REG, DEST = EA

Immediate Operand to Memory or Register Operand:

100000 s w	mod 010 r/m	data	data if s:w=01

LSRC = EA, RSRC = data, DEST = EA

Immediate Operand to Accumulator:

0001010 w	data	data if w=1

if w = 0 then LSRC = AL, RSRC = data, DEST = AL
else LSRC = AX, RSRC = data, DEST = AX

ADC Operands	Clocks*	Transfers	Bytes	ADC Coding Examples
register, register	3	—	2	ADC AX, SI
register, memory	9(13) + EA	1	2-4	ADC DX, BETA [SI]
memory, register	16(24) + EA	2	2-4	ADC ALPHA [BX] [SI], DI
register, immediate	4	—	3-4	ADC BX, 256
memory, immediate	17(25) + EA	2	3-6	ADC GAMMA, 30H
accumulator, immediate	4	—	2-3	ADC AL, 5

*b(w): where b denotes the number of clock cycles for byte operands and
w denotes the number of clock cycles for word operands.

ADD

ADDITION

ADD

Operation:

(DEST) ← (LSRC) + (RSRC)

Flags Affected:

AF, CF, OF, PF, SF, ZF

Description:

ADD *destination,source*

The sum of the two operands, which may be bytes or words, replaces the destination operand. Both operands may be signed or unsigned binary numbers (see AAA and DAA). ADD updates AF, CF, OF, PF, SF and ZF.

ADD   ADDITION   ADD

Encoding:

Memory or Register Operand with Register Operand:

0 0 0 0 0 0 d w	mod reg r/m

if d = 1 then LSRC = REG, RSRC = EA, DEST = REG
else LSRC = EA, RSRC = REG, DEST = EA

Immediate Operand to Memory or Register Operand:

1 0 0 0 0 0 s w	mod 0 0 0 r/m	data	data if s:w=01

LSRC = EA, RSRC = data, DEST = EA

Immediate Operand to Accumulator:

0 0 0 0 0 1 0 w	data	data if w=1

if w = 0 then LSRC = AL, RSRC = data, DEST = AL
else LSRC = AX, RSRC = data, DEST = AX

ADD Operands	Clocks*	Transfers	Bytes	ADD Coding Examples
register, register	3	—	2	ADD CX, DX
register, memory	9(13) + EA	1	2-4	ADD DI, [BX].ALPHA
memory, register	16(24) + EA	2	2-4	ADD TEMP, CL
register, immediate	4	—	3-4	ADD CL, 2
memory, immediate	17(25) + EA	2	3-6	ADD ALPHA, 2
accumulator, immediate	4	—	2-3	ADD AX, 200

*b(w): where b denotes the number of clock cycles for byte operands and
w denotes the number of clock cycles for word operands.

AND   AND LOGICAL   AND

Operation:

(DEST) ← (LSRC) & (RSRC)
(CF) ← 0
(OF) ← 0

Flags Affected:

CF, OF, PF, SF, ZF.
AF undefined

Description:

AND *destination,source*

AND performs the logical "and" of the two
operands (byte or word) and returns the result
to the destination operand. A bit in the result
is set if both corresponding bits of the original
operands are set; otherwise the bit is cleared.

Encoding:

Memory or Register Operand with Register Operand:

0 0 1 0 0 0 d w	mod reg r/m

if d = 1 then LSRC = REG, RSRC = EA, DEST = REG
else LSRC = EA, RSRC = REG, DEST = EA

Immediate Operand to Memory or Register Operand:

1 0 0 0 0 0 0 w	mod 1 0 0 r/m	data	data if w=1

LSRC = EA, RSRC = data, DEST = EA

Immediate Operand to Accumulator:

0 0 1 0 0 1 0 w	data	data if w=1

if w = 0 then LSRC = AL, RSRC = data, DEST = AL
else LSRC = AX, RSRC = data, DEST = AX

AND Operands	Clocks*	Transfers	Bytes	AND Coding Examples
register, register	3	—	2	AND AL, BL
register, memory	9(13) + EA	1	2-4	AND CX, FLAG__WORD
memory, register	16(24) + EA	2	2-4	AND ASCII [DI], AL
register, immediate	4	—	3-4	AND CX, 0F0H
memory, immediate	17(25) + EA	2	3-6	AND BETA, 01H
accumulator, immediate	4	—	2-3	AND AX, 01010000B

*b(w): where b denotes the number of clock cycles for byte operands and w denotes the number of clock cycles for word operands.

CALL   CALL PROCEDURE   CALL

Operation:

if Inter-Segment then
    (SP) ← (SP) - 2
    ((SP) + 1:(SP)) ← (CS)
    (CS) ← SEG
(SP) ← (SP) - 2
((SP) + 1:(SP)) ← (IP)
(IP) ← DEST

Flags Affected:

None

Description:

CALL *procedure-name*

CALL activates an out-of-line procedure, saving information on the stack to permit a RET (return) instruction in the procedure to transfer control back to the instruction following the CALL. The assembler generates a different type of CALL instruction depending on whether the programmer has defined the procedure name as NEAR or FAR. For control to return properly, the type of CALL instruction must match the type of RET instruction that exits from the procedure. (The potential for a mismatch exists if the procedure and the CALL are contained in separately assembled programs.) Different forms of the CALL instruction allow the address of the target procedure to be obtained from the instruction itself (direct CALL) or from a memory location or register referenced by the instruction (indirect CALL). In the following descriptions, bear in mind that the processor automatically adjusts IP to point to the next instruction to be *executed* before saving it on the stack.

For an intrasegment direct CALL, SP (the stack pointer) is decremented by two and IP is pushed onto the stack. The target procedure's relative displacement (up to ±32k) from the CALL instruction is then added to the instruction pointer. This CALL instruction form is "self-relative" and appropriate for position-independent (dynamically relocatable) routines in which the CALL and its target are moved together in the same segment.

An intrasegment indirect CALL may be made through memory or a register. SP is decremented by two; IP is pushed onto the stack. The target procedure offset is obtained from the memory word or 16-bit general register referenced in the instruction and replaces IP.

For an intersegment direct CALL, SP is decremented by two, and CS is pushed onto the stack. CS is replaced by the segment word contained in the instruction. SP again is decremented by two. IP is pushed onto the stack and replaced by the offset word in the instruction.

For an intersegment indirect CALL (which only may be made through memory), SP is decremented by two, and CS is pushed onto the stack. CS is then replaced by the content of the second word of the doubleword memory pointer referenced by the instruction. SP again is decremented by two, and IP is pushed onto the stack and replaced by the content of the first word of the doubleword pointer referenced by the instruction.

CALL   CALL PROCEDURE   CALL

Encoding:

Intra-segment direct:

1 1 1 0 1 0 0 0	disp-low	disp-high

DEST = (IP) + disp

Intra-Segment Indirect:

1 1 1 1 1 1 1 1	mod 0 1 0 r/m

DEST = (EA)

Inter-Segment Direct:

1 0 0 1 1 0 1 0	offset-low	offset-high
	seg-low	seg-high

DEST = offset, SEG = seg

Inter-Segment Indirect:

1 1 1 1 1 1 1 1	mod 0 1 1 r/m

DEST = (EA), SEG = (EA + 2)

CALL Operands	Clocks	Transfers	Bytes	CALL Coding Examples
near-proc	(23)	1	3	CALL NEAR_PROC
far-proc	(36)	2	5	CALL FAR_PROC
memptr 16	(29) + EA	2	2-4	CALL PROC_TABLE [SI]
regptr 16	(24)	1	2	CALL AX
memptr 32	(53) + EA	4	2-4	CALL [BX].TASK [SI]

CBW   CONVERT BYTE TO WORD   *CBW*

Operation:

if (AL) < 80H then (AH) ← 0 else (AH) < FFH

Flags Affected:

None

Description:

CBW (Convert Byte to Word) extends the sign of the byte in register AL throughout register AH. CBW does not affect any flags. CBW can be used to produce a double-length (word) dividend from a byte prior to performing byte division.

Encoding:

```
10011000
```

CBW Operands	Clocks	Transfers	Bytes	CBW Coding Example
(no operands)	2	—	1	CBW

CLC CLEAR CARRY CLC

Operation:

(CF) ← 0

Flags Affected:

CF

Description:

CLC (Clear Carry flag) zeroes the carry flag (CF) and affects no other flags. It (and CMC and STC) is useful in conjunction with the RCL and RCR instructions.

Encoding:

| 1 1 1 1 1 0 0 0 |

CLC Operands	Clocks	Transfers	Bytes	CLC Coding Example
(no operands)	2	—	1	CLC

CLD   CLEAR DIRECTION FLAG   CLD

Operation:

(DF)← 0

Flags Affected:

DF

Description:

CLD (Clear Direction flag) zeroes DF causing the string instructions to auto-increment the SI and/or DI index registers. CLD does not affect any other flags.

Encoding:

| 1 1 1 1 1 1 0 0 |

CLD Operands	Clocks	Transfers	Bytes	CLD Coding Example
(no operands)	2	—	1	CLD

CLI CLEAR INTERRUPT-ENABLE FLAG CLI

Operation:

(IF)← 0

Flags Affected:

IF

Description:

CLI (Clear Interrupt-enable flag) zeroes IF. When the interrupt-enable flag is cleared, the 8086 and 8088 do not recognize an external interrupt request that appears on the INTR line; in other words maskable interrupts are disabled. A non-maskable interrupt appearing on the NMI line, however, is honored, as is a software interrupt. CLI does not affect any other flags.

Encoding:

```
11111010
```

CLI Operands	Clocks	Transfers	Bytes	CLI Coding Example
(no operands)	2	—	1	CLI

CMC COMPLEMENT CARRY FLAG CMC

Operation:

if (CF) = 0 then (CF) ← 1 else (CF) ← 0

Flags Affected:

CF

Description:

CMC (Complement Carry flag) "toggles" CF to its opposite state and affects no other flags.

Encoding:

| 1 1 1 1 0 1 0 1 |

CMC Operands	Clocks	Transfers	Bytes	CMC Coding Example
(no operands)	2	—	1	CMC

CMP COMPARE CMP

Operation:

(LSRC) - (RSRC)

Flags Affected:

AF, CF, OF, PF, SF, ZF

Description:

CMP destination,source

CMP (Compare) subtracts the source from the destination, which may be bytes or words, but does not return the result. The operands are unchanged, but the flags are updated and can be tested by a subsequent conditional jump instruction. CMP updates AF, CF, OF, PF, SF and ZF. The comparison reflected in the flags is that of the destination to the source. If a CMP instruction is followed by a JG (jump if greater) instruction, for example, the jump is taken if the destination operand is greater than the source operand.

Encoding:

Memory or Register Operand with Register Operand:

0 0 1 1 1 0 d w	mod reg r/m

if d = 1 then LSRC = REG, RSRC = EA
else LSRC = EA, RSRC = REG

Immediate Operand with Memory or Register Operand:

1 0 0 0 0 0 s w	mod 1 1 1 r/m	data	data if s:w=01

LSRC = EA, RSRC = data

Immediate Operand with Accumulator:

0 0 1 1 1 1 0 w	data	data if w=1

if w = 0 then LSRC = AL, RSRC = data
else LSRC = AX, RSRC = data

CMP Operands	Clocks*	Transfers	Bytes	CMP Coding Examples
register, register	3	—	2	CMP BX, CX
register, memory	9(13) + EA	—	2-4	CMP DH, ALPHA
memory, register	9(13) + EA	—	2-4	CMP [BP + 2], SI
register, immediate	4	—	3-4	CMP BL, 02H
memory, immediate	10(14) + EA	—	3-6	CMP [BX].RADAR [DI], 3420H
accumulator, immediate	4	—	2-3	CMP AL, 00010000B

*b(w): where b denotes the number of clock cycles for byte operands and w denotes the number of clock cycles for word operands.

CMPS COMPARE STRING (BYTE OR WORD) CMPS

Operation:

(LSRC) - (RSRC)
if (DF) = 0 then
   (SI) ← (SI) + DELTA
   (DI) ← (DI) + DELTA
else
   (SI) ← (SI) - DELTA
   (DI) ← (DI) - DELTA

Flags Affected:

AF, CF, OF, PF, SF, ZF

Description:

CMPS destination-string,source-string

CMPS (Compare String) subtracts the destination byte or word (addressed by DI) from the source byte or word (addressed by SI). CMPS affects the flags but does not alter either operand, updates SI and DI to point to the next string element and updates, AF, CF, OF, PF, SF and ZF to reflect the relationship of the destination element to the source element. For example, if a JG (Jump if Greater) instruction follows CMPS, the jump is taken if the destination element is greater than the source element. If CMPS is prefixed with REPE or REPZ, the operation is interrupted as "compare while not end-of-string (CX not zero) and strings are equal (ZF = 1)." If CMPS is preceded by REPNE or REPNZ, the operation is interrupted as "compare while not end-of-string (CX not zero) and strings are not equal (ZF = 0)." Thus, CMPS can be used to find matching or differing string elements.

Encoding:

```
1 0 1 0 0 1 1 w
```

if w = 0 then LSRC = (SI), RSRC = (DI), DELTA = 1
else LSRC = (SI) + 1:(SI), RSRC = (DI) + 1:(DI), DELTA = 2

CMPS Operands	Clocks*	Transfers	Bytes	CMPS CodingExamples
dest-string, source-string	22(30)	2	1	CMPS BUFF1, BUFF2
(repeat) dest-string, source-string	9 + 22(30)/rep	2/rep	1	REP COMPS ID, KEY

*b(w): where b denotes the number of clock cycles for byte operands and w denotes the number of clock cycles for word operands.

CWD CONVERT WORD TO DOUBLEWORD CWD

Operation:

if (AX) < 8000H then (DX) ← 0
else (DX) ← FFFFH

Flags Affected:

None

Description:

CWD (Convert Word to Doubleword) extends
the sign of the word in register AX throughout
register DX. CWD does not affect any flags.
CWD can be used to produce a double-length
(doubleword) dividend from a word prior to
performing word division.

Encoding:

| 10011001 |

CWD Operands	Clocks	Transfers	Bytes	CWD Coding Example
(no operands)	5	—	1	CWD

DAA DECIMAL ADJUST FOR ADDITION DAA

Operation:

if ((AL) & 0FH) > 9 or (AF) = 1 then
    (AL) ← (AL) + 6
    (AF) ← 1
if (AL) > 9FH or (CF) = 1 then
    (AL) ← (AL) + 60H
    (CF) ← 1

Flags Affected:

AF, CF, PF, SF, ZF
OF undefined

Description:

DAA (Decimal Adjust for Addition) corrects the result of previously adding two valid packed decimal operands (the destination operand must have been register AL). DAA changes the content of AL to a pair of valid packed decimal digits. It updates AF, CF, PF, SF and ZF; the content of OF is undefined following execution of DAA.

Encoding:

```
00100111
```

DAA Operands	Clocks	Transfers	Bytes	DAA Coding Example
(no operands)	4	—	1	DAA

DAS   DECIMAL ADJUST
FOR SUBTRACTION   DAS

Operation:

if ((AL) & 0FH) >9 or (AF) = 1 then
   (AL) ← (AL) - 6
   (AF) ← 1
if (AL) > 9FH or (CF) = 1 then
   (AL) ← (AL) - 60H
   (CF) ← 1

Flags Affected:

AF, CF, PF, SF, ZF.
0F undefined

Description:

DAS (Decimal Adjust for Subtraction) corrects the result of a previous subtraction of
two valid packed decimal operands (the destination operand must have been specified as
register AL). DAS changes the content of AL
to a pair of valid packed decimal digits. DAS
updates AF, CF, PF, SF and ZF; the content
of OF is undefined following execution of
DAS.

Encoding:

```
00101111
```

DAS Operands	Clocks	Transfers	Bytes	DAS Coding Example
(no operands)	4	—	1	DAS

DEC   DECREMENT   DEC

Operation:

(DEST) ← (DEST) - 1

Flags Affected:

AF, OF, PF, SF, ZF

Description:

DEC (Decrement) subtracts one from the destination operand. The operand may be a byte or a word and is treated as an unsigned binary number (see AAA and DAA). DEC updates AF, OF, PF, SF and ZF; it does not affect CF.

Encoding:

Memory or Register Operand:

| 1 1 1 1 1 1 1 w | mod 0 0 1 r/m |

DEST = EA

16-Bit Register Operand:

| 0 1 0 0 1 reg |

DEST = REG

DEC Operands	Clocks*	Transfers	Bytes	DEC Coding Example
reg16	2	—	1	DEC AX
reg8	3	—	2	DEC AL
memory	15(23) + EA	2	2-4	DEC ARRAY [SI]

*b(w): where b denotes the number of clock cycles for byte operands and w denotes the number of clock cycles for word operands.

DIV   DIVIDE   DIV

Operation:

(temp) ← (NUMR)
if (temp) / (DIVR) > MAX then the
   following, in sequence
   (QUO), (REM) undefined
   (SP) ← (SP) - 2
   ((SP) + 1:(SP)) ← FLAGS
   (IF) ← 0
   (TF) ← 0
   (SP) ← (SP) - 2
   ((SP) + 1:(SP)) ← (CS)
   (CS) ← (2) i.e., the contents of
      memory locations 2 and 3
   (SP) ← (SP) - 2
   ((SP) + 1:(SP)) ← (IP)
   (IP) ← (0) i.e., the contents of
      locations 0 and 1
else
   (QUO) ← (temp) / (DIVR), where
      / is unsigned division
   (REM) ← (temp) % (DIVR) where
      % is unsigned modulo

Flags Affected:

AF, CF, OF, PF, SF, ZF undefined

Description:

DIV *source*

DIV (divide) performs an unsigned division of the accumulator (and its extension) by the source operand. If the source operand is a byte, it is divided into the two-byte dividend assumed to be in registers AL and AH. The byte quotient is returned in AL, and the byte remainder is returned in AH. If the source operand is a word, it is divided into the two-word dividend in registers AX and DX. The word quotient is returned in AX, and the word remainder is returned in DX. If the quotient exceeds the capacity of its destination register (FFH for byte source, FFFFH for word source), as when division by zero is attempted, a type 0 interrupt is generated, and the quotient and remainder are undefined. Nonintegral quotients are truncated to integers. The content of AF, CF, OF, PF, SF and ZF is undefined following execution of DIV.

DIV DIVIDE DIV

Encoding:

| 1111011w | mod 110 r/m |

if w = 0 then NUMR = AX, DIVR = EA, QUO = AL, REM = AH, MAX = FFH
else NUMR = DX:AX, DIVR = EA, QUO = AX, REM = DX, MAX = FFFFH

DIV Operands	Clocks	Transfers	Bytes	DIV Coding Example
reg8	80-90	—	2	DIV CL
reg16	144-162	—	2	DIV BX
mem8	(86-96) + EA	1	2-4	DIV ALPHA
mem16	(154-172) + EA	1	2-4	DIV TABLE [SI]

ESC   ESCAPE   ESC

Operation:

if mod ≠ 11 then data bus ← (EA)

Flags Affected:

None

Description:

The ESC (Escape) instruction provides a mechanism by which other processors (coprocessors) may receive their instructions from the 8086 or 8088 instruction stream and make use of the 8086 or 8088 addressing modes. The CPU (8086 or 8088) does a no operation (NOP) for the ESC instruction other than to access a memory operand and place it on the bus.

Encoding:

1 1 0 1 1 x	mod x r/m

ESC Operands	Clocks*	Transfers	Bytes	ESC Coding Example
immediate, memory	8(12) + EA	1	2-4	ESC 6,ARRAY [SI]
immediate, register	2	—	2	ESC 20,AL

*b(w): where b denotes the number of clock cycles for byte operands and w denotes the number of clock cycles for word operands.

HLT

HALT

HLT

Operation:

None

Flags Affected:

None

Description:

HLT (Halt) causes the CPU to enter the halt state. The processor leaves the halt state upon activation of the RESET line, upon receipt of a non-maskable interrupt request on NMI, or, if interrupts are enabled, upon receipt of a mask- able interrupt request on INTR. HLT does not affect any flags. It may be used as an alterna- tive to an endless software loop in situations where a program must wait for an interrupt.

Encoding:

```
11110100
```

HLT Operands	Clocks	Transfers	Bytes	HLT Coding Example
(no operands)	2	—	1	HLT

IDIV INTEGER DIVIDE IDIV

Operation:

(temp) ← (NUMR)
if (temp) / (DIVR) > 0 and (temp)
 / (DIVR) > MAX
or (temp) / (DIVR) < 0 and (temp)
 / (DIVR) < 0 - MAX - 1 then
 (QUO), (REM) undefined
 (SP) ← (SP) - 2
 ((SP) + 1:(SP)) ← FLAGS
 (IF) ← 0
 (TF) ← 0
 (SP) ← (SP) - 2
 ((SP) + 1:(SP)) ← (CS)
 (CS) ← (2)
 (SP) ← (SP) - 2
 ((SP) + 1:(SP)) ← (IP)
 (IP) ← (0)
else
 (QUO) ← (temp) / (DIVR), where
 / is signed division
 (REM) ← (temp) % (DIVR) where
 % is signed modulo

Flags Affected:

AF, CF, OF, PF, SF, ZF undefined

Description:

IDIV source

IDIV (Integer Divide) performs a signed division of the accumulator (and its extension) by the source operand. If the source operand is a byte, it is divided into the double-length dividend assumed to be in registers AL and AH; the single-length quotient is returned in AL, and the single-length remainder is returned in AH. For byte integer division, the maximum positive quotient is +127 (7FH) and the minimum negative quotient is −127 (81H). If the source operand is a word, it is divided into the double-length dividend in registers AX and DX; the single-length quotient is returned in AX, and the single-length remainder is returned in DX. For word integer division, the maximum positive quotient is +32,767 (7FFFH) and the minimum negative quotient is −32,767 (8001H). If the quotient is positive and exceeds the maximum, or is negative and is less than the minimum, the quotient and remainder are undefined, and a type 0 interrupt is generated. In particular, this occurs if division by 0 is attempted. Nonintegral quotients are truncated (toward 0) to integers, and the remainder has the same sign as the dividend. The content of AF, CF, OF, PF, SF and ZF is undefined following IDIV.

IDIV INTEGER DIVIDE IDIV

Encoding:

1111011w	mod 111 r/m

if w = 0 then NUMR = AX, DIVR = EA, QUO = AL, REM = AH, MAX = 7FH
else NUMR = DX:AX, DIVR = EA, QUO = AX, REM = DX, MAX = 7FFFH

IDIV Operands	Clocks	Transfers	Bytes	IDIV Coding Example
reg8	101-112	—	2	IDIV BL
reg16	165-184	—	2	IDIV CX
mem8	(107-118) + EA	1	2-4	IDIV DIVISOR__BYTE [SI]
mem16	(175-194) + EA	1	2-4	IDIV [BX].DIVISOR__WORD

IMUL INTEGER MULTIPLY IMUL

Operation:

(DEST) ← (LSRC) * (RSRC) where
   * is signed multiply
if (ext) = sign-extension of (LOW)
   then (CF) ← 0
else (CF) ← 1;
(OF) ← (CF)

Flags Affected:

CF, OF
AF, PF, SF, ZF undefined

Description:

IMUL *source*

IMUL (Integer Multiply) performs a signed multiplication of the source operand and the accumulator. If the source is a byte, then it is multiplied by register AL, and the double-length result is returned in AH and AL. If the source is a word, then it is multiplied by register AX, and the double-length result is returned in registers DX and AX. If the upper half of the result (AH for byte source, DX for word source) is not the sign extension of the lower half of the result, CF and OF are set; otherwise they are cleared. When CF and OF are set, they indicate that AH or DX contains significant digits of the result. The content of AF, PF, SF and ZF is undefined following execution of IMUL.

Encoding:

| 1 1 1 1 0 1 1 w | mod 1 0 1 r/m |

if w = 0 then LSRC = AL, RSRC = EA, DEST = AH, EXT = AH, LOW = AL
else LSRC = AX, RSRC = EA, DEST = DX:AX, EXT = DX, LOW = AX

IMUL Operands	Clocks	Transfers	Bytes	IMUL Coding Example
reg8	80-98	—	2	IMUL CL
reg16	128-154	—	2	IMUL BX
mem8	(86-104) + EA	1	2-4	IMUL RATE__BYTE
mem16	(138-164) + EA	1	2-4	IMUL RATE__WORD [BP] [DI]

IN INPUT BYTE OR WORD IN

Operation:

(DEST) ← (SRC)

Flags Affected:

None

Description:

IN *accumulator,port*

IN transfers a byte or a word from an input port to the AL register or the AX register, respectively. The port number may be specified either with an immediate byte constant, allowing access to ports numbered 0 through 255, or with a number previously placed in the DX register, allowing variable access (by changing the value in DX) to ports numbered from 0 through 65,535.

Encoding:

Fixed Port:

1 1 1 0 0 1 0 w	port

if w = 0 then SRC = port, DEST = AL
else SRC = port + 1:port, DEST = AX

Variable Port:

1 1 1 0 1 1 0 w

if w = 0 then SRC = (DX), DEST = AL
else SRC = (DX) + 1:(DX), DEST = AX

IN Operands	Clocks*	Transfers	Bytes	IN Coding Example
accumulator, immed8	10(14)	1	2	IN AL,0EAH
accumulator, DX	8(12)	1	1	IN AX, DX

*b(w): where b denotes the number of clock cycles for byte operands and w denotes the number of clock cycles for word operands.

INCREMENT

Operation:

(DEST) ← (DEST) + 1

Flags Affected:

AF, OF, PF, SF, ZF

Description:

INC destination

INC (Increment) adds one to the destination operand. The operand may be a byte or a word and is treated as an unsigned binary number (see AAA and DAA). INC updates AF, OF, PF, SF and ZF; it does not affect CF.

Encoding:

Memory or Register Operand:

| 1 1 1 1 1 1 1 w | mod 0 0 0 r/m |

DEST = EA

16-Bit Register Operand:

| 0 1 0 0 0 reg |

DEST = REG

INC Operands	Clocks*	Transfers	Bytes	INC Coding Example
reg16	2	—	1	INC CX
reg8	3	—	2	INC BL
memory	15(23) + EA	2	2-4	INC ALPHA [DI] [BX]

*b(w): where b denotes the number of clock cycles for byte operands and w denotes the number of clock cycles for word operands.

INT INTERRUPT INT

Operation:

$(SP) \leftarrow (SP) - 2$
$((SP) + 1:(SP)) \leftarrow FLAGS$
$(IF) \leftarrow 0$
$(TF) \leftarrow 0$
$(SP) \leftarrow (SP) - 2$
$((SP) + 1:(SP)) \leftarrow (CS)$
$(CS) \leftarrow (TYPE * 4 + 2)$
$(SP) \leftarrow (SP) - 2$
$((SP) + 1:(SP)) \leftarrow (IP)$
$(IP) \leftarrow (TYPE * 4)$

Flags Affected:

IF, TF

Description:

INT *interrupt-type*

INT (Interrupt) activates the interrupt procedure specified by the interupt-type operand. INT decrements the stack pointer by two, pushes the flags onto the stack, and clears the trap (TF) and interrupt-enable (IF) flags to disable single-step and maskable interrupts. The flags are stored in the format used by the PUSHF instruction. SP is decremented again by two, and the CS register is pushed onto the stack. The address of the interrupt pointer is calculated by multiplying interrupt-type by four; the second word of the interrupt pointer replaces CS. SP again is decremented by two, and IP is pushed onto the stack and is replaced by the first word of the interrupt pointer. If interrupt-type = 3, the assembler generates a short (1 byte) form of the instruction, known as the breakpoint interrupt.

Software interrupts can be used as "supervisor calls," i.e., requests for service from an operating system. A different interrupt-type can be used for each type of service that the operating system could supply for an application program. Software interrupts also may be used to check out interrupt service procedures written for hardware-initiated interrupts.

Encoding:

| 1 1 0 0 1 1 0 v | type if v= 1 |

if v = 0 then TYPE = 3
else TYPE = type

INT Operands	Clocks	Transfers	Bytes	INT Coding Example
immed8 (type = 3)	(72)	5	1	INT 3
immed8 (type ≠ 3)	(71)	5	2	INT 67

INTO

INTERRUPT ON OVERFLOW

INTO

Operation:

if (OF) = 1 then
  (SP) ← (SP) - 2
  ((SP) + 1:(SP)) ← FLAGS
  (IF) ← 0
  (TF) ← 0
  (SP) ← (SP) - 2
  ((SP) + 1:(SP)) ← (CS)
  (CS) ← (12H)
  (SP) ← (SP) - 2
  ((SP) + 1:(SP)) ← (IP)
  (IP) ← (10H)

Flags Affected:

None

Description:

INTO (Interrupt on Overflow) generates a software interrupt if the overflow flag (OF) is set; otherwise control proceeds to the following instruction without activating an interrupt procedure. INTO addresses the target interrupt procedure (its type is 4) through the interrupt pointer at location 10H; it clears the TF and IF flags and otherwise operates like INT. INTO may be written following an arithmetic or logical operation to activate an interrupt procedure if overflow occurs.

Encoding:

| 11001110 |

INTO Operands	Clocks	Transfers	Bytes	INTO Coding Example
(no operands)	(73) or 4	5	1	INTO

IRET   INTERRUPT RETURN   IRET

Operation:

(IP) ← ((SP)+1:(SP))
(SP) ← (SP) + 2
(CS) ← ((SP)+1:(SP))
(SP) ← (SP) + 2
FLAGS ← ((SP) + 1:(SP))
(SP) ← (SP) + 2

Flags Affected:

All

Description:

IRET (Interrupt Return) transfers control back to the point of interruption by popping IP, CS and the flags from the stack. IRET thus affects all flags by restoring them to previously saved values. IRET is used to exit any interrupt procedure, whether activated by hardware or software.

Encoding:

```
11001111
```

IRET Operands	Clocks	Transfers	Bytes	IRET Coding Example
(no operands)	(44)	3	1	IRET

JA   JUMP ON ABOVE   JA

JNBE   JUMP ON NOT BELOW   JNBE
OR EQUAL

Operation:

if (CF) & (ZF) = 0 then
(IP) ← (IP) + disp (sign-extended
to 16-bits)

Flags Affected:

None

Description:

Jump on Above (JA)/Jump on Not Below or
Equal (JNBE) transfers control to the target
operand (IP + displacement) if CF and ZF = 0.

Encoding:

01110111	disp

JA/JNBE Operands	Clocks	Transfers	Bytes	JA Coding Example
short-label	16 or 4	—	2	JA ABOVE
				JNBE Coding Example
				JNBE ABOVE

JAE
JNB

JUMP ON ABOVE OR EQUAL
JUMP ON NOT BELOW

JAE
JNB

Operation:

if (CF) = 0 then
   (IP) ← (IP) + disp (sign-extended
     to 16-bits)

Flags Affected:

None

Description:

JAE (Jump on Above or Equal)/JNB (Jump on Not Below) transfers control to the target operand (IP + displacement) if CF = 0.

Encoding:

01110011	disp

JAE/JNB Operands	Clocks	Transfers	Bytes	JAE Coding Example
short-label	16 or 4	—	2	JAE ABOVE__EQUAL

JB
JNAE

JUMP ON BELOW

JUMP ON NOT ABOVE OR EQUAL

JB
JNAE

Operation:

if (CF) = 1 then
   (IP) ← (IP) + disp (sign-extended
      to 16-bits)

Flags Affected:

None

Description:

JB (Jump on Below)/JNAE (Jump on Not Above or Equal) transfers control to the target operand (IP + displacement) if CF = 1.

Encoding:

01110010	disp

JB/JNAE Operands	Clocks	Transfers	Bytes	JB Coding Example
short-label	16 or 4	—	2	JB BELOW

JBE JUMP ON BELOW OR EQUAL JBE

JNA JUMP ON NOT ABOVE JNA

Operation:

IF (CF) or (ZF) = 1 then
  (IP) ← (IP) + disp (sign-extended
    to 16-bits)

Flags Affected:

None

Description:

JBE (Jump on Below or Equal)/JNA (Jump on Not Above) transfers control to the target operand (IP + displacement) if CF or ZF = 1.

Encoding:

01110110	disp

JBE/JNA Operands	Clocks	Transfers	Bytes	JNA Coding Example
short-label	16 or 4	—	2	JNA NOT__ABOVE

JC   JUMP ON CARRY   JC

Operation:

if (CF) = 1 then
  (IP) ← (IP) + disp (sign-extended
    to 16-bits)

Flags Affected:

None

Description:

JC (Jump on Carry) transfers control to the
target operand (IP + displacement) on the condition CF = 1.

Encoding:

01110010	disp

JC Operands	Clocks	Transfers	Bytes	JC Coding Example
short-label	16 or 4	—	2	JC CARRY__SET

JCXZ   JUMP IF CX REGISTER ZERO   JCXZ

Operation:

if (CX) = 0 then
   (IP) ← (IP) + disp (sign-extended
     to 16-bits)

Flags Affected:

None

Description:

JCXZ *short-label*

JCXZ (Jump if CX Zero) transfers control to
the target operand if CX is 0. This instruction
is useful at the beginning of a loop to bypass
the loop if CX has a zero value, i.e., to execute
the loop zero times.

Encoding:

11100011	disp

JCXZ Operands	Clocks	Transfers	Bytes	JCXZ Coding Example
short-label	18 or 6	—	2	JCXZ COUNT__DONE

JE
JZ

JUMP ON EQUAL
JUMP ON ZERO

JE
JZ

Operation:

if (ZF) = 1 then
   (IP) ← (IP) + disp (sign-extended
    to 16-bits)

Flags Affected:

None

Description:

JE (Jump on Equal)/JZ (Jump on Zero) transfers control to the target operand (IP + displacement) if ZF = 1.

Encoding:

01110100	disp

JE/JZ Operands	Clocks	Transfers	Bytes	JZ Coding Example
short-label	16 or 4	—	2	JZ ZERO

JG

JNLE

JUMP ON GREATER

JUMP ON NOT LESS OR EQUAL

JG

JNLE

Operation:

if ((SF) = (OF)) or (ZF) = 0 then
(IP) ← (IP) + disp (sign-extended
to 16-bits)

Flags Affected:

None

Description:

JG (Jump on Greater Than)/JNLE (Jump on Not Less Than or Equal) transfers control to the target operand (IP + displacement) if the conditions ((SF XOR OF) or ZF = 0) are greater than/not less than or equal to the tested value.

Encoding:

01111111	disp

JG/JNLE Operands	Clocks	Transfers	Bytes	JG Coding Example
short-label	16 or 4	—	2	JG GREATER

JGE   JUMP ON GREATER   JGE
              OR EQUAL

JNL   JUMP ON NOT LESS   JNL

Operation:

if (SF) = (OF) then
   (IP) ← (IP) + disp (sign-extended
    to 16-bits)

Flags Affected:

None

Description:

JGE (Jump on Greater Than or Equal)/JNL
(Jump on Not Less Than) transfers control to
the target operand (IP + displacement) if the
condition (SF XOR OF = 0) is greater than or
equal/not less than the tested value.

Encoding:

01111101	disp

JGE/JNL Operands	Clocks	Transfers	Bytes	JGE Coding Example
short-label	16 or 4	—	2	JGE GREATER_EQUAL

JL JUMP ON LESS JL

JNGE JUMP ON NOT GREATER OR EQUAL JNGE

Operation:

if (SF) ≠ (OF) then
   (IP) ← (IP) + disp (sign-extended
      to 16-bits)

Flags Affected:

None

Description:

JL (Jump on Less Than)/JNGE (Jump on Not Greater Than or Equal), transfers control to the target operand if the condition (SF XOR OF = 1) is less than/not greater than or equal to the tested value.

Encoding:

01111100	disp

JL/JNGE Operands	Clocks	Transfers	Bytes	JL Coding Example
short-label	16 or 4	—	2	JL LESS

JLE

JNG

JUMP ON LESS OR EQUAL

JUMP ON NOT GREATER

JLE

JNG

Operation:

if ((SF) ≠ (OF)) or ((ZF) = 1) then
   (IP) ← (IP) + disp (sign-extended
      to 16-bits)

Flags Affected:

None

Description:

JLE (Jump on Less Than or Equal to)/JNG
(Jump on Not Greater Than) transfers control
to the target operand (IP + displacement) if
the conditions tested ((SF XOR OF) or ZF = 1)
are less than or equal to/not greater than the
tested value.

Encoding:

01111110	disp

JLE/JNG Operands	Clocks	Transfers	Bytes	JNG Coding Example
short-label	16 or 4	—	2	JNG NOT__GREATER

JMP JUMP UNCONDITIONALLY JMP

Operation:

if Inter-Segment then (CS) ← SEG
(IP) ← DEST

Flags Affected:

None

Description:

JMP *target*

JMP unconditionally transfers control to the target location. Unlike a CALL instruction, JMP does not save any information on the stack; no return to the instruction following the JMP is expected. Like CALL, the address of the target operand may be obtained from the instruction itself (direct JMP), or from memory or a register referenced by the instruction (indirect JMP).

An intrasegment direct JMP changes the instruction pointer by adding the relative displacement of the target from the JMP instruction. If the assembler can determine that the target is within 127 bytes of the JMP, it automatically generates a two-byte instruction form called a SHORT JMP; otherwise, it generates a NEAR JMP that can address a target within ±32k. Intrasegment direct JMPS are self-relative and appropriate in position-

independent (dynamically relocatable) routines in which the JMP and its target are moved together in the same segment.

An intrasegment indirect JMP may be made either through memory or a 16-bit general register. In the first case, the word content referenced by the instruction replaces the instruction pointer. In the second case, the new IP value is taken from the register named in the instruction.

An intersegment direct JMP replaces IP and CS with values contained in the instruction.

An intersegment indirect JMP may be made only through memory. The first word of the doubleword pointer referenced by the instruction replaces IP and the second word replaces CS.

JMP JUMP UNCONDITIONALLY JMP

Encoding:

Intra-Segment Direct:

11101001	disp-low	disp-high

DEST = (IP) + disp

Intra-Segment Direct Short:

11101011	disp

DEST = (IP) + disp sign extended to 16-bits

Intra-Segment Indirect:

11111111	mod 1 0 0 r/m

DEST = (EA)

Inter-Segment Direct:

11101010	offset-low	offset-high
	seg-low	seg-high

DEST = offset, SEG = seg

Inter-Segment Indirect:

11111111	mod 1 0 1 r/m

DEST = (EA), SEG = (EA + 2)

JMP Operands	Clocks	Transfers	Bytes	JMP Coding Example
short-label	15	—	2	JMP SHORT
near-label	15	—	3	JMP WITHIN__SEGMENT
far-label	15	—	5	JMP FAR__LABEL
memptr16	18 + EA	—	2-4	JMP [BX].TARGET
regptr16	11	—	2	JMP CX
memptr32	24 + EA	—	2-4	JMP OTHER.SEG [SI]

JNC JUMP ON NOT CARRY JNC

Operation:

if (CF) = 0 THEN
  (IP) ← (IP) + disp (sign-extended
    to 16-bits)

Flags Affected:

None

Description:

JNC (Jump on Not Carry) transfers control to
the target operand (IP + displacement) on the
condition CF = 0.

Encoding:

01110011	disp

JNC Operands	Clocks	Transfers	Bytes	JNC Coding Example
short-label	16 or 4	—	2	JNC NO__CARRY

JNE JUMP ON NOT EQUAL JNE
JNZ JUMP ON NOT ZERO JNZ

Operation:

if (ZF) = 0 then
   (IP) ← (IP) + disp (sign-extended
    to 16-bits)

Flags Affected:

None

Description:

JNE (Jump on Not Equal to)/ JNZ (Jump on Not Zero) transfers control to the target operand (IP + displacement) if the condition tested (ZF = 0) is true.

Encoding:

01110101	disp

JNE/JNZ Operands	Clocks	Transfers	Bytes	JNE Coding Example
short-label	16 or 4	—	2	JNE NOT__EQUAL

JNO JUMP ON NOT OVERFLOW JNO

Operation:

if (OF) = 0 then
    (IP) ← (IP) + disp (sign-extended
        to 16-bits)

Flags Affected:

None

Description:

JNO (Jump on Not Overflow) transfers control to the target operand (IP + displacement)
if the condition tested (OF = 0) is true.

Encoding:

01110001	disp

JNO Operands	Clocks	Transfers	Bytes	JNO Coding Example
short-label	16 or 4	—	2	JNO NO__OVERFLOW

Operation:

if (SF) = 0 then
   (IP) ← (IP) + disp (sign-extended
     to 16-bits)

Flags Affected:

None

Description:

JNS (Jump on Not Sign) transfers control to
the target operand (IP + displacement) when
the tested condition (SF = 0) is true.

Encoding:

01111001	disp

JNS Operands	Clocks	Transfers	Bytes	JNS Coding Example
short-label	16 or 4	—	2	JNS POSITIVE

JNP JUMP ON NOT PARITY JNP

JPO JUMP ON PARITY ODD JPO

Operation:

if (PF) = 0 then
(IP) ← (IP) + disp (sign-extended
to 16-bits)

Flags Affected:

None

Description:

JNP (Jump on Not Parity)/JPO (Jump on Parity Odd) transfers control to the target operand if the condition tested (PF = 0) is true.

Encoding:

01111011	disp

JNP/JPO Operands	Clocks	Transfers	Bytes	JPO Coding Example
short-label	16 or 4	—	2	JPO ODD__PARITY

Operation:

if (OF) = 1 then
   (IP) ← (IP) + disp (sign-extended
     to 16-bits)

Flags Affected:

None

Description:

JO (Jump on Overflow) transfers control to the target operand (IP + displacement) if the tested condition (OF = 1) is true.

Encoding:

01110000	disp

JO Operands	Clocks	Transfers	Bytes	JO Coding Example
short-label	16 or 4	—	2	JO SIGNED__OVERFLOW

JP	**JUMP ON PARITY**	JP
JPE	**JUMP ON PARITY EQUAL**	JPE

Operation:

if (PF) = 1 then
   (IP) ← (IP) + disp (sign-extended
     to 16-bits)

Flags Affected:

None

Description:

JP (Jump on Parity)/JPE (Jump on Parity Equal) transfers control to the target operand (IP + displacement) if the condition tested (PF = 1) is true.

Encoding:

01111010	disp

JP/JPE Operands	Clocks	Transfers	Bytes	JPE Coding Example
short-label	16 or 4	—	2	JPE EVEN__PARITY

JS JUMP ON SIGN JS

Operation:

if (SF) = 1 then
  (IP) ← (IP) + disp (sign-extended
    to 16-bits)

Flags Affected:

None

Description:

JS (Jump on Sign) transfers control to the
target operand (IP + displacement) if the
tested condition (SF = 1) is true.

Encoding:

01111000	disp

JS Operands	Clocks	Transfers	Bytes	JS Coding Example
short-label	16 or 4	—	2	JS NEGATIVE

LAHF LOAD REGISTER AH LAHF
FROM FLAGS

Operation:

(AH) ← (SF):(ZF):X:(AF):X:(PF):X:(CF)

Flags Affected:

None

Description:

LAHF (load register AH from flags) copies SF, ZF, AF, PF and CF (the 8080/8085 flags) into bits 7, 6, 4, 2 and 0, respectively, of register AH. The content of bits 5, 3 and 1 is undefined; the flags themselves are not affected. LAHF is provided primarily for converting 8080/8085 assembly language programs to run on an 8086 or 8088.

Encoding:

```
10011111
```

LAHF Operands	Clocks	Transfers	Bytes	LAHF Coding Example
(no operands)	4	—	1	LAHF

LDS LOAD POINTER USING DS LDS

Operation:

(REG) ← (EA)
(DS) ← (EA + 2)

Flags Affected:

None

Description:

LDS destination,source

LDS (load pointer using DS) transfers a 32-bit pointer variable from the source operand, which must be a memory operand, to the destination operand and register DS. The offset word of the pointer is transferred to the destination operand, which may be any 16-bit general register. The segment word of the pointer is transferred to register DS. Specifying SI as the destination operand is a convenient way to prepare to process a source string that is not in the current data segment (string instructions assume that the source string is located in the current data segment and that SI contains the offset of the string).

Encoding:

| 11000101 | mod reg r/m |

if mod = 11 then undefined operation

LDS Operands	Clocks	Transfers	Bytes	LDS Coding Example
reg16, mem32	24 + EA	2	2-4	LDS SI,DATA.SEG [DI]

LEA LOAD EFFECTIVE ADDRESS LEA

Operation:

(REG) ← EA

Flags Affected:

None

Description:

LEA *destination,source*

LEA (load effective address) transfers the offset of the source operand (rather than its value) to the destination operand. The source operand must be a memory operand, and the destination operand must be a 16-bit general register. LEA does not affect any flags. The XLAT and string instructions assume that certain registers point to operands; LEA can be used to load these registers (e.g., loading BX with the address of the translate table used by the XLAT instruction).

Encoding:

| 10001101 | mod reg r/m |

if mod = 11 then undefined operation

LEA Operands	Clocks	Transfers	Bytes	LEA Coding Example
reg16, mem16	2 + EA	—	2-4	LEA BX,[BP] [DI]

LES LOAD POINTER USING ES LES

Operation:

(REG) ← (EA)
(ES) ← (EA + 2)

Flags Affected:

None

Description:

LES *destination,source*

LES (load pointer using ES) transfers a 32-bit pointer variable from the source operand, which must be a memory operand, to the destination operand and register ES. The offset word of the pointer is transferred to the destination operand, which may be any 16-bit general register. The segment word of the pointer is transferred to register ES. Specifying DI as the destination operand is a convenient way to prepare to process a destination string that is not in the current extra segment. (The destination string must be located in the extra segment, and DI must contain the offset of the string.)

Encoding:

| 11000100 | mod reg r/m |

if mod = 11 then undefined operation

LES Operands	Clocks	Transfers	Bytes	LES Coding Example
reg16, mem32	24 + EA	2	2-4	LES DI,[BX].TEXT_BUFF

LOCK   LOCK THE BUS   LOCK

Operation:

None

Flags Affected:

None

Description:

LOCK is a one-byte prefix that causes the 8088 (configured in maximum mode) to assert its bus LOCK signal while the following instruction executes. LOCK does not affect any flags.

The instruction most useful in this context is an exchange register with memory. A simple software lock may be implemented with the following code sequence:

```
Check:    MOV    AL,1      ;set AL to 1 (implies locked)
   LOCK   XCHG   Sema,AL   ;test and set lock
          TEST   AL,AL     ;set flags based on AL
          JNZ    Check     ;retry if lock already set

          MOV    Sema,0    ;clear the lock when done
```

The LOCK prefix may be combined with the segment override and/or REP prefixes.

Encoding:

```
11110000
```

LOCK Operands	Clocks	Transfers	Bytes	LOCK Coding Example
(no operands)	2	—	1	LOCK XCHG FLAG,AL

LODS   LOAD STRING (BYTE OR WORD)   LODS

Operation:

(DEST) ← (SRC)
if (DF) = 0 then (SI) ← (SI) + DELTA
else (SI) ← (SI) - DELTA

Flags Affected:

None

Description:

LODS source-string

LODS (Load String) transfers the byte or word string element addressed by SI to register AL or AX, and updates SI to point to the next element in the string. This instruction is not ordinarily repeated since the accumulator would be overwritten by each repetition, and only the last element would be retained. However, LODS is very useful in software loops as part of a more complex string function built up from string primitives and other instructions.

Encoding:

```
1010110 w
```

if w = 0 then SRC = (SI), DEST = AL, DELTA = 1
else SRC = (SI) + 1:(SI), DEST = AX, DELTA = 2

LODS Operands	Clocks*	Transfers	Bytes	LODS Coding Example
source-string	12(16)	1	1	LODS CUSTOMER__NAME
(repeat) source-string	9 + 13(17)/rep	1/rep	1	REP LODS NAME

*b(w): where b denotes the number of clock cycles for byte operands and w denotes the number of clock cycles for word operands.

LOOP

LOOP **LOOP**

Operation:

(CX) ← (CX) - 1
if (CX) ≠ 0 then
  (IP) ← (IP) + disp (sign-extended
    to 16-bits)

Flags Affected:

None

Description:

LOOP *short-label*

LOOP decrements CX by 1 and transfers control to the target operand if CX is not 0; otherwise the instruction following LOOP is executed.

Encoding:

11100010	disp

LOOP Operands	Clocks	Transfers	Bytes	LOOP Coding Example
short-label	17/5	—	2	LOOP AGAIN

LOOPE LOOP WHILE EQUAL LOOPE

LOOPZ LOOP WHILE ZERO LOOPZ

Operation:

(CX) ← (CX) - 1
if (ZF) = 1 and (CX) ≠ 0 then
  (IP) ← (IP) + disp (sign-extended
    to 16-bits)

Flags Affected:

None

Description:

LOOPE/LOOPZ *short-label*

LOOPE and LOOPZ (Loop While Equal and Loop While Zero) are different mnemonics for the same instruction (similar to the REPE and REPZ repeat prefixes). CX is decremented by 1, and control is transferred to the target operand if CX is not 0 and if ZF is set; otherwise the instruction following LOOPE/ LOOPZ is executed.

Encoding:

11100001	disp

LOOPE/LOOPZ Operands	Clocks	Transfers	Bytes	LOOPE Coding Example
short-label	18 or 6	—	2	LOOPE AGAIN

LOOPNZ LOOP WHILE NOT ZERO LOOPNZ

LOOPNE LOOP WHILE NOT EQUAL LOOPNE

Operation:

$(CX) \leftarrow (CX) - 1$
if $(ZF) = 0$ and $(CX) \neq 0$ then
   $(IP) \leftarrow (IP) + disp$ (sign-extended
     to 16-bits)

Flags Affected:

None

Description:

LOOPNE/LOOPNZ *short-label*

LOOPNE and LOOPNZ (Loop While Not Equal and Loop While Not Zero) are also synonyms for the same instruction. CX is decremented by 1, and control is transferred to the target operand if CX is not 0 and if ZF is clear; otherwise the next sequential instruction is executed.

Encoding:

11100000	disp

LOOPNE/LOOPNZ Operands	Clocks	Transfers	Bytes	LOOPNE Coding Example
short-label	19 or 5	—	2	LOOPNE AGAIN

MOV MOVE (BYTE OR WORD) MOV

Operation:

(DEST) ← (SRC)

Flags Affected:

None

Description:

MOV *destination,source*

MOVE transfers a byte or a word from the source operand to the destination operand.

Encoding:

Memory or Register Operand to/from Register Operand:

1 0 0 0 1 0 d w	mod reg r/m

if d = 1 then SRC = EA, DEST = REG
else SRC = REG, DEST = EA

Immediate Operand to Memory or Register Operand:

1 1 0 0 0 1 1 w	mod 0 0 0 r/m	data	data if w=1

SRC = data, DEST = EA

Immediate Operand to Register:

1 0 1 1 w reg	data	data if w=1

SRC = data, DEST = REG

MOV MOVE (BYTE OR WORD) MOV

Encoding:

Memory Operand to Accumulator:

| 1 0 1 0 0 0 0 w | addr-low | addr-high |

if w = 0 then SRC = addr, DEST = AL
else SRC = addr + 1:addr, DEST = AX

Accumulator to Memory Operand:

| 1 0 1 0 0 0 1 w | addr-low | addr-high |

if w = 0 then SRC = AL, DEST = addr
else SRC = AX, DEST = addr + 1:addr

Memory or Register Operand to Segment Register:

| 1 0 0 0 1 1 1 0 | mod 0 reg r/m |

if reg ≠ 01 then SRC = EA, DEST = REG
else undefined operation

Segment Register to Memory or Register Operand:

| 1 0 0 0 1 1 0 0 | mod 0 reg r/m |

SRC = REG, DEST = EA

MOV Operands	Clocks*	Transfers	Bytes	MOV Coding Example
memory, accumulator	10(14)	1	3	MOV ARRAY AL
accumulator, memory	10(14)	1	3	MOV AX, TEMP__RESULT
register, register	2	—	2	MOV AX,CX
register, memory	8(12) + EA	1	2-4	MOV BP, STACK__TOP
memory, register	9(13) + EA	1	2-4	MOV COUNT [DI], CX
register, immediate	4	—	2-3	MOV CL, 2
memory, immediate	10(14) + EA	1	3-6	MOV MASK [BX] [SI], 2CH
seg-reg, reg16	2	—	2	MOV ES, CX
seg-reg, mem16	(12) + EA	1	2-4	MOV DS, SEGMENT__BASE
reg16, seg-reg	2	—	2	MOV BP, SS
memory, seg-reg	(13) + EA	1	2-4	MOV [BX].SEG__SAVE, CS

*b(w): where b denotes the number of clock cycles for byte operands and
w denotes the number of clock cycles for word operands.

MOVS   MOVE STRING   MOVS

Operation:

(DEST) ← (SRC)

Flags Affected:

None

Description:

MOVS *destination-string,source-string*

MOVS (Move String) transfers a byte or a word from the source string (addressed by SI) to the destination string (addressed by DI) and updates SI and DI to point to the next string element. When used in conjunction with REP, MOVS performs a memory-to-memory block transfer.

Encoding:

```
1010010 w
```

if w = 0 then SRC = (SI), DEST = AL, DELTA = 1
else SRC = (SI) + 1:(SI), DEST = AX, DELTA = 2

MOVS Operands	Clocks*	Transfers	Bytes	MOVS Coding Example
dest-string, source-string	18(26)	2	1	MOVS LINE__EDIT__DATA
(repeat) dest-string, source-string	9 + 17(25) / rep	2/rep	1	REP MOVS SCREEN, BUFFER

*b(w): where b denotes the number of clock cycles for byte operands and w denotes the number of clock cycles for word operands.

MUL   MULTIPLY   MUL

Operation:

(DES) ← (LSRC) * (RSRC), where *
   is unsigned multiply
if (EXT) = 0 then (CF) ← 0
else (CF) ← 1;
(OF) ← (CF)

Flags Affected:

CF, OF.
AF, PF, SF, ZF undefined

Description:

MUL *source*

MUL (Multiply) performs an unsigned multiplication of the source operand and the accumulator. If the source is a byte, then it is multiplied by register AL, and the double-length result is returned in AH and AL. If the source operand is a word, then it is multiplied by register AX, and the double-length result is returned in registers DX and AX. The operands are treated as unsigned binary numbers (see AAM). If the upper half of the result (AH for byte source, DX for word source) is non-zero, CF and OF are set; otherwise they are cleared. When CF and OF are set, they indicate that AH or DX contains significant digits of the result. The content of AF, PF, SF and ZF is undefined following execution of MUL.

Encoding:

| 1 1 1 1 0 1 1 w | mod 1 0 0 r/m |

if w = 0 then LSRC = AL, RSRC = EA, DEST = AX, EXT = AH
else LSRC = AX, RSRC = EA, DEST = DX:AX, EXT = DX

MUL Operands	Clocks	Transfers	Bytes	MUL Coding Example
reg8	70-77	—	2	MUL BL
reg16	118-113	—	2	MUL CX
mem8	(76-83) + EA	1	2-4	MUL MONTH [SI]
mem16	(128-143) + EA	1	2-4	MUL BAUD__RATE

NEG   NEGATE   NEG

Operation:

(EA) ← SRC - (EA)
(EA) ← (EA) + 1 (affecting flags)

Flags Affected:

AF, CF, OF, PF, SF, ZF

Description:

NEG *destination*

NEG (Negate) subtracts the destination operand, which may be a byte or a word, from 0 and returns the result to the destination. This forms the two's complement of the number, effectively reversing the sign of an integer. If the operand is zero, its sign is not changed.

Attempting to negate a byte containing −128 or a word containing −32,768 causes no change to the operand and sets OF. NEG updates AF, CF, OF, PF, SF and ZF. CF is always set except when the operand is zero, in which case it is cleared.

Encoding:

```
1 1 1 1 0 1 1 w   mod 0 1 1 r/m
```

if w = 0 then SRC = FFH
else SRC = FFFFH

NEG Operands	Clocks*	Transfers	Bytes	NEG Coding Example
register	3	—	2	NEG AL
memory	16(24) + EA	2	2-4	NEG MULTIPLIER

*b(w): where b denotes the number of clock cycles for byte operands and w denotes the number of clock cycles for word operands.

NOP   NO OPERATION   NOP

Operation:

None

Flags Affected:

None

Description:

NOP

NOP (No Operation) causes the CPU to do nothing. NOP does not affect any flags.

Encoding:

```
10010000
```

NOP Operands	Clocks	Transfers	Bytes	NOP Coding Example
(no operands)	3	—	1	NOP

NOT LOGICAL NOT NOT

Operation:

(EA) ← SRC - (EA)

Flags Affected:

None

Description:

NOT *destination*

NOT inverts the bits (forms the one's complement) of the byte or word operand.

Encoding:

| 1 1 1 1 0 1 1 w | mod 0 1 0 r/m |

if w = 0 then SRC = FFH
else SRC = FFFFH

NOT Operands	Clocks*	Transfers	Bytes	NOT Coding Example
register	3	—	—	NOT AX
memory	16(24) + EA	2	—	NOT CHARACTER

*b(w): where b denotes the number of clock cycles for byte operands and
w denotes the number of clock cycles for word operands.

OR LOGICAL OR OR

Operation:

(DEST) ← (LSRC) OR (RSRC)
(CF) ← 0
(OF) ← 0

Flags Affected:

CF, OF, PF, SF, ZF.
AF undefined

Description:

OR *destination,source*

OR performs the logical "inclusive or" of the
two operands (byte or word) and returns the
result to the destination operand. A bit in the
result is set if either or both corresponding bits
in the original operands are set; otherwise the
result bit is cleared.

LOGICAL OR

Encoding:

Memory or Register Operand with Register Operand:

0 0 0 0 1 0 d w	mod reg r/m

if d = 1 then LSRC = REG, RSRC = EA, DEST = REG
else LSRC = EA, RSRC = REG, DEST = EA

Immediate Operand to Memory or Register Operand:

1 0 0 0 0 0 0 w	mod 0 0 1 r/m	data	data if w=1

LSRC = EA, RSRC = data, DEST = EA

Immediate Operand to Accumulator:

0 0 0 0 1 1 0 w	data	data if w=1

if w = 0 then LSRC = AL, RSRC = data, DEST = AL
else LSRC = AX, RSRC = data, DEST = AX

OR Operands	Clocks*	Transfers	Bytes	OR Coding Example
register, register	3	—	2	OR AL, BL
register, memory	9(13) + EA	1	2-4	OR DX, PORT__ID [DI]
memory, register	16(24) + EA	2	2-4	OR FLAG__BYTE, CL
accumulator, immediate	4	—	2-3	OR AL, 01101100B
register, immediate	4	—	3-4	OR CX,01H
memory, immediate	17(25) + EA	2	3-6	OR [BX].CMD__WORD,0CFH

*b(w): where b denotes the number of clock cycles for byte operands and w denotes the number of clock cycles for word operands.

Operation:

(DEST) ← (SRC)

Flags Affected:

None

Description:

OUT *port,accumulator*

OUT transfers a byte or a word from the AL register or the AX register, respectively, to an output port. The port number may be specified either with an immediate byte constant, allowing access to ports numbered 0 through 255, or with a number previously placed in register DX, allowing variable access (by changing the value in DX) to ports numbered from 0 through 65,535.

Encoding:

Fixed Port:

1 1 1 0 0 1 1 w	port

if w = 0 then SRC = AL, DEST = port
else SRC = AX, DEST = port + 1:port

Variable Port:

1 1 1 0 1 1 1 w

if w = 0 then SRC = AL, DEST = (DX)
else SRC = AX, DEST = (DX) + 1:(DX)

OUT Operands	Clocks*	Transfers	Bytes	OUT Coding Example
immed8, accumulator	10(14)	1	2	OUT 44, AX
DX, accumulator	8(12)	1	1	OUT DX, AL

*b(w): where b denotes the number of clock cycles for byte operands and w denotes the number of clock cycles for word operands.

POP POP POP

Operation:

(DEST) ← ((SP) + 1:(SP))
(SP) ← (SP) + 2

Flags Affected:

None

Description:

POP *destination*

POP transfers the word at the current top of stack (pointed to by SP) to the destination operand, and then increments SP by two to point to the new top of stack. POP can be used to move temporary variables from the stack to registers or memory.

POP POP POP

Encoding:

Memory or Register Operand:

| 1 0 0 0 1 1 1 1 | mod 0 0 0 r/m |

DEST = EA

Register Operand:

| 0 1 0 1 1 reg |

DEST = REG

Segment Register:

| 0 0 0 reg 1 1 1 |

if reg ≠ 01 then DEST = REG
else undefined operation

POP Operands	Clocks	Transfers	Bytes	POP Coding Example
register	12	1	1	POP DX
seg-reg (CS illegal)	12	1	1	POP DS
memory	25 + EA	2	2-4	POP PARAMETER

POPF   POP FLAGS   POPF

Operation:

Flags ← ((SP) + 1:(SP))
(SP) ← (SP) + 2

Flags Affected:

All

Description:

POPF

POPF transfers specific bits from the word at the current top of stack (pointed to by register SP) into the 8086/8088 flags, replacing whatever values the flags previously contained (see figure 2-32). SP is then incremented by two to point to the new top of stack. PUSHF and POPF allow a procedure to save and restore a calling program's flags. They also allow a program to change the setting of TF (there is no instruction for updating this flag directly). The change is accomplished by pushing the flags, altering bit 8 of the memory-image and then popping the flags.

Encoding:

```
10011101
```

POPF Operands	Clocks	Transfers	Bytes	POPF Coding Example
(no operands)	12	1	1	POPF

PUSH   PUSH   PUSH

Operation:

(SP) ← (SP) - 2
((SP) + 1:(SP)) ← (SRC)

Flags Affected:

None

Description:

PUSH *source*

PUSH decrements SP (the stack pointer) by
two and then tranfers a word from the source
operand to the top of stack now pointed to by
SP. PUSH often is used to place parameters
on the stack before calling a procedure; more
generally, it is the basic means of storing temporary data on the stack.

PUSH   PUSH   PUSH

Encoding:

Memory or Register Operand:

| 1 1 1 1 1 1 1 1 | mod 1 1 0 r/m |

SRC = EA

Register Operand:

| 0 1 0 1 0 reg |

SRC = REG

Segment Register:

| 0 0 0 reg 1 1 0 |

SRC = REG

PUSH Operands	Clocks	Transfers	Bytes	PUSH Coding Example
register	15	1	1	PUSH SI
seg-reg (CS legal)	14	1	1	PUSH ES
memory	24 + EA	2	2-4	PUSH RETURN__CODE [SI]

PUSHF   PUSH FLAGS   PUSHF

Operation:

(SP) ← (SP) - 2
((SP) + 1:(SP)) ← Flags

Flags Affected:

None

Description:

PUSHF

PUSHF decrements SP (the stack pointer) by
two and then transfers all flags to the word at
the top of stack pointed to by SP. The flags
themselves are not affected.

Encoding:

| 1 0 0 1 1 1 0 0 |

PUSHF Operands	Clocks	Transfers	Bytes	PUSHF Coding Example
(no operands)	14	1	1	PUSHF

RCL

ROTATE THROUGH CARRY LEFT

RCL

Operation:

(temp) ← COUNT
do while (temp) ≠ 0
   (tmpcf) ← (CF)
   (CF) ← high-order bit of (EA)
   (EA) ← (EA) * 2 + (tmpcf)
   (temp) ← (temp) - 1
if COUNT = 1 then
   if high-order bit of (EA) ≠ (CF)
     then (OF) ← 1
   else (OF) ← 0
else (OF) undefined

Flags Affected:

CF, OF

Description:

RCL *destination,count*

RCL (Rotate through Carry Left) rotates the
bits in the byte or word destination operand to
the left by the number of bits specified in the
count operand. The carry flag (CF) is treated
as "part of" the destination operand; that is,
its value is rotated into the low-order bit of the
destination, and itself is replaced by the high-
order bit of the destination.

RCL ROTATE THROUGH CARRY LEFT RCL

Encoding:

| 1 1 0 1 0 0 v w | mod 0 1 0 r/m |

if v = 0 then COUNT = 1
else COUNT = (CL)

RCL Operands	Clocks*	Transfers	Bytes	RCL Coding Example
register 1,	2	—	2	RCL CX, 1
register, CL	8 + 4/bit	—	2	RCL AL, CL
memory, 1	15(23) + EA	2	2-4	RCL ALPHA, 1
memory, CL	20(28) + EA + 4/bit	2	2-4	RCL [BP].PARAM,CL

*b(w): where b denotes the number of clock cycles for byte operands and
w denotes the number of clock cycles for word operands.

RCR ROTATE THROUGH CARRY RIGHT RCR

Operation:

(temp) ← COUNT
do while (temp) ≠ 0
  (tmpcf) ← (CF)
  (CF) ← low-order bit of (EA)
  (EA) ← (EA) / 2
  high-order bit of (EA) ← (tmpcf)
  (temp) ← (temp) - 1
if COUNT = 1 then
  if high-order bit of (EA) ≠ next-
    to-high-order bit of (EA)
    then (OF) ← 1
  else (OF) ← 0
else (OF) undefined

Flags Affected:

CF, OF

Description:

RCR *destination,count*

RCR (Rotate through Carry Right) operates exactly like RCL except that the bits are rotated right instead of left.

Encoding:

| 1 1 0 1 0 0 v w | mod 0 1 1 r/m |

if v = 0 then COUNT = 1
else COUNT = (CL)

RCR Operands	Clocks	Transfers	Bytes	RCR Coding Example
register, 1	2	—	2	RCR BX, 1
register, CL	8 + 4/bit	—	2	RCR BL, CL
memory, 1	15(23) + EA	2	2-4	RCR [BX].STATUS, 1
memory, CL	20(28) + EA + 4/bit	2	2-4	RCR ARRAY [DI], CL

*b(w): where b denotes the number of clock cycles for byte operands and w denotes the number of clock cycles for word operands.

REP   REPEAT   REP

REPE/REPZ   REPE/REPZ
REPEAT WHILE EQUAL/
REPEAT WHILE ZERO

REPNE/REPNZ REPNE/REPNZ
REPEAT WHILE NOT EQUAL/
REPEAT WHILE NOT ZERO

Operation:

do while (CX) ≠ 0
   service pending interrupt (if
   any) execute primitive string
      operation in succeeding byte
   (CX) ← (CX) - 1
   if primitive operation is CMPB,
   CMPW, SCAB, or SCAW and
   (ZF) ≠ z then exit from
   while loop

Flags Affected:

None

REP   REPEAT   REP

REPE/REPZ   REPE/REPZ
REPEAT WHILE EQUAL/
REPEAT WHILE ZERO

REPNE/REPNZ REPNE/REPNZ
REPEAT WHILE NOT EQUAL/
REPEAT WHILE NOT ZERO

Description:

REP/REPE/REPZ/REPNE/REPNZ

Repeat, Repeat While Equal, Repeat While Zero, Repeat While Not Equal and Repeat While Not Zero are mnemonics for two forms of the prefix byte that controls subsequent string instruction repetition. The different mnemonics are provided to improve program clarity. The repeat prefixes do not affect the flags.

REP is used in conjunction with the MOVS (Move String) and STOS (Store String) instructions and is interpreted as "repeat while not end-of-string" (CX not 0). REPE and REPZ operate identically and are physically the same prefix byte as REP. These instructions are used with the CMPS (Compare String) and SCAS (Scan String) instructions and require ZF (posted by these instructions) to be set before initiating the next repetition. REPNE and REPNZ are mnemonics for the same prefix byte. These instructions function the same as REPE and REPZ except that the zero flag must be cleared or the repetition is terminated. ZF does not need to be initialized before executing the repeated string instruction.

Repeated string sequences are interruptable; the processor will recognize the interrupt before processing the next string element. System interrupt processing is not affected in any way. Upon return from the interrupt, the repeated operation is resumed from the point of interruption. However, execution does *not* resume properly if a second or third prefix (i.e., segment override or LOCK) has been specified in addition to any of the repeat prefixes. At interrupt time, the processor "remembers" only the prefix that immediately precedes the string instruction. After returning from the interrupt, processing resumes, but any additional prefixes specified are not in effect. If more than one prefix must be used with a string instruction, interrupts may be disabled for the duration of the repeated execution. However, this will not prevent a non-maskable interrupt from being recognized. Also, the time that the system is unable to respond to interrupts may be unacceptable if long strings are being processed.

REP REPEAT REP
REPE/REPZ REPE/REPZ
REPEAT WHILE EQUAL/
REPEAT WHILE ZERO

REPNE/REPNZ REPNE/REPNZ
REPEAT WHILE NOT EQUAL/
REPEAT WHILE NOT ZERO

Encoding:

```
1111001z
```

REP Operands	Clocks	Transfers	Bytes	REP Coding Example
(no operands)	2	—	1	REP MOVS DEST, SRCE
REPE/REPZ Operands	Clocks	Transfers	Bytes	REPE Coding Example
(no operands)	2	—	1	REPE CMPS DATA, KEY
REPNE/REPNZ Operands	Clocks	Transfers	Bytes	REPNE Coding Example
(no operands)	2	—	1	REPNE SCAS INPUT__LINE

RET RETURN RET

Operation:

$(IP) \leftarrow ((SP) + 1:(SP))$
$(SP) \leftarrow (SP) + 2$
if Inter-Segment then
  $(CS) \leftarrow ((SP) + 1:(SP))$
  $(SP) \leftarrow (SP) + 2$
if Add Immediate to Stack Pointer
  then $(SP) \leftarrow (SP) + data$

Flags Affected:

None

Description:

RET *optional-pop-value*

RET (Return transfers control from a procedure back to the instruction following the CALL that activated the procedure. The assembler generates an intrasegment RET if the programmer has defined the procedure NEAR, or an intersegment RET if the procedure has been defined as FAR. RET pops the word at the top of the stack (pointed to by register SP) into the instruction pointer and increments SP by two. If RET is intersegment, the word at the new top of stack is popped into the CS register, and SP is again incremented by two. If an optional pop value has been specified, RET adds that value to SP. This feature may be used to discard parameters pushed onto the stack before the execution of the CALL instruction.

RET RETURN RET

Encoding:

Intra-Segment:

| 1 1 0 0 0 0 1 1 |

Intra-Segment and Add Immediate to Stack Pointer:

| 1 1 0 0 0 0 1 0 | data-low | data-high |

Inter-Segment:

| 1 1 0 0 1 0 1 1 |

Inter-Segment and Add Immediate to Stack Pointer:

| 1 1 0 0 1 0 1 0 | data-low | data-high |

RET Operands	Clocks	Transfers	Bytes	RET Coding Example
(intra-segment, no pop)	20	1	1	RET
(intra-segment, pop)	24	1	3	RET 4
(inter-segment, no pop)	34	2	1	RET
(inter-segment, pop)	33	2	3	RET 2

ROL ROTATE LEFT ROL

Operation:

(temp) ← COUNT
do while (temp) ≠ 0
  (CF) ← high-order bit of (EA)
  (EA) ← (EA) * 2 + (CF)
  (temp) ← (temp) - 1
if COUNT = 1 then
  if high-order bit of (EA) ≠ (CF)
    then (OF) ← 1
  else (OF) ← 0
else (OF) undefined

Flags Affected:

CF, OF

Description:

ROL *destination,count*

ROL (Rotate Left) rotates the destination byte or word left by the number of bits specified in the count operand.

Encoding:

| 1 1 0 1 0 0 v w | mod 0 0 0 r/m |

if v = 0 then COUNT = 1
else COUNT = (CL)

ROL Operands	Clocks*	Transfers	Bytes	ROL Coding Example
register, 1	2	—	2	ROL BX, 1
register, CL	8 + 4/bit	—	2	ROL DI, CL
memory, 1	15(23) + EA	2	2-4	ROL FLAG__BYTE [DI], 1
memory, CL	20(28) + EA + 4/bit	2	2-4	ROL ALPHA, CL

*b(w): where b denotes the number of clock cycles for byte operands and w denotes the number of clock cycles for word operands.

ROR ROTATE RIGHT ROR

Operation:

(temp) ← COUNT
do while (temp) ≠ 0
  (CF) ← low-order bit of (EA)
  (EA) ← (EA) / 2
  high-order bit of (EA) ← (CF)
  (temp) ← (temp) - 1
if COUNT = 1 then
  if high-order bit of (EA) ≠ next-
to-high-order bit of (EA)
then (OF) ← 1
  else (OF) ← 0
else (OF) undefined

Flags Affected:

CF, OF

Description:

ROR *destination,count*

ROR (Rotate Right) operates similar to ROL
except that the bits in the destination byte or
word are rotated right instead of left.

Encoding:

| 1 1 0 1 0 0 v w | mod 0 0 1 r/m |

if v = 0 then COUNT = 1
else COUNT = (CL)

ROR Operand	Clocks*	Transfers	Bytes	ROR Coding Example
register, 1	2	—	2	ROR AL, 1
register, CL	8 + 4/bit	—	2	ROR BX, CL
memory, 1	15(23) + EA	2	2-4	ROR PORT__STATUS, 1
memory, CL	20(28) + EA + 4/bit	2	2-4	ROR CMD__WORD, CL

*b(w): where b denotes the number of clock cycles for byte operands and
  w denotes the number of clock cycles for word operands.

SAHF STORE REGISTER AH INTO FLAGS SAHF

Operation:

$(SF):(ZF):X:(AF):X:(PF):X:(CF) \leftarrow (AH)$

Flags Affected:

AF, CF, PF, SF, ZF

Description:

SAHF

SAHF (store register AH into flags) transfers bits 7, 6, 4, 2 and 0 from register AH into SF, ZF, AF, PF and CF, respectively, replacing whatever values these flags previously had. OF, DF, IF and TF are not affected. This instruction is provided for 8080/8085 compatibility.

Encoding:

```
10011110
```

SAHF Operands	Clocks	Transfers	Bytes	SAHF Coding Example
(no operands)	4	—	1	SAHF

SAL SHIFT ARITHMETIC LEFT SAL

SHL SHIFT LOGICAL LEFT SHL

Operation:

(temp) ← COUNT
do while (temp) ≠ 0
  (CF) ← high-order bit of (EA)
  (EA) ← (EA) * 2
  (temp) ← (temp) - 1
if COUNT = 1 then
  if high-order bit of (EA) ≠ (CE)
    then (OF) ← 1
  else (OF) ← 0
else (OF) undefined

Flags Affected:

CF, OF, PF, SF, ZF.
AF undefined

Description:

SHL/SAL *destination,count*

SHL and SAL (Shift Logical Left and Shift Arithmetic Left) perform the same operation and are physically the same instruction. The destination byte or word is shifted left by the number of bits specified in the count operand. Zeros are shifted in on the right. If the sign bit retains its original value, then OF is cleared.

SAL SHIFT ARITHMETIC LEFT SAL
SHL SHIFT LOGICAL LEFT SHL

Encoding:

110100vw	mod100r/m

if v = 0 then COUNT = 1
else COUNT = (CL)

SAL/SHL Operands	Clocks*	Transfers	Bytes	SAL/SHLCoding Example
register, 1	2	—	2	SAL AH, 1
register, CL	8 + 4/bit	—	2	SHL DI, CL
memory, 1	15(23) + EA	2	2-4	SHL [BX].OVERDRAW, 1
memory, CL	20(28) + EA + 4/bit	2	2-4	SAL STORE_COUNT, CL

*b(w): where b denotes the number of clock cycles for byte operands and
 w denotes the number of clock cycles for word operands.

SAR SHIFT ARITHMETIC RIGHT SAR

Operation:

(temp) ← COUNT
do while (temp) ≠ 0
  (CF) ← low-order bit of (EA)
  (EA) ← (EA) / 2, where / is
    equivalent to signed division,
    rounding down
  (temp) ← (temp) - 1
if COUNT = 1 then
  if high-order bit of (EA) ≠ next-
    to-high-order bit of (EA)
    then (OF) ← 1
  else (OF) ← 0
else (OF) ← 0

Flags Affected:

CF, OF, PF, SF, ZF.
AF undefined

Description:

SAR destination,count

SAR (Shift Arithmetic Right) shifts the bits in the destination operand (byte or word) to the right by the number of bits specified in the count operand. Bits equal to the original high-order (sign) bit are shifted in on the left, preserving the sign of the original value. Note that SAR does not produce the same result as the dividend of an "equivalent" IDIV instruc-

tion if the destination operand is negative and 1-bits are shifted out. For example, shifting −5 right by one bit yields −3, while integer division −5 by 2 yields −2. The difference in the instructions is that IDIV truncates all numbers toward zero, while SAR truncates positive numbers toward zero and negative numbers toward negative infinity.

SAR SHIFT ARITHMETIC RIGHT SAR

SAR

Encoding:

1 1 0 1 0 0 v w	mod 1 1 1 r/m

if v = 0 then COUNT = 1
else COUNT = (CL)

SAR Operands	Clocks*	Transfers	Bytes	SAR Coding Example
register, 1	2	—	2	SAR DX, 1
register, CL	8 + 4/bit	—	2	SAR DI, CL
memory, 1	15(23) + EA	2	2-4	SAR N__BLOCKS, 1
memory, CL	20(28) + EA + 4/bit	2	2-4	SAR N__BLOCKS, CL

*b(w): where b denotes the number of clock cycles for byte operands and w denotes the number of clock cycles for word operands.

SUBTRACT WITH BORROW

Operation:

if (CF) = 1 then (DEST) = (LSRC) - (RSRC) - 1
else (DEST) ← (LSRC) - (RSRC)

Flags Affected:

AF, CF, OF, PF, SF, ZF

Description:

SBB destination,source

SBB (Subtract with Borrow) subtracts the source from the destination, subtracts one if CF is set, and returns the result to the destination operand. Both operands may be bytes or words. Both operands may be signed or unsigned binary numbers (see AAS and DAS). SBB updates AF, CF, OF, PF, SF, and ZF. Since it incorporates a borrow from a previous operation, SBB may be used to write routines that subtract numbers longer than 16 bits.

SBB   SUBTRACT WITH BORROW   SBB

Encoding:

Memory or Register Operand and Register Operand:

0 0 0 1 1 0 d w	mod reg r/m

if d = 1 then LSRC = REG, RSRC = EA, DEST = REG
else LSRC = EA, RSRC = REG, DEST = EA

Immediate Operand from Memory or Register Operand:

1 0 0 0 0 0 s w	mod 0 1 1 r/m	data	data if s:w=01

LSRC = EA, RSRC = data, DEST = EA

Immediate Operand from Accumulator:

0 0 0 1 1 1 0 w	data	data if w=1

if w = 0 then LSRC = AL, RSRC = data, DEST = AL
else LSRC = AX, RSRC = data, DEST = AX

SBB Operands	Clocks*	Transfers	Bytes	SBB Coding Example
register, register	3	—	2	SBB BX, CX
register, memory	9(13) + EA	1	2-4	SBB DI, [BX].PAYMENT
memory, register	16(24) + EA	2	2-4	SBB BALANCE, AX
accumulator, immediate	4	—	2-3	SBB AX, 2
register, immediate	4	—	3-4	SBB CL, 1
memory, immediate	17(25) + EA	2	3-6	SBB COUNT [SI], 10

*b(w): where b denotes the number of clock cycles for byte operands and
w denotes the number of clock cycles for word operands.

SCAS SCAN (BYTE OR WORD) STRING SCAS

Operation:

(LSRC) − (RSRC)
if (DF) = 0 then (DI) ← (DI) + DELTA
else (DI) ← (DI) - DELTA

Flags Affected:

AF, CF, OF, PF, SF, ZF

Description:

SCAS *destination-string*

SCAS (Scan String) subtracts the destination string element (byte or word) addressed by DI from the content of AL (byte string) or AX (word string) and updates the flags, but does not alter the destination string or the accumulator. SCAS also updates DI to point to the next string element and AF, CF, OF, PF, SF and ZF to reflect the relationship of the scan value in AL/AX to the string element. If SCAS is prefixed with REPE or REPZ, the operation is interpreted as "scan while not end-of-string (CX not 0) and string-element = scan-value (ZF = 1)." This form may be used to scan for departure from a given value. If SCAS is prefixed with REPNE or REPNZ, the operation is interpreted as "scan while not end-of-string (CX not 0) and string-element is not equal to scan-value (ZF = 0)." This form may be used to locate a value in a string.

Encoding:

```
1010111w
```

if w = 0 then LSRC = AL, RSRC = (DI), DELTA = 1
else LSRC = AX, RSRC = (DI) + 1:(DI), DELTA = 2

SCAS Operands	Clocks*	Transfers	Bytes	SCAS Coding Example
dest-string	15(19)	1	1	SCAS INPUT__LINE
(repeat) dest-string	9 + 15(19)/rep	1/rep	1	REPNE SCAS BUFFER

*b(w): where b denotes the number of clock cycles for byte operands and w denotes the number of clock cycles for word operands.

SHR   SHIFT LOGICAL RIGHT   SHR

Operation:

(temp) ← COUNT
do while (temp) ≠ 0
  (CF) ← low-order bit of (EA)
  (EA) ← (EA) / 2, where / is
    equivalent to unsigned
    division
  (temp) ← (temp) - 1
if COUNT = 1 then
  if high-order bit of (EA) ≠ next-
    to-high-order bit of (EA)
    then (OF) ← 1
  else (OF) ← 0
else (OF) undefined

Flags Affected:

CF, OF, PF, SF, ZF.
AF undefined

Description:

SHR *destination, source*

SHR (Shift Logical Right) shifts the bits in the
destination operand (byte or word) to the right
by the number of bits specified in the count
operand. Zeros are shifted in on the left. If the
sign bit retains its original value, then OF is
cleared.

SHR   SHIFT LOGICAL RIGHT   SHR

Encoding:

```
110100vw  mod101r/m
```

if v = 0 then COUNT = 1
else COUNT = (CL)

SHR Operands	Clocks*	Transfers	Bytes	SHR Coding Example
register, 1	2	—	2	SHR SI, 1
register, CL	8 + 4/bit	—	2	SHR SI, CL
memory, 1	15(23) + EA	2	2-4	SHR ID__BYTE [SI] [BX], 1
memory, CL	20(28) + EA + 4/bit	2	2-4	SHR INPUT__WORD, CL

*b(w): where b denotes the number of clock cycles for byte operands and w denotes the number of clock cycles for word operands.

STC   SET CARRY   STC

Operation:

(CF) ← 1

Flags Affected:

CF

Description:

STC

STC (Set Carry flag) sets CF to 1 and affects
no other flags.

Encoding:

| 11111001 |

STC Operands	Clocks	Transfers	Bytes	STC Coding Example
(no operands)	2	—	1	STC

Operation:

(DF) ← 1

Flags Affected:

DF

Description:

STD

STD (Set Direction flag) sets DF to 1 causing the string instructions to auto-decrement the SI and/or DI index registers. STD does not affect any other flags.

Encoding:

| 1 1 1 1 1 1 0 1 |

Timing: 2 clocks

STD Operands	Clocks	Transfers	Bytes	STD Coding Example
(no operands)	2	—	1	STD

STI   SET INTERRUPT-
ENABLE FLAG   STI

Operation:

(IF) ← 1

Flags Affected:

IF

Description:

STI (Set Interrupt-enable flag) sets IF to 1, enabling processor recognition of maskable interrupt requests appearing on the INTR line. Note however, that a pending interrupt will not actually be recognized until the instruction following STI has executed. STI does not affect any other flags.

Encoding:

| 11111011 |

STI Operands	Clocks	Transfers	Bytes	STI Coding Example
(no operands)	2	—	1	STI

STOS   STORE (BYTE/OR/ WORD) STRING   STOS

Operation:

(DEST) ← (SRC)
if (DF) = 0 then (DI) ← (DI) + DELTA
else (DI) ← (DI) - DELTA

Flags Affected:

None

Description:

STOS *destination-string*

STOS (Store String) transfers a byte or word from register AL or AX to the string element addressed by DI and updates DI to point to the next location in the string. As a repeated operation, STOS provides a convenient way to initialize a string to a constant value (e.g., to blank out a print line).

Encoding:

```
1 0 1 0 1 0 1 w
```

if w = 0 then SRC = AL, DEST = (DI), DELTA = 1
else SRC = AX, DEST = (DI) + 1:(DI), DELTA = 2

STOS Operands	Clocks*	Transfers	Bytes	STOS Coding Example
dest-string	11(15)	1	1	STOS PRINT__LINE
(repeat) dest-string	9 + 10(14)/rep	1/rep	1	REP STOS DISPLAY

*b(w): where b denotes the number of clock cycles for byte operands and w denotes the number of clock cycles for word operands.

SUB SUBTRACT SUB

Operation:

(DEST) ← (LSRC) - (RSRC)

Flags Affected:

AF, CF, OF, PF, SF, ZF

Description:

SUB destination,source

The source operand is subtracted from the destination operand, and the result replaces the destination operand. The operands may be bytes or words. Both operands may be signed or unsigned binary numbers (see AAS and DAS). SUB updates AF, CF, OF, PF, SF and ZF.

SUB   SUBTRACT   SUB

Encoding:

Memory or Register Operand and Register Operand:

0 0 1 0 1 0 d w	mod reg r/m

if d = 1 then LSRC = REG, RSRC = EA, DEST = REG
else LSRC = EA, RSRC = REG, DEST = EA

Immediate Operand from Memory or Register Operand:

1 0 0 0 0 0 s w	mod 1 0 1 r/m	data	data if s:w=01

LSRC = EA, RSRC = data, DEST = EA

Immediate Operand from Accumulator:

0 0 1 0 1 1 0 w	data	data if w=1

if w = 0 then LSRC = AL, RSRC = data, DEST = AL
else LSRC = AX, RSRC = data, DEST = AX

SUB Operands	Clocks*	Transfers	Bytes	SUB Coding Example
register, register	3	—	2	SUB CX, BX
register, memory	9(13) + EA	1	2-4	SUB DX, MATH_TOTAL [SI]
memory, register	16(24) + EA	2	2-4	SUB [BP + 2], CL
accumulator, immediate	4	—	2-3	SUB AL, 10
register, immediate	4	—	3-4	SUB SI, 5280
memory, immediate	17(25) + EA	2	3-6	SUB [BP].BALANCE, 1000

*b(w): where b denotes the number of clock cycles for byte operands and
w denotes the number of clock cycles for word operands.

TEST   TEST   TEST

Operation:

(LSRC) & (RSRC)
(CF) ← 0
(OF) ← 0

Flags Affected:

CF, OF, PF, SF, ZF.
AF undefined

Description:

TEST *destination,source*

TEST performs the logical "and" of the two
operands (byte or word), updates the flags, but
does not return the result, i.e., neither operand
is changed. If a TEST instruction is followed
by a JNZ (jump if not zero) instruction, the
jump will be taken if there are any corresponding 1-bits in both operands.

Encoding:

Memory or Register Operand with Register Operand:

1 0 0 0 0 1 0 w	mod reg r/m

LSRC = REG, RSRC = EA

Immediate Operand with Memory or Register Operand:

1 1 1 1 0 1 1 w	mod 0 0 0 r/m	data	data if w=1

LSRC = EA, RSRC = data

Immediate Operand with Accumulator:

1 0 1 0 1 0 0 w	data	data if w=1

if w = 0 then LSRC = AL, RSRC = data
else LSRC = AX, RSRC = data

TEST Operands	Clocks*	Transfers	Bytes	TEST Coding Example
register, register	3	—	2	TEST SI, DI
register, memory	9(13) + EA	1	2-4	TEST SI, END_COUNT
accumulator, immediate	4	—	2-3	TEST AL, 00100000B
register, immediate	5	—	3-4	TEST BX, 0CC4H
memory, immediate	11(15) + EA	1	3-6	TEST RETURN_CODE, 01H

*b(w): where b denotes the number of clock cycles for byte operands and w
denotes the number of clock cycles for word operands.

WAIT WAIT WAIT

Operation:

None

Flags Affected:

None

Description:

WAIT causes the CPU to enter the wait state
while its TEST line is not active. WAIT does
not affect any flags.

Encoding:

| 10011011 |

WAIT Operands	Clocks	Transfers	Bytes	WAIT Coding Example
(no operands)	3 + 5n	—	1	WAIT

XCHG EXCHANGE XCHG

Operation:

(temp) ← (DEST)
(DEST) ← (SRC)
(SRC) ← (temp)

Flags Affected:

None

Description:

XCHG *destination,source*

XCHG (exchange) switches the contents of the source and destination (byte or word) operands. When used in conjunction with the LOCK prefix, XCHG can test and set a semaphore that controls access to a resource shared by multiple processors (see section 2.5).

Encoding:

Memory or Register Operand with Register Operand:

| 1 0 0 0 0 1 1 w | mod reg r/m |

SRC = EA, DEST = REG

Register Operand with Accumulator:

| 1 0 0 1 0 reg |

SRC = REG, DEST = AX

XCHG Operands	Clocks*	Transfers	Bytes	XCHG Coding Example
accumulator, reg16	3	—	1	XCHG AX, BX
memory, register	17(25) + EA	2	2-4	XCHG SEMAPHORE, AX
register, register	4	—	2	XCHG AL, BL

*b(w): where b denotes the number of clock cycles for byte operands and w denotes the number of clock cycles for word operands.

XLAT TRANSLATE XLAT

Operation:

AL ← ((BX) + (AL))

Flags Affected:

None

Description:

XLAT *translate-table*

XLAT (translate) replaces a byte in the AL register with a byte from a 256-byte, user-coded translation table. Register BX is assumed to point to the beginning of the table. The byte in AL is used as an index into the table and is replaced by the byte at the offset in the table corresponding to AL's binary value.

The first byte in the table has an offset of 0. For example, if AL contains 5H, and the sixth element of the translation table contains 33H, then AL will contain 33H following the instruction. XLAT is useful for translating characters from one code to another, the classic example being ASCII to EBCDIC or the reverse.

Encoding:

| 11010111 |

XLAT Operands	Clocks	Transfers	Bytes	XLAT Coding Example
source-table	11	1	1	XLAT ASCII__TAB

XOR EXCLUSIVE OR XOR

Operation:

(DEST) ← (LSRC) XOR (RSRC)
(CF) ← 0
(OF) ← 0

Flags Affected:

CF, OF, PF, SF, ZF.
AF undefined

Description:

XOR destination,source

XOR (Exclusive Or) performs the logical "exclusive or" of the two operands and returns the result to the destination operand. A bit in the result is set if the corresponding bits of the original operands contain opposite values (one is set, the other is cleared); otherwise the result bit is cleared.

XOR   EXCLUSIVE OR   XOR

Encoding:

Memory or Register Operand with Register Operand:

0 0 1 1 0 0 d w	mod reg r/m

if d = 1 then LSRC = REG, RSRC = EA, DEST = REG
else LSRC = EA, RSRC = REG, DEST = EA

Immediate Operand to Memory or Register Operand:

1 0 0 0 0 0 0 w	mod 1 1 0 r/m	data	data if w=1

LSRC = EA, RSRC = data, DEST = EA

Immediate Operand to Accumulator:

0 0 1 1 0 1 0 w	data	data if w=1

if w = 0 then LSRC = AL, RSRC = data, DEST = AL
else LSRC = AX, RSRC = data, DEST = AX

XOR Operands	Clocks*	Transfers	Bytes	XOR Coding Example
register, register	3	—	2	XOR CX, BX
register, memory	9(13) + EA	1	2-4	XOR CL, MASK__BYTE
memory, register	16(24) + EA	2	2-4	XOR ALPHA [SI], DX
accumulator, immediate	4	—	2-3	XOR AL, 01000010B
register, immediate	4	—	3-4	XOR SI, 00C2H
memory, immediate	17(25) + EA	2	3-6	XOR RETURN__CODE, 0D2H

*b(w): where b denotes the number of clock cycles for byte operands and w denotes the number of clock cycles for word operands.

iAPX 88 Hardware Design

CHAPTER 3
HARDWARE DESIGN

INTRODUCTION

This chapter discusses the hardware design of iAPX 88 systems. First, the pins and signals of the 8088 CPU are functionally described for simple, but powerful iAPX 88 systems.

The timings of 8088 signals are explained, and how they cleanly interface the 8088 CPU with the rest of the system.

Other parts of the iAPX 88 system are discussed including, the clock generator, reset and wait state circuits.

Interrupt handling follows, leading into a description of maximum mode iAPX 88 systems.

8088 CPU Pin Functions

The functions of the 8088 CPU pins, are categorized by these groups (Fig. 3-1):

1) Address
2) Data
3) Control and Status
4) Timing
5) Power/Ground

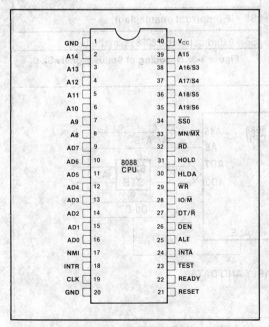

Figure 3-1. 8088 CPU Pins

The number of pins in each group varies. The only pin in the Timing group is the clock, while others, such as the Address and Data groups, use many pins and are multiplexed with other functions.

The 8088 pins and their functions are briefly described here. For more information, consult the iAPX 88/10 data sheet (see pg. 37 of Appendix) and the iAPX 86, 88 Family User's Manual.

ADDRESS AND DATA

The 8088 CPU uses 20 pins to directly address up to one million bytes of memory. Some address pins are multiplexed to also function as data or status pins. Thus, the 8088 provides all necessary signals from a 40-pin package.

The address pins are discussed below in these three groups:

1) AD_0-AD_7. Drives the lower eight address bits and also the iAPX 88's 8-bit data bus.
2) A_8-A_{15}. Address bits 8-15.
3) A_{16}-A_{19}. Drives the upper 4 bits of the iAPX 88's 20 bit address bus; also generates status signals.

AD_0-AD_7

Pins AD_0 through AD_7 are time-multiplexed in the iAPX 88 system to serve as both address and data lines (Fig. 3-2). At the beginning of every machine cycle, the lower 8 address bits are driven on these pins. Later in the machine cycle, these pins function as the 8-bit data bus. At this time, AD_0-AD_7 may be inputs or outputs, depending on whether the 8088 is reading or writing data to or from the system.

These lines float to 3-state OFF during interrupt acknowledge and local bus "hold acknowledge."

A_8-A_{15}

These pins drive the next 8 address bits on the address bus. They are not multiplexed with other signals and are valid during the entire machine cycle.

These lines float to 3-state OFF during interrupt acknowledge and local bus "hold acknowledge".

A_{16}-A_{19}

A_{16} through A_{19} have two sets of functions. First, at the beginning of each machine cycle, these pins drive the upper 4 bits of the iAPX 88's 20-bit address bus. These 4 address bits, (not provided by other 8-bit microprocessors), together with the other 16-bits of address, enable the iAPX 88 to directly address 1 megabyte of memory. This is 16 times more than 8080, 8085, Z80,* MC6800** and MC6809**.

The second function of these four pins is to provide status information. After the address has been latched, pins A_{16} and A_{17} change their function to status signals S3 and S4. These two signals can be decoded to determine which memory segment is being accessed by the 8088 during the current machine cycle (Fig. 3-3). This information could be used to enable memory, such that each of the

4 segments could have its own megabyte of memory, extending the iAPX 88 memory space to 4 megabytes.

Status line S5 gives the state of the interrupt flag. S6 is always low. These status signals are not necessary for normal operation of most systems, but they can be useful for diagnostics.

These lines float to 3-state OFF during local bus "hold acknowledge." During interrupt acknowledge, the address information is indeterminate, but the status information is valid.

POWER

The 8088 should have pin 40 connected to +5V, and pins 1 and 20 are ground. Decou-

S3	S4	
0	0	Alternate (relative to the ES segment)
1	0	Stack (relative to the SS segment)
0	1	Code/None (relative to the CS segment or a default of zero)
1	1	Data (relative to the DS segment)
S5 = IF (interrupt enable flag)		
S6 = 0 (indicates the 8088 is on the bus)		

Figure 3-3. Decoding of Status Signals S_3-S_6

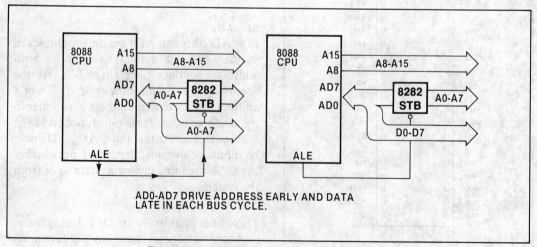

ADO-AD7 DRIVE ADDRESS EARLY AND DATA LATE IN EACH BUS CYCLE.

Figure 3-2. Time Multiplexing of Address and Data

*Z80 is a registered trademark of Zilog Corporation.
**MC6800 and MC6809 are registered trademarks of Motorola Corporation.

pling capacitors are recommended to reduce the noise on the power and ground lines.

TIMING
Pin 19 is the clock input for basic timing of the 8088. The maximum clock frequency is 5 MHz for the 8088, and 8 MHz for the 8088-2. The clock signal is usually generated by the 8284A (see pg. 3-13).

CONTROL STATUS
These lines specify the type of machine cycle occurring and control external logic.

$\overline{RD}$. The Read line is an active LOW output, which indicates when the CPU is reading data from a memory or I/O device.

This signal floats to 3-state OFF during "hold acknowledge".

$\overline{WR}$. The Write signal is an active LOW output, which indicates that the CPU is outputting data onto the data bus to write it into a memory or I/O device.

This signal floats to 3-state OFF during "hold acknowledge".

ALE. Address Latch Enable is an output that latches the addresses on the iAPX 88's address bus. This signal is usually connected to the STB input of an 8282 latch, (Fig. 3-5).

The falling edge of ALE latches the address on the system address bus to hold it throughout the entire machine cycle, even though some of the 8088's address pins will change their functions during this time. ALE never floats.

$IO/\overline{M}$. This output specifies whether the current machine cycle will address an I/O or a memory device (HIGH = I/O, LOW = Memory). This signal is valid during the entire machine cycle, and floats to 3-state OFF during "hold acknowledge".

RESET. Providing an orderly way to start or restart an iAPX 88 system, reset is an active HIGH input to the 8088, synchronized by the 8284A.

Reset causes the processor to immediately terminate its present activity and to condition the bus as shown in Fig. 3-15. When reset returns LOW, the 8088 will begin executing from memory location $FFFF0_{16}$.

During reset the processor is initialized to the following conditions:

1) The Flag register is reset to 0000. This disables interrupts and the single step mode.

2) The DS, ES, SS and IP registers are reset to 0000.

3) The CS register is set to $FFFF_{16}$.

$Mn/\overline{Mx}$. This input configures the 8088 in the minimum mode when HIGH, and in the maximum mode when LOW. This manual focuses on minimum mode systems. Refer to pg. 3-24 for a discussion of maximum mode systems.

The pins and signals described above are sufficient to completely control a small multiplexed bus system (Fig. 3-4). Larger systems, however, use latches and transceivers for demultiplexing and increasing the drive of the busses. Control signals for handling these latches and for other functions are described below as they are used in the iAPX 88 larger system (Fig. 3-5).

$DT/\overline{R}$. Data Transmit/Receive is an output, controlling the direction in which the data bus transceivers (8286s or 8287s) drive the data on the data bus. When HIGH, data is transmitted onto the system data bus from the 8088. When LOW, data is received from the system bus to be read by the 8088. This signal floats to 3-state OFF during "hold acknowledge".

$\overline{DEN}$. The Data Enable output drives the output enable of the 8286/8287 data bus transceivers. This prevents bus contention by disabling the data bus transceivers while the 8088 is driving addresses on the address/data bus.

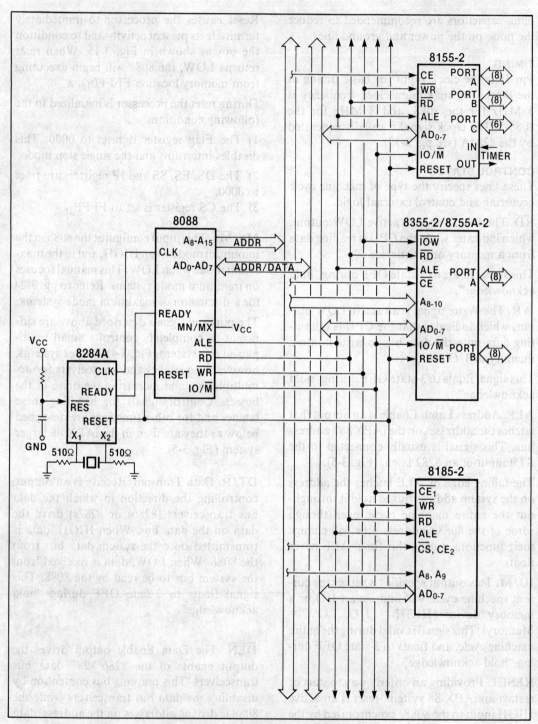

Figure 3-4. iAPX 88 Multiplexed Bus System

This signal floats to 3-state OFF during "hold acknowledge" (Fig. 3-5).

INTR. Interrupt Request is a level-triggered active HIGH input, sampled during the last clock cycle of each instruction. It tells the 8088 to stop what it is currently doing and service an I/O or peripheral device.

When INTR is detected HIGH, the 8088 jumps to an interrupt service routine via an interrupt vector table in system memory.

INTR can be internally masked through software by resetting the interrupt enable bit in the Flag register. **INTR** is internally synchronized.

INTA. Used as a read strobe during interrupt acknowledge cycles, $\overline{\text{INTA}}$ is active LOW during T2, T3, and T4 of each interrupt acknowledge cycle. $\overline{\text{INTA}}$ is never floated.

SSO. This is a status output. When decoded with IO/$\overline{\text{M}}$ and DR/R, $\overline{\text{SS0}}$ specifies the type of bus activity in progress (Fig.3-6).

IO/$\overline{\text{M}}$	DT/$\overline{\text{R}}$	$\overline{\text{SSO}}$	
1(HIGH)	0	0	Interrupt Acknowledge
1	0	1	Read I/O port
1	1	0	Write I/O port
1	1	1	Halt
0(LOW)	0	0	Code access
0	0	1	Read memory
0	1	0	Write memory
0	1	1	Passive

Figure 3-6. iAPX 88 Status Decoding

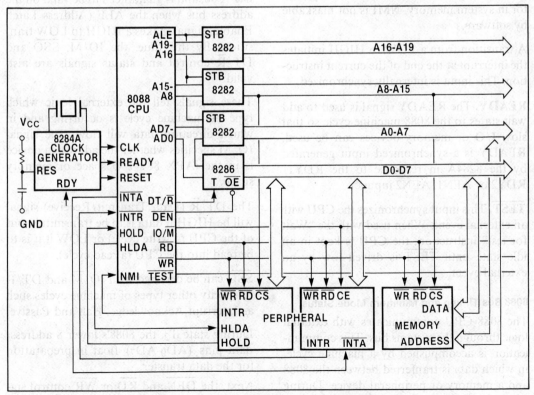

Figure 3-5. iAPX 88 with Buffered Demultiplexed Busses

HOLD/HLDA. Hold indicates that another master is requesting control of the local bus. To be acknowledged, HOLD must be in its active HIGH state.

The processor receiving the "HOLD" request will issue HLDA (HIGH) at the end of the current data transfer operation. A data transfer operation is one bus cycle for a byte operation and two bus cycles for a word operation or interrupt acknowledge.

After HOLD is detected as LOW, the processor LOWers HLDA, and when the processor needs to run another cycle, it will again drive the local bus and control lines.

NMI. Non-Maskable Interrupt is an edge-triggered input causing a type 2 interrupt.

A subroutine is activated via an interrupt vector in system memory. NMI is not maskable by software.

A transition from a LOW to HIGH initiates the interrupt at the end of the current instruction. This input is internally synchronized.

READY. The READY signal is used to add wait states to the 8088 machine cycle so that slow I/O or memory devices can be used. READY is a synchronized input generated by the 8284A in response to the RDY1/RDY2 or $\overline{AEN1}/\overline{AEN2}$ inputs.

TEST. This input synchronizes the CPU with an external event. When used with the "Wait for test" instruction, the CPU is kept in an idle state until $\overline{TEST}$ is driven low by an external event.

8088 Bus Timing and Minimum Mode Status

The 8088 CPU communicates with external logic through the systems bus. This communication is accomplished by a machine cycle, in which data is tranferred between the 8088 and a memory or peripheral device. During this machine cycle, the 8088 first generates an address to select the proper memory or peripheral device. Then the 8088 activates the read or write control-line, and the data is either transferred *into* the 8088 from the selected memory or peripheral device (a read cycle) or *out of* the 8088 to the selected memory or peripheral device (a write cycle).

On termination of the cycle, the data is latched by the 8088 (read), or the selected device (write), and the control signal is deactivated.

The basic machine cycle of the 8088 consists of four clock periods or *T-states*, T_1, T_2, T_3 and T_4. (Fig. 3-7)

During the first T state (T_1), the CPU places an address on the 20-bit address/data/status bus. This address specifies a unique location in the memory or I/O address spaces of the iAPX 88, and is guaranteed to be valid on the address bus when the ALE (Address Latch Enable) signal makes a HIGH to LOW transition. By this time, the $IO/\overline{M}$, $\overline{SSO}$ and $DT/\overline{R}$ control and status signals are also valid.

These signals tell the external logic which type of machine cycle is occurring and in which direction data will flow. The signal $IO/\overline{M}$ specifies whether the addressed device is in the iAPX 88's I/O space or memory space.

The $DT/\overline{R}$ (Data Transmit/Receive) signal will be HIGH if data is to be transmitted out of the CPU (a write cycle) or LOW if it is to be read into the CPU (a read cycle).

$\overline{SSO}$ can be decoded with $IO/\overline{M}$ and $DT/\overline{R}$ to specify other types of machine cycles such as Interrupt Acknowledge, Halt and Passive.

During state T_2, the 8088's lower 8 address/data pins (AD_0-AD_7) float in preparation for the data transfer.

Next, the $\overline{DEN}$ and $\overline{RD}$ or $\overline{WR}$ control signals become valid, to enable the data onto the bus for the transfer. This data will be read into, or out of, the 8088 through pins AD_0-AD_7, which now function as the data bus. Also at this time the upper 4 address lines switch from address (A_{16}-A_{19}) to status ($S3$-$S6$). The status information available from decoding these lines is primarily for diagnostics monitoring.

However, S3 and S4 can be decoded to determine which of the four segments is being accessed by that particular machine cycle. This information can be used to select one of the four memory segments (Code, Data, Stack or Extra) being addressed by the iAPX 88. This technique allows memory partitioning by segment to expand memory addressing up to four megabytes.

Decoding S3 and S4 can also provide a degree of memory protection, by preventing erroneous writes into overlapping segments.

During T_3 the CPU continues to assert write data or sample read data on the lower 8 bus lines (AD_0-AD_7) and to provide status information on the upper 4 bus lines (A_{16}/$S3$-A_{19}/$S6$). This state allows time for the data to stabilize on the bus and be read by the 8088 or the selected memory or peripheral.

At the beginning of T_4 the $\overline{RD}$ or $\overline{WR}$ line goes inactive (HIGH) and the data is latched into the 8088 or the selected device. The $\overline{DEN}$ and $DT/\overline{R}$ signals also go HIGH and the memory or peripheral is deselected from the bus.

Extending Machine Cycle

If the memory or I/O device cannot transfer data at maximum CPU transfer rate, the

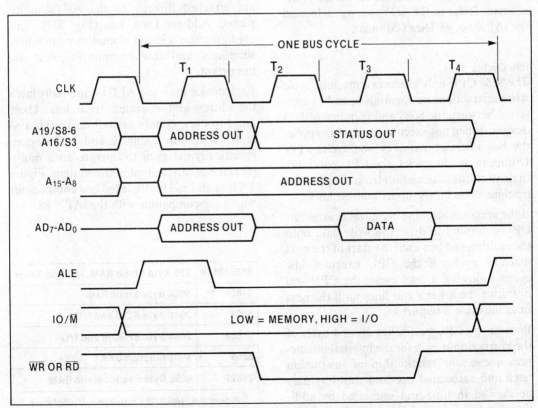

Figure 3-7. iAPX 88 Basic Machine Cycle

device must tell the CPU that the data transfer is not complete and that the machine cycle must be extended. It does this by bringing the READY input LOW before the beginning of T_3. This forces the 8088 to insert additional clock cycles (Wait States or Tw's) between T_3 and T_4.

Bus activity during Tw is the same as T_3. The address and control signals remain on the bus, allowing time to complete the data transfer. When the selected device has completed the transfer, it brings the READY pin HIGH, allowing the CPU to continue from the Tw states into T_4.

The CPU will then latch the data on the bus during T_4, as it would during a normal machine cycle. The machine cycle is then terminated in T_4 when the command lines are disabled, and the external device is deselected. Refer to READY, see pg. 3-16, and the iAPX 86, 88 User's Manual.

Idle Cycles

The 8088 CPU only executes a machine cycle when instructions or operands must be transferred between the 8088 and memory or I/O devices. When not executing a machine cycle, the bus interface executes idle cycles (T_1). During these idle cycles, the CPU continues to drive status information from the previous machine cycle on the upper address lines.

If the previous machine cycle was a write, the CPU continues to drive the write data onto the multiplexed bus until the start of the next machine cycle. If the CPU executes idle cycles following a read cycle, the CPU will not drive the lower 8 bus lines until the next machine cycle is required.

Because the CPU prefetches up to 4 bytes of the instruction stream for the internal instruction queue, the relationship of instruction fetch and associated operand transfers may be skewed in time and separated by additional instruction fetches.

In general, if a given instruction is fetched into the 8088's internal instruction queue, several additional instructions may be fetched before the given instruction is removed from the queue and executed.

If the instruction being executed is a jump or other control transfer instruction, any instructions remaining in the queue are discarded without execution.

Bus Interface

The bus interface of an iAPX 88 can be structured in a number of ways. The best configuration for a particular application depends on system size, and the type of memory, and I/O devices used.

The simplest bus interface for an iAPX 88 system uses the "multiplexed bus" configuration. In this system, memory and I/O devices are attached directly to the 8088's multiplexed Address/Data Bus (Fig. 3-4). This configuration is ideal for small systems where simplicity and low component-count are important.

Each device must use ALE to internally latch the address and separate it from data. There are, however, certain limitations to this system. First, only memory and I/O devices specifically designed to operate on a multiplexed bus can be used in this system. Figure 3-8 lists all Intel multiplexed bus components which are compatible with the iAPX 88.

8155/8156	256 Byte Static RAM, I/O and Timer
8185	1024 Byte Static Ram
8355	2048 Byte ROM and I/O
8755A	2048 Byte EPROM and I/O
8256	Multifunction UART
21821	4096 Byte Pseudostatic RAM

Figure 3-8. iAPX 88 Compatible Multiplexed Bus Components

Secondly, a multiplexed system is necessarily small — usually less than 15 components — due to the limited drive capability of the MOS parts which directly drive the bus.

Larger iAPX 88 systems will normally use a demultiplexed and buffered bus configuration, (Fig. 3-5). In this configuration, the 8282 is used to latch the address and hold it on the address bus throughout the entire machine cycle. The 8286 octal transceiver buffers the data bus to provide the higher drive capability necessary for large systems. Small systems could eliminate this transceiver and the latch on address lines A_8-A_{15}.

Memory and Peripheral Interface

The 8088 uses address, data and control information to control and communicate with system memory and peripheral components. Some components connect directly to the multiplexed Address/Data Bus, while others have separate address and data pins and must connect to a *demultiplexed* bus. Some interfacing methods for both multiplexed and demultiplexed busses follow.

MULTIPLEXED BUS SYSTEMS

The connection of two multiplexed bus components (the 8755A and 8185) is given in Figure 3-9. These components receive both address and data on the same pins. The address is internally latched by the ALE control signal.

The data then flows in (write), or out (read) if the device has been enabled using the CS (chip select) and CE (chip enable) inputs.

Note that the $\overline{RD}$, $\overline{WR}$, IO/$\overline{M}$ and ALE control signals from the 8088 CPU connect *directly* to these chips.

Linear Chip Select

Connecting A_{19} to CE2 of the 8755A in Fig. 3-9 enables this device whenever A_{19} is HIGH. CE1 is grounded so it is always valid.

The 8185 is enabled whenever A_{11} is LOW and A_{12} is HIGH by connecting CS to A_{11}, CE2 to A_{12}, and $\overline{CE1}$ to ground.

Recall that address lines A_8-A_{15} are held stable throughout the machine cycle and thus can be connected directly to the chip enable or chip select lines.

Linear chip select is a method that reduces system chip complexity and chip count. At the same time, linear chip selection reduces available address space in the system. For instance a 2K memory device, the 8755A, is enabled by any address between 80000_{16} and $FFFFF_{16}$ (a 512K byte logical address space) (Fig. 3-9). This is usually not a problem because most systems using the multiplexed bus configuration are small enough that the 1 megabyte address space of the iAPX 88 is far larger than necessary.

DE-MULTIPLEXED BUS SYSTEMS

Most system memories and peripherals require the address to be stable for the entire machine cycle, therefore requiring address to be latched and held on a separate de-multiplexed address bus. Figure 3-10 shows this system, with address lines A_0-A_7 latched by an 8282 octal latch, which drives the lower 8 bits of the de-multiplexed address bus.

Note that the data bus is still multiplexed. This brings up two things to consider.

First, multiplexed bus parts can still be used in this system, provided they are connected to the data bus.

Second, any devices connected to the data bus must guarantee not to drive data onto this bus before the ALE signal has latched the address into the 8282 and the 8088 has 3-stated its lower 8 address drivers in preparation for reading the data. If a device were to drive the data bus as soon as its address is generated, bus contention would occur because the 8088 is still driving the address on this bus. This could cause an incorrect address to be latched into the 8282 address latch.

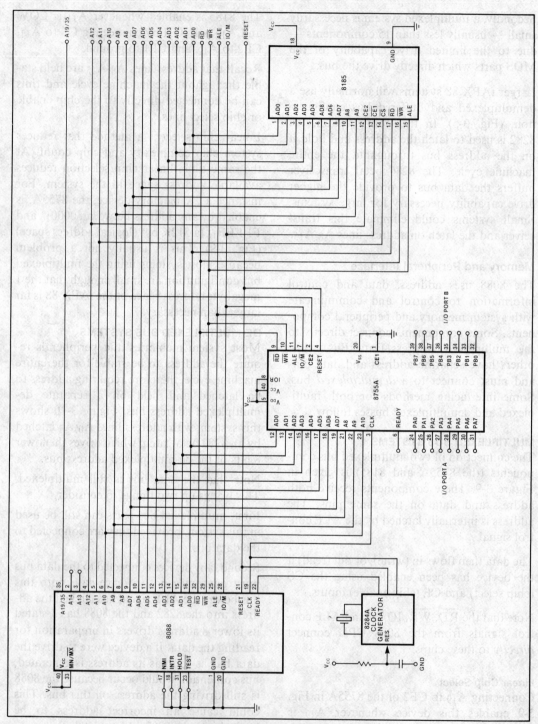

Figure 3-9. Multiplexed Bus Connections

Conveniently, most Intel peripherals, EPROMs and RAMs in the iAPX 88 family provide output enable or read inputs which prevent this from happening.

Observe how some memory and peripheral components are connected in this system configuration. A 2716 2K x 8 EPROM and two 2114 RAMs are connected in an iAPX 88 system with a demultiplexed address bus (Fig. 3-10). Address lines A_0-A_{10} from the demultiplexed address bus are connected to the address inputs A_0-A_{10} of the 2716.

The multiplexed data bus is connected to the data output of the 2716. The $\overline{CE}$ (chip enable) input is driven from an address decoder. This could be either a decoder PROM or a TTL decoder such as a 74LS139.

Another possibility is to use a linear chip select, described previously.

The output enable ($\overline{OE}$) of the 2716 is driven by the 8088's $\overline{RD}$ control line. This enables the output data onto the data bus from the 2716 with the proper timing to prevent bus contention problems.

The connections for a 2114 RAM are a little different from a 2716 because the 2114 is a 1K x 4 memory, and because it can be written-to as well as read. Also, because it does not have an output enable, care must be taken to not cause bus contention by driving the data bus too early.

The address pins of the 2114 are directly connected to A_0-A_9 on the de-multiplexed address bus. The data pins I/O_1-I/O_4 are connected to the multiplexed data bus.

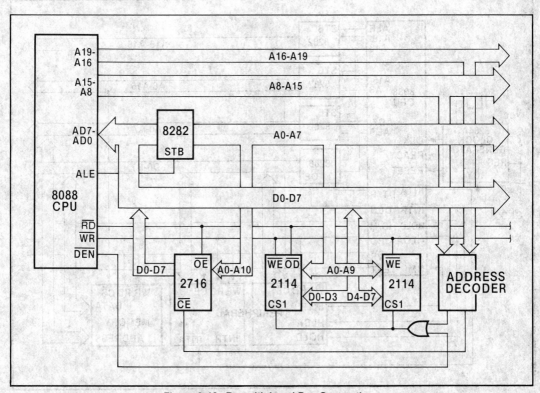

Figure 3-10. Demultiplexed Bus Connections

Because the 2114 is a 1K x 4 memory, we need two 2114's to make an 8-bit wide memory. The two 2114s are connected to the data bus so that one drives data lines D_0-D_3, and the other drives D_4-D_7. Any read or write to the 2114s will enable both chips at the same time to move the 8-bit data byte.

The chip select input cannot be connected directly to the output of the address decoder, as was done with the 2716, because the 2114 has no output enable pin. Instead, $\overline{CS}$ is delayed by ORing the chip select with the $\overline{DEN}$ output of the 8088. This delays the 2114s from outputting the data until after the address has been latched by the falling edge of ALE and the 8088 has tri-stated its address/data bus.

LARGE DE-MULTIPLEXED BUS SYSTEMS

The bus configuration in Figure 3-10 is fine for medium-sized systems, but if too many components are connected to the busses, the 8088's outputs will not be able to drive the system.

Figure 3-5 shows a system where 8282 latches have been added to lines A_8-A_{15} and A_{16}-A_{19}, and an 8286 octal transceiver has been added to the multiplexed data bus. This accomplishes two things.

First, address bits A_{16}-A_{19} are multiplexed with status bits $S3$-$S6$ and therefore must be latched like lines AD_0-AD_7 if they are to be used in addressing.

Second, the 8286 on the data bus, and the 8282s on the address bus, can drive much higher loads than the 8088 can. With the 8088

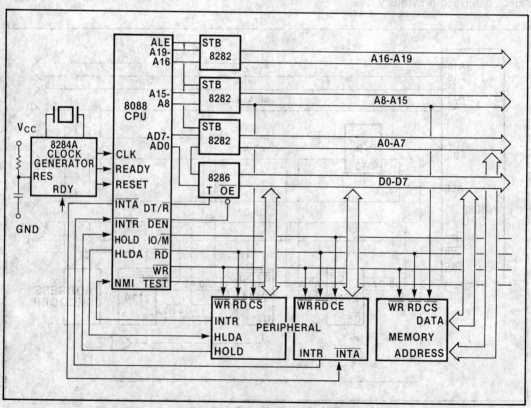

Figure 3-11. iAPX 88 with Buffered Demultiplexed Busses

drive specified to drive 2.0mA and 100pF, a system with 5 peripheral components and 10 memory components would overload the bus.

The 8282 non-inverting and 8283 inverting octal latches plus the 8286 non-inverting and 8287 inverting octal transceivers can drive loads up to 32mA and 300pF. The 8282/8283 are directly controlled by connecting ALE to the STB (strobe) input and grounding $\overline{OE}$. The 8286/8287 is controlled by connecting the 8088's $\overline{DEN}$ and DT/$\overline{R}$ signals to the 8286/8287's EN (enable) and T (transmit inputs). These signals provide the proper timing to guarantee that the address is latched properly and that the 8286/8287 drives data in the correct direction for read and write cycles.

Note that adding these latches and transceivers increases the chip count and adds propagation delays (25ns for the 8283 and 8287 and 35ns for the 8282 and 8286) that subtract from the read or write access time of the system's memory and peripheral devices. For complete specifications of the 8283/8282 and 8286/8287 see the data sheets in the Appendix.

Memory Operands

The iAPX 88 directly operates on 8- or 16-bit memory based variables. This means that a variable may occupy one or two bytes of memory (each byte is 8-bits). Consequently, 8-bit operands are read or written in one machine cycle, while 16-bit operands require two bus cycles.

16-bit operands are stored in memory, with the least significant byte (LSB) first and the most significant byte (MSB) in the next location. Figure 3-12 shows that when the 16-bit operand 6543 was moved from the AX register to memory location 3, the LSB (43) was moved into location 3 by the first machine cycle, and the MSB (65) was moved to location 4 in the next machine cycle.

Clock Generation

The 8088 requires a clock signal with fast rise and fall times (10ns maximum) between low and high voltages.

The maximum clock frequency of the 8088 is 5 MHz, and 8 MHz for the 8088-2. The recommended method for generating this signal is to use Intel's 8284A clock generator.

USING 8284A

Either an external frequency source or a series resonant crystal may be selected to drive the 8284A. The selected source must oscillate at 3X the desired CPU frequency.

To select the crystal inputs of the 8284A as the frequency source for clock generation, the F/$\overline{C}$ input to the 8284A must be strapped to ground. The crystal should be connected using the configuration shown in Figure 3-13.

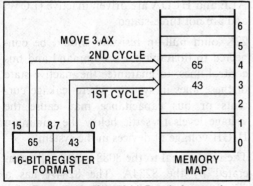

Figure 3-12. How 16-bit Data is Arranged within 8-bit memory

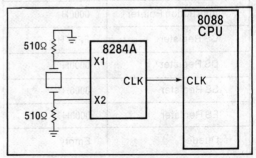

Figure 3-13. Generating Clock Signal with 8284A

If a high-accuracy frequency source, externally-variable frequency source, or a common source for driving multiple 8284A's is desired, the External Frequency Input (EFI) of the 8284A can be selected by strapping the $F/\overline{C}$ input HIGH through a pull-up resistor (~ 1K ohms). The external frequency source should be TTL compatible, have a 50% duty cycle, and oscillate at 3 times the desired CPU operating frequency.

The 8284A has several other functions, including RESET and READY generation (see pg. 3-16). For complete details on iAPX 88 clock generation, refer to the iAPX 88/10 and 8284A data sheets.

Reset

The 8088 RESET line provides an orderly way to start or restart an iAPX 88 system.

When the processor detects the positive-going edge of a pulse on RESET, it terminates all activities until the signal goes LOW, at which time the internal CPU registers are initialized to the reset condition (Fig. 3-14).

Upon RESET, the code segment register and the instruction pointer are initialized to $FFFF_{16}$ and 0 respectively. Therefore, the 8088 executes its first instruction following system reset from absolute memory location FFFF0H. This location normally contains an intersegment direct JMP instruction whose target is the actual beginning of the system program.

As external (maskable) interrupts are disabled by system reset, the system software should re-enable interrupts as soon as the system is initialized, to the point where interrupts can be processed.

The 8088 requires an active HIGH reset, with minimum pulse width of 4 clocks, except after power-on which requires a 50 μs reset pulse.

Since the CPU internally synchronizes reset with the clock, the reset is internally active for up to one clock period after the external reset.

Non-Maskable interrupts (NMI) or hold requests occurring during the internal reset are not acknowledged. A hold request active immediately after the internal reset will be honored before the first instruction fetch.

Upon reset the 8088 will condition the system busses in the following manner (Fig. 3-15):

The address bus will float to the three-state condition upon detection of reset by the CPU. It floats until the CPU comes out of reset and begins fetching code from $FFFF0_H$.

Other signals which three-state will be driven HIGH for one clock low period prior to entering three-state (Fig. 3-16).

ALE and HLDA are driven inactive (LOW) and are not three-stated.

22K ohm pull-up resistors should be connected to floatable CPU command and bus control lines, to guarantee the inactive state of these lines in systems where leakage currents or bus capacitance may cause the voltage levels to settle below the minimum HIGH voltage of devices in the system.

The reset signal to the 8088 is normally generated by the 8284A. The 8284A has a schmitt trigger input (RES) for generating reset from a LOW active external reset.

CPU COMPONENT	CONTENT
FLAGS	Clear
Instruction Pointer	0000H
CS Register	FFFFH
DS Register	0000H
SS Register	0000H
ES Register	0000H
Queue	Empty

Figure 3-14. CPU State Following Reset

The hysteresis specified in the 8284A data sheet implies that at least 0.25 volts will separate the logic 0 and 1 switching point of the 8284A reset input. Inputs without hysteresis switch from LOW to HIGH and HIGH to LOW at approximately the same voltage threshold. The inputs are guaranteed to switch at specified LOW and HIGH voltages (V_{IL} and V_{IH}), but the actual switching point is anywhere in between.

Since V_{IL} min. is specified at 0.8 volts, the hysteresis guarantees that the reset will be active until the input reaches at least 1.05 volts. A reset will not be recognized until the input drops at least 0.25 volts below the reset inputs V_{IH} of 2.6 volts.

To guarantee reset from power up, the reset input must remain below 1.05 volts for 50 μs after V_{CC} has reached the minimum supply voltage of 4.5 volts. The hysteresis allows the reset input to be driven by a simple RC circuit (Fig. 3-17).

The calculated RC value does not include time for the power supply to reach 4.5 volts, or the charge accumulated during this interval. Without the hysteresis, the reset output might oscillate as the input voltage passes through the switching voltage of the input. The calculated RC value provides the minimum required reset period of 50 μs for 8284A's that switch at the 1.05 volt level, and a reset period of approximately 162 μs for 8284A's that switch at the 2.6 volt level.

SIGNAL	CONDITION
AD0-AD7 * A8-A15	FLOAT
SS0 * IO/M * DT/R * DEN * WR * RD * INTA	DRIVEN HIGH, THEN FLOAT
ALE * HLDA	LOW

Figure 3-15. iAPX 88 Bus Condition During Reset

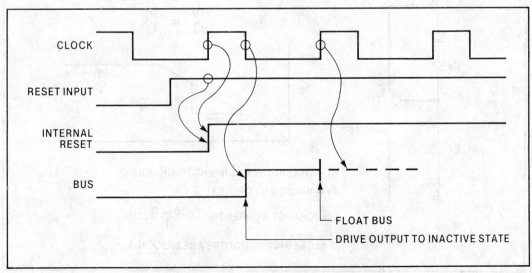

Figure 3-16. iAPX 88 Bus During Reset

If tighter tolerance between the minimum and maximum reset times is necessary, the reset circuit shown in Figure 3-18 might be used rather than the simple RC circuit. This circuit provides a constant current source and a linear charge rate on the capacitor, rather than the inverse exponential charge rate of the RC circuit. The maximum reset period for this implementation is 124 μs.

The 8284A synchronizes the reset input with the CPU clock to generate the RESET signal to the CPU. This output is also available as a general reset to the entire system. Reset has no effect on any clock circuits in the 8284A.

READY IMPLEMENTATION AND TIMING

As discussed previously, the ready signal is used in the iAPX 88 system to generate wait states to accommodate slow memory and I/O devices. Ready is also used in multiprocessor systems to force the CPU to wait for access to the system bus.

The 8284A can be set up for systems using synchronous or asynchronous ready signals by strapping the $\overline{\text{ASYNCH}}$ input HIGH (synchronous) or LOW (asynchronous). To use the synchronous configuration, the designer must analyze the ready timing to insure that the setup and hold requirements

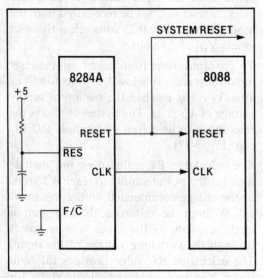

Figure 3-17. 8284A Reset Circuit

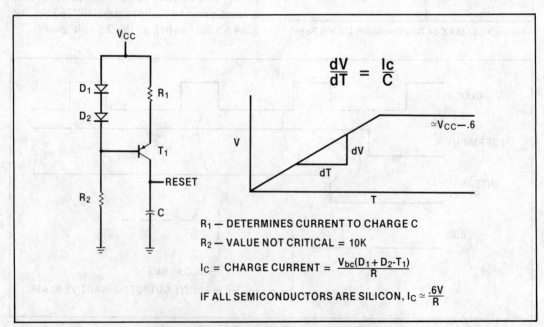

$$\frac{dV}{dT} = \frac{Ic}{C}$$

$\simeq V_{CC} - .6$

R₁ — DETERMINES CURRENT TO CHARGE C

R₂ — VALUE NOT CRITICAL = 10K

I_C = CHARGE CURRENT = $\dfrac{V_{bc}(D_1 + D_2 - T_1)}{R}$

IF ALL SEMICONDUCTORS ARE SILICON, $I_C \simeq \dfrac{.6V}{R}$

Figure 3-18. Constant Current on Reset Circuit

are always met by the 8284A's RDY and $\overline{\text{AEN}}$ inputs. If this can not be guaranteed, the asynchronous configuration must be used.

Asynchronous System

To insert a wait state in the asynchronous configuration, the RDY inputs must be valid at least 35ns before the rising edge of the clock in state T_2. The $\overline{\text{AEN}}$ must be valid 50ns before that edge.

If RDY or $\overline{\text{AEN}}$ make a transition later than these setup times, the 8284A may not recognize the change in time to cause the READY output to change until after the next clock cycle. For a *normally not READY* system, this simply causes an extra wait state to be added. In *normally READY* systems, this must be avoided because it results in premature termination of the machine cycle.

Synchronous Systems

In synchronous systems, setup times for the 8284A's RDY and $\overline{\text{AEN}}$ inputs are specified from the *falling* edge of the clock in state T_2. In this configuration ($\overline{\text{ASYNCH}}$ strapped LOW), transitions must not occur during the RDY or $\overline{\text{AEN}}$ setup time to insure proper operation of the 8284A.

Depending on the size and characteristics of the system, ready implementation may use either the *normally READY* or the *normally not READY* approach.

Normally Ready Systems

In *normally READY* systems, all devices are assumed to operate at the maximum CPU bus bandwidth. Devices that do not meet this requirement must disable READY as noted above to guarantee the insertion of wait states (Fig. 3-19). This implementation is typically used in small single-CPU systems. It reduces the logic required to control the READY signal. Since a device requiring wait states may fail to disable READY in time to be recognized, resulting in premature termination of the machine cycle, the system timing must be carefully analyzed when using this approach.

Normally Not Ready Systems

An alternate ready implementation is to have the system normally not READY. When the selected device receives the command ($\overline{\text{RD}}/$ $\overline{\text{WR}}/\overline{\text{INTA}}$) and has had sufficient time to complete the data transfer, it activates READY to the CPU, allowing the CPU to terminate the machine cycle (Fig. 3-20). This implementation is characteristic of large multiprocessor systems, multibus systems, or where propagation delays, bus access delays and device characteristics inherently slow the system down. For maximum system performance, devices that can run with no wait states must return "READY" within the previously described time. Failure to respond in

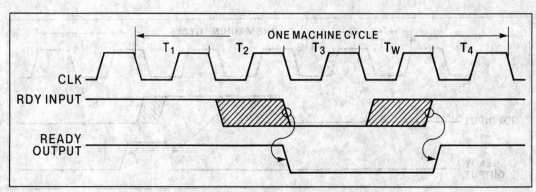

Figure 3-19. Normally READY Wait State Timing

time will only result in the insertion of one or more wait states.

RDY1 and RDY2

To generate a stable READY signal to satisfy the 8088's setup hold times, the 8284A provides two separate system ready inputs (RDY1 and RDY2) and a single synchronized ready output (READY) for the CPU.

The RDY inputs are enabled with separate active LOW access enables ($\overline{AEN1}$, $\overline{AEN2}$) to select one of the two ready signals. The system ready inputs to the 8284A (RDY1, RDY2) must be valid 35ns (TR1VCL) before T_3 and $\overline{AEN}$ must be valid 60ns before T_3.

For a system using only one RDY input, the associated $\overline{AEN}$ is tied to ground while the other $\overline{AEN}$ is connected to 5 volts through 1K ohms (Fig. 3-21). If the system generates a LOW active ready signal, it can be connected to one of the 8284A's $\overline{AEN}$ inputs, if the additional setup time required by the $\overline{AEN}$ input is satisfied. In this case, the associated RDY input would be tied HIGH (Fig. 3-22).

Single Wait State Generator

Most memory and peripheral devices that fail to operate at the maximum CPU frequency typically require only one wait state.

The circuit in Figure 3-23 is an example of a simple wait state generator. The system ready line is driven low whenever a device requiring

one wait state is selected. The flip-flop is cleared by ALE, enabling RDY to the 8284A.

If no wait states are required, the flip-flop remains HIGH. If the system ready is driven LOW, the flip-flop toggles on the LOW to HIGH clock transition of T_2 to force one wait state. The next LOW to HIGH clock transition toggles the flip-flop again to indicate ready, and allow completion of the machine cycle. Further changes in the state of the flip-flop will not affect the machine cycle. The cycle allows approximately 100ns for chip select decode and conditioning of the system ready.

Interrupts

The iAPX 88 has a simple and versatile interrupt system. Interrupts may be triggered by devices external to the CPU or by software interrupt instructions or, under certain conditions, by the CPU itself.

Every interrupt is assigned a *type code* that identifies it to the CPU. The type code is used by the CPU to point to a location in the memory based *interrupt vector table* containing the address of the interrupt routine.

This interrupt vector table can contain up to 256 vectors for different interrupt types (Fig. 3-25).

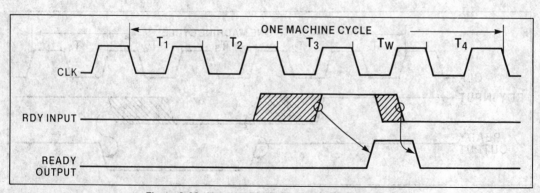

Figure 3-20. Normally Not READY Wait State Timing

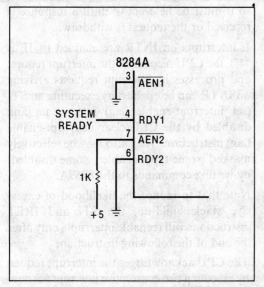

Figure 3-21. Using RDY1/RDY2 to Generate READY

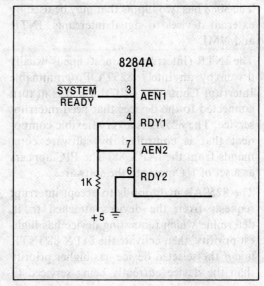

Figure 3-22. Using $\overline{\text{AEN1}}/\overline{\text{AEN2}}$ to Generate READY

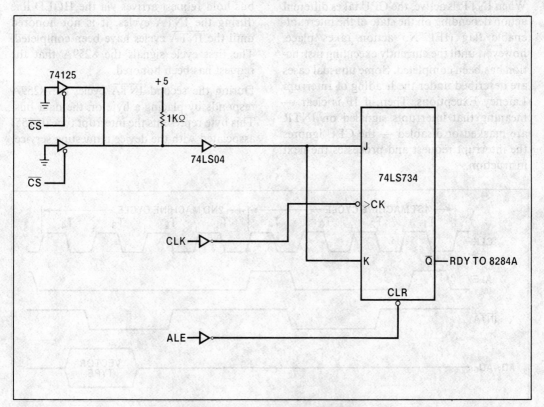

Figure 3-23. Single Wait State Generator

EXTERNAL INTERRUPTS

The 8088 has two inputs that may be used by external devices to signal interrupts, INTR and NMI.

The INTR (Interrupt Request) line is usually driven by an Intel® 8259A Programmable Interrupt Controller (PIC), which is in turn connected to the devices that need interrupt service. The 8259A is a very flexible component that is controlled by software commands from the iAPX 88. The PIC appears as a set of I/O ports to the software.

The 8259A's main job is to accept interrupt requests from the devices attached to it, determine which requesting device has highest priority, then activate the iAPX 88 INTR line *if* the selected device has higher priority than the device currently being serviced (if any).

When INTR is active, the CPU takes different action depending on the state of the interrupt-enable flag (IF). No action takes place, however, until the currently executing instruction has been completed. Some unusual cases are described under the heading of Interrupt Latency Exceptions. Then, if IF is clear — meaning that interrupts signaled on INTR are masked or disabled — the CPU ignores the interrupt request and processes the next instruction.

The INTR signal is not latched by the CPU, so it must be held active until a response is received or the request is withdrawn.

If interrupts on INTR are enabled (if IF is "1"), the CPU recognizes the interrupt request and processes it. Interrupt requests arriving on INTR can be enabled by executing an STI (set interrupt-enable flag) instruction, and disabled by the CLI (clear interrupt-enable flag) instruction. They also may be selectively masked (some types enabled, some disabled) by writing commands to the 8259A.

Note that to reduce the likelihood of excessive stack build-up, the STI and IRET instructions will reenable interrupts only after the end of the following instruction.

The CPU acknowledges the interrupt request by executing two consecutive interrupt acknowledge (INTA) machine cycles (Fig. 3-24). If a bus hold request arrives via the HOLD line during the INTA cycles, it is not honored until the INTA cycles have been completed. The first cycle signals the 8259A that the request has been honored.

During the second INTA cycle, the 8259A responds by placing a byte on the data bus. This byte represents the interrupt type (0-255) associated with the device requesting service.

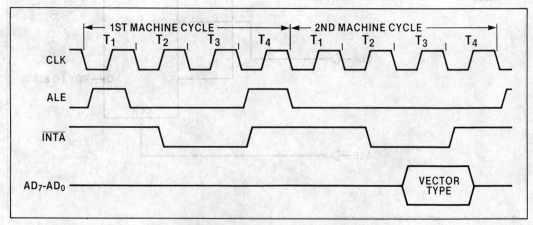

Figure 3-24. Interupt Acknowledge Sequence

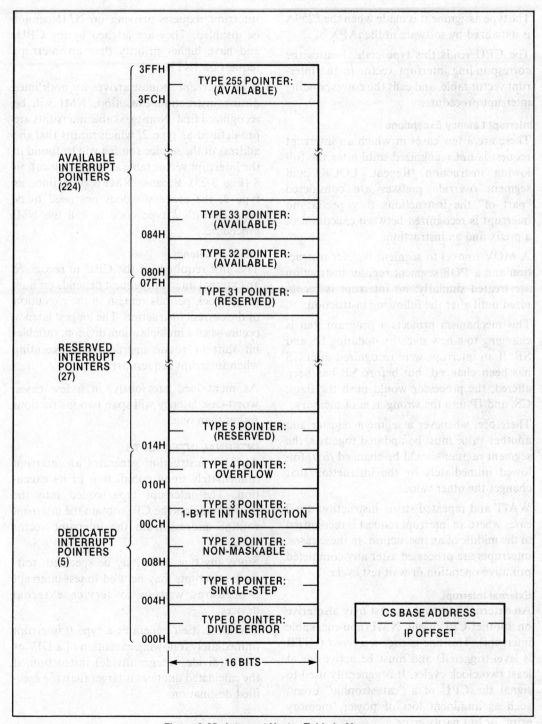

Figure 3-25. Interrupt Vector Table in Memory

Within the figure:

3FFH
TYPE 255 POINTER: (AVAILABLE)
3FCH

AVAILABLE INTERRUPT POINTERS (224)

084H
TYPE 33 POINTER: (AVAILABLE)

080H
TYPE 32 POINTER: (AVAILABLE)

07FH
TYPE 31 POINTER: (RESERVED)

RESERVED INTERRUPT POINTERS (27)

014H
TYPE 5 POINTER: (RESERVED)

010H
TYPE 4 POINTER: OVERFLOW

00CH
TYPE 3 POINTER: 1-BYTE INT INSTRUCTION

008H
TYPE 2 POINTER: NON-MASKABLE

DEDICATED INTERRUPT POINTERS (5)

004H
TYPE 1 POINTER: SINGLE-STEP

000H
TYPE 0 POINTER: DIVIDE ERROR

← 16 BITS →

CS BASE ADDRESS
IP OFFSET

The type assignment is made when the 8259A is initialized by software in the iAPX 88.

The CPU reads this type code, locates the corresponding interrupt vector in the interrupt vector table, and calls the corresponding interrupt procedure.

Interrupt Latency Exceptions

There are a few cases in which an interrupt request is not recognized until after the following instruction. Repeat, LOCK, and segment override prefixes are considered "part of" the instructions they prefix; no interrupt is recognized between execution of a prefix and an instruction.

A MOV (move) to segment register instruction and a POP segment register instruction are treated similarly: no interrupt is recognized until after the following instruction.

This mechanism protects a program that is changing to a new stack by updating SS and SP. If an interrupt were recognized after SS has been changed, but before SP has been altered, the processor would push the flags, CS, and IP into the wrong area of memory.

Therefore, whenever a segment register and another value must be updated together, the segment register should be changed *first*, followed immediately by the instruction that changes the other value.

WAIT and repeated string instruction are 2 cases where an interrupt request is recognized in the middle of an instruction. In these cases, interrupts are processed after any completed primitive operation or wait test cycle.

External Interrupt

An external interrupt request may also arive on another CPU input, NMI (non-maskable interrupt). This line is *edge-triggered* (INTR is level-triggered) and must be active for at least two clock cycles. It is generally used to signal the CPU of a "catastrophic" event, such as imminent loss of power, memory error, or bus parity error.

Interrupt requests arriving on NMI cannot be disabled. They are latched by the CPU, and have higher priority than an interrupt request on INTR.

If an interrupt request arrives on both lines during instruction execution, NMI will be recognized first. Non-maskable interrupts are pre-defined as type 2, which means that the address of the service routine will be found in the interrupt vector table at memory location 8 (Fig. 3-25). Because NMI is predefined as type 2, the processor does not need to be supplied with a type code to call the NMI procedure.

Interrupt Latency

The time required for the CPU to recognize an external interrupt request depends on how many clock periods remain in the execution of the current instruction. The longest latency occurs when a multiplication, division, variable-bit shift or rotate instruction is executing when interrupt request arrives.

As mentioned previously, in a few cases, worst-case latency will span two instructions rather than one.

INTERNAL INTERRUPTS

An INT instruction generates an interrupt immediately upon completion of its execution. The interrupt type, coded into the instruction, lets the CPU obtain the interrupt routine address from the interrupt vector table.

Since any type code may be specified, software interrupts may be used to test interrupt procedures written to service external devices.

The CPU itself generates a type 0 interrupt immediately following execution of a DIV or IDIV (divide, integer divide) instruction, if the calculated quotient is larger than the specified destination.

SINGLE-STEP EXECUTION

If the trap flag (TF) is set, the CPU automatically generates a type 1 interrupt following every instruction. Single-step execution is a powerful debugging tool.

If the overflow flag (OF) is set, an INTO (interrupt on overflow) instruction generates a type 4 interrupt immediately upon completion of its execution.

All internal interrupts, INT n, INTO, divide error, and single-step share these characteristics:

1) The interrupt type code is either contained in the instruction or is predefined.
2) No INTA machine cycles are run.
3) Internal interrupts cannot be disabled, except for single-step.
4) Any internal interrupt (except single-step) has higher priority than any external interrupt (Fig. 3-26). If interrupt requests arrive on NMI and/or INTR during execution of an instruction that causes an internal interrupt (e.g., divide error), the internal interrupt is processed first.

INTERRUPT VECTOR TABLE

The interrupt vector table is the link between an interrupt type code and the procedure designated to service interrupts associated with that code (Fig. 3-25).

The interrupt vector table occupies up to the first 1K bytes of low memory. There may be up to 256 entries in that table, one for each

INTERRUPT	PRIORITIES
Divide error, INT n, INT0	highest
NMI	
INTR	
Single-step	lowest

Figure 3-26. Interrupt Priorities

interrupt type that can occur in the system. Each entry in the table is a double word pointer containing the address of the procedure that is to service interrupts of that type.

The higher-addressed word of the pointer contains the base address of the code segment containing the procedure. The lower-addressed word contains the procedure's offset from the beginning of the segment. These two word pointers will be placed in the CS and IP registers, respectively, to cause the CPU to execute the interrupt service routine.

Since each entry is four bytes long, the CPU can calculate the location of the corresponding entry for a given interrupt type by simply multiplying (type $\cdot$ 4).

Unused space at the high end of the interrupt vector table may be used for other purposes. The dedicated and reserved portions of the interrupt pointer table (locations OH—7FH), however, should not be used for any other purpose, to insure proper operation and compatibility with future Intel hardware and software products.

INTERRUPT ACKNOWLEDGE SEQUENCE

When a maskable interrupt is acknowledged, the CPU executes two interrupt acknowledge machine cycles (Fig. 3-24). The CPU will not recognize a hold request from another bus master until the full interrupt acknowledge sequence is completed.

During the first machine cycle, the CPU floats the address/data bus and activates the INTA (Interrupt Acknowledge) command output during states T_2 through T_4.

During the second machine cycle, the CPU again activates its INTA command output. The external interrupt system (e.g., an Intel® 8259A Programmable Interrupt Controller) responds to this by placing a byte on the data bus that identifies the interrupt source, the vector type. This byte is read by the CPU, multiplied by four, and used as a pointer into the interrupt vector table.

Before calling the corresponding interrupt routine, the CPU saves the machine status by pushing the flag's register onto the stack.

The CPU then clears the interrupt enable and trap bits in the flag's register to prevent subsequent maskable and single-step interrupts. The CPU also establishes the interrupt routine return linkage by pushing the current CS and IP register contents onto the stack, before loading the new CS and IP register values from the interrupt vector table.

Bus Control Transfer

In most iAPX 88 designs, the system busses are normally controlled by the 8088 CPU. This means that address and control signals are driven by the 8088, and that data is driven by the 8088 or by a device being read by the 8088.

HOLD AND HLDA

In some cases, however, another device can take control of the system bus and drive it while the 8088 is forced into the inactive state, called "HOLD".

This occurs when a device such as Intel's 8237A or 8257 DMA Controller requests control of the iAPX 88 system by driving the 8088's HOLD input HIGH. The DMA controller must then wait until the 8088 responds by raising the HLDA (Hold Acknowledge) output. This signals the DMA controller that the 8088 has completed the machine cycle in progress when the HOLD request occurred and floated its busses as listed in Figure 3-27.

The 8088 remains in the HOLD state until the DMA controller releases it by bringing the HOLD line LOW. Then the DMA controller floats the bus and control goes back to the 8088 after its HLDA output goes LOW.

Figure 3-28 gives a general interconnect diagram for an iAPX 88 system with an 8237A-5 DMA controller. This is a typical

configuration in which the HOLD/HLDA sequence would be used.

The handshake timing for transfer of bus control is shown in Figure 3-29. Note that the 8237A-5 drives the system only when the 8088 is in HOLD, and that HLDA and the 8237A AEN output can be used to properly enable and disable other components to assure a clean transfer of control.

Maximum Mode Systems

In addition to the minimum mode systems described, the iAPX 88 can also be configured in the maximum mode.

Maximum mode systems are intended primarily for larger multi-board and multi-processor systems because they provide a more sophisticated set of bus control signals.

SIGNAL	CONDITION
AD0-AD7	
A8-A15	
A16/S3-A19S6	
$\overline{RD}$	
IO/$\overline{M}$	FLOAT
$\overline{WR}$	
$\overline{INTA}$	
DT/$\overline{R}$	
$\overline{DEN}$	
ALE	LOW
HLDA	HIGH

Figure 3-27. iAPX 88 Bus Condition During HOLD

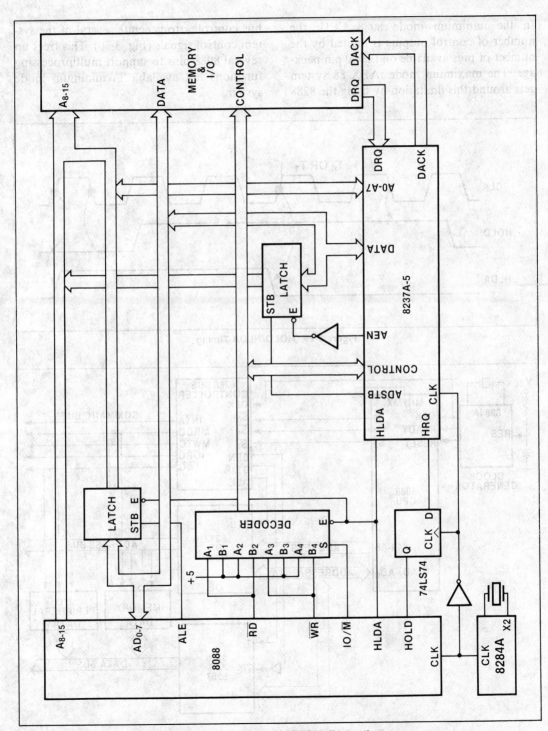

Figure 3-28. iAPX 88 and 8237A Connections

In the minimum mode 8088 CPU, the number of control outputs is limited by the number of pins available on the 40 pin package. The maximum mode iAPX 88 system gets around this limitation by using the 8288 bus controller to generate several of the system control signals (Fig. 3-30). This frees up several 8088 pins to support multiprocessing functions not available in minimum mode systems.

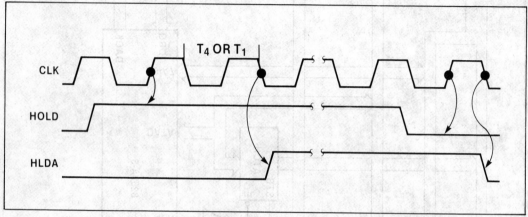

Figure 3-29. HOLD/HLDA Timing

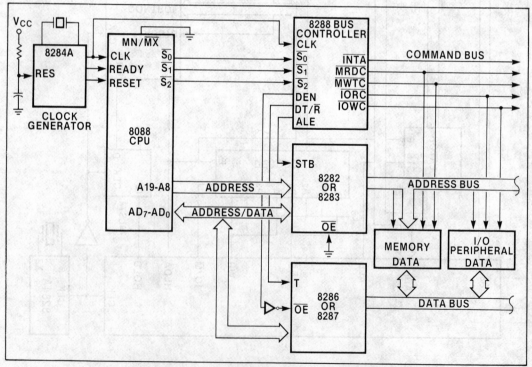

Figure 3-30. iAPX 88 Using Maximum Mode

Pins with different functions in minimum and maximum modes are listed in Fig. 3-31.

Pins 26, 27 and 28, which were DEN, DT/$\overline{R}$ and IO/$\overline{M}$ in the minimum mode, are replaced by the status lines S0, S1 and S2.

These three status lines are used by the 8288 to produce seven bus control functions, enabling the 8088 to redefine pins 24, 25 and 29.

Pins 24 and 25 are now used to track the status of the 8088's queue (listed in Fig. 3-32). Pin 29 provides a function called $\overline{LOCK}$ which is used to prevent other processors from using a shared resource while it is being used by the 8088.

Pins 31 and 30 now implement functions called Request/Grant 0 and Request/Grant 1. These have the same function as HOLD/HLDA, but both functions are implemented on one bi-directional line. This enables the maximum mode iAPX 88 system to directly support three bus masters — the 8088 and two more — instead of the two supported in the minimum mode. Figure 3-33 shows the timing for the Request/Grant function.

In Figure 3-34, an iAPX 88 system is configured in the maximum mode. Status lines S0, S1 and S2 from the 8088 are connected to the 8288, which then produces the system command and control signals and interface to the multibus.

The Request/Grant lines can interface to the 8087 and 8089 co-processors as shown.

The 8284A clock generator is used the same way as in minimum mode systems. The 8289 Bus Arbiter, also included, coordinates the use of system resources. For a complete discussion of maximum mode systems, see Intel's iAPX 88, 86 User's Manual.

Pin	Mode	
	Minimum	Maximum
31	HOLD	$\overline{RQ}/\overline{GT0}$
30	HLDA	$\overline{RQ}/\overline{GT1}$
29	$\overline{WR}$	$\overline{LOCK}$
28	IO/$\overline{M}$	$\overline{S2}$
27	DT/$\overline{R}$	$\overline{S1}$
26	$\overline{DEN}$	$\overline{S0}$
25	ALE	QS0
24	$\overline{INTA}$	QS1
34	SS0	High State

Figure 3-31. Minimum/Maximum Mode Pin Assignments

QS1	QS0	FUNCTION
0 (LOW)	0	No operation
0	1	First byte of opcode from queue
1 (HIGH)	0	Empty the queue
1	1	Subsequent byte from queue

Figure 3-32. Queue Status Decoding

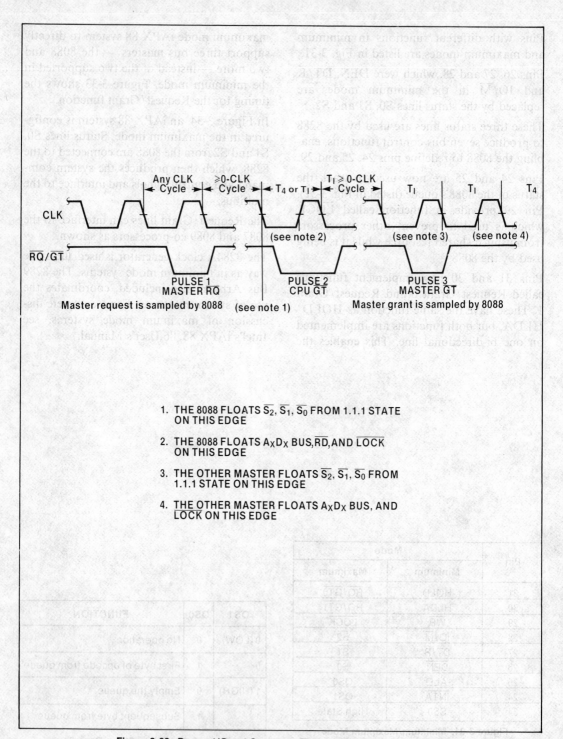

1. THE 8088 FLOATS $\overline{S_2}$, $\overline{S_1}$, $\overline{S_0}$ FROM 1.1.1 STATE ON THIS EDGE

2. THE 8088 FLOATS A_XD_X BUS, $\overline{RD}$, AND $\overline{LOCK}$ ON THIS EDGE

3. THE OTHER MASTER FLOATS $\overline{S_2}$, $\overline{S_1}$, $\overline{S_0}$ FROM 1.1.1 STATE ON THIS EDGE

4. THE OTHER MASTER FLOATS A_XD_X BUS, AND $\overline{LOCK}$ ON THIS EDGE

Figure 3-33. Request/Grant Sequence Timing (Maximum Mode Only)

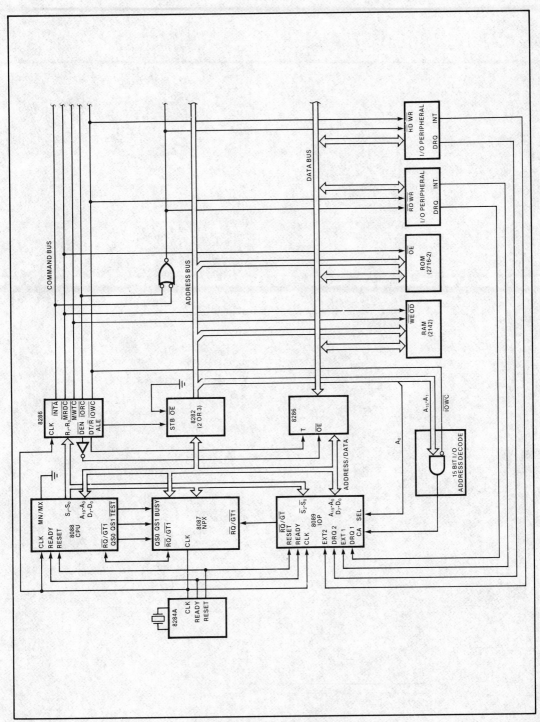

Figure 3-34. iAPX 88/21 Configuration

Application **E**xamples

4

CHAPTER 4
APPLICATION EXAMPLES

INTRODUCTION

This chapter describes some iAPX 88 system design examples, ranging from a simple seven-chip system, to a larger system with multiple CPU's and coprocessors. The iAPX nomenclature is used for configurations using the 8088 or 8086 with 8089s and 8087s.

MULTIPLEXED SYSTEM

The first iAPX 88 design example is a simple multiplexed bus system, complete with 8088 CPU, 8284A clock generator, and — depending on the amount of memory and I/O desired — 2-5 multiplexed bus components. This system demonstates the power, simplicity, and density possible in iAPX 88 designs.

In its smallest configuration, this system consists of only 4 chips:

8088	CPU
8284A	Clock Generator
8755A-2	2K Bytes EPROM, 16 Lines I/O
8185	1K Bytes RAM

The configuration we will discuss has 7 chips:

8088	CPU
8284A	Clock Generator
2 x 8755A-2	4K Bytes EPROM, 32 I/O Lines
2 x 8185	2K Bytes RAM
8155-2	256 Bytes RAM, 22 I/O Lines, Timer/Counter

This system is built on a 95 mm X 105 mm printed circuit board. It draws 400 — 600 mA from a single 5V power supply and includes an RS-232C interface, an LED for visual communication, a RESET switch, and JUMPER options. A small monitor and two programs — CHESS and TINY BASIC —are available to demonstrate system capabilities.

This system uses the 5MHz 8088 CPU. Its memory and I/O components are connected directly to the 8088's multiplexed address/data bus, and no wait states are required.

Address Decoding

The memory and I/O address spaces are decoded using upper address lines for linear chip selects. Address lines A10-A13 are connected directly to the CS (chip select) and CE (chip enable) inputs of the memory and I/O components. This eliminates the need for special decoding PROMs or TTL, reducing component count and system complexity.

The address decoding table (Fig. 4-1) lists address line usage for memory and I/O address decoding.

CAUTION: For most systems using linear chip selects, some addresses enable more than one memory or I/O device at the same time. For instance, the 8755A-2 in location E3 is enables any time A11 is HIGH. Another device, the 8185 at E6 is enabled, when A13 is LOW and A10 is HIGH. Although the 8755A-2 is uniquely selected by address locations F800H-FFFFH and the 8185 is uniquely selected by 14H-17FFH, both components are enabled by memory addresses from COOH to FFFH. Therefore, the programmer must NOT use this range of addresses.

I/O

This system provides 54 I/O lines, some dedicated to the RS232C interface, the LED output, and the 8155's timer/counter. The other I/O lines are available for general purpose I/O. The two 8755As provide 32 I/O lines, individually programmable as inputs or outputs. Three of these lines, PA7, PB0 and PB7 of E3, implement the RS232C RECEIVE-DATA and TRANSMIT-DATA functions, and the LED output.

The implementation of the RS232C interface will be explained for a few interesting tricks

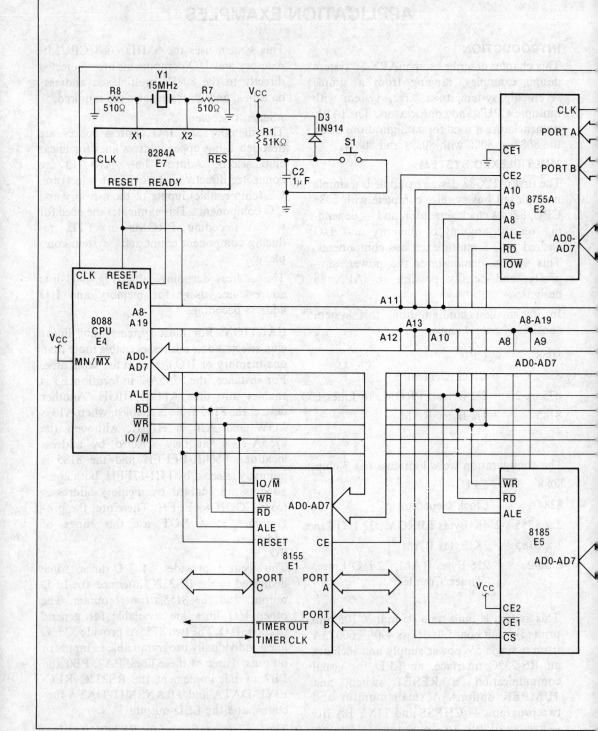

Figure 4-0. iAPX 88 Multiplexed System

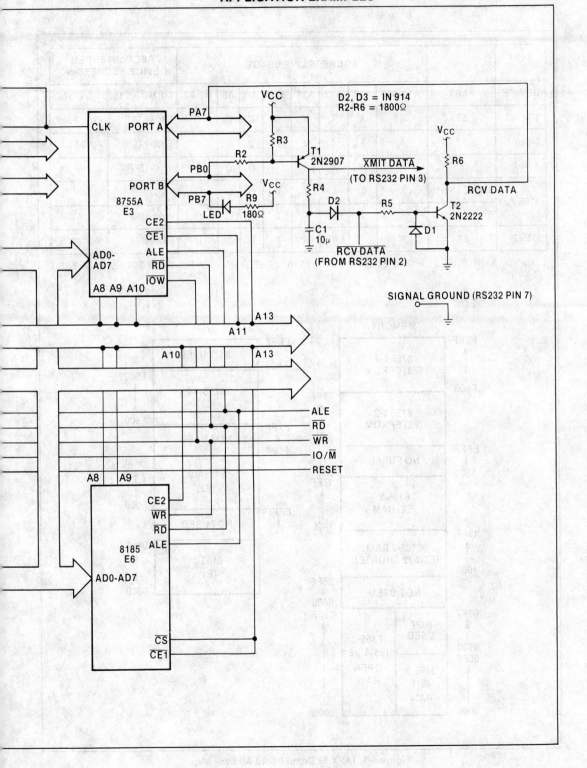

DEVICE	PART	ADDRESS LINE USAGE								RECOMMENDED DEVICE ADDRESSING	
		A14-A19	A13	A12	A11	A10	A9	A8	A7-A0	MEMORY 16	I/O 16
8755A-2	E3	X	X	X	1	D	D	D	D	F800-FFFF	F800-F803
8755A-2	E2	X	1	X	0	D	D	D	D	F000-F7FF	F000-F003
8185-2	E6	X	0	X	X	1	D	D	D	1400-17FF	—
8185-2	E5[1](J2 short)	X	0	1	X	0	D	D	D	1000-13FF	—
	E5[2](J2 open)	X	0	X	X	0	D	D	D	0000-03FF	—
8155-2	E1	X	X	0	X	X	X	X	D	0000-00FF	0000-0005

LEGEND : X=NOT USED ; 0=CHIP SELECT ON 0 ; 1=CHIP SELECT ON 1 : D=FULLY DECODED ADDRESS
[1]J2 short
[2]J2 open

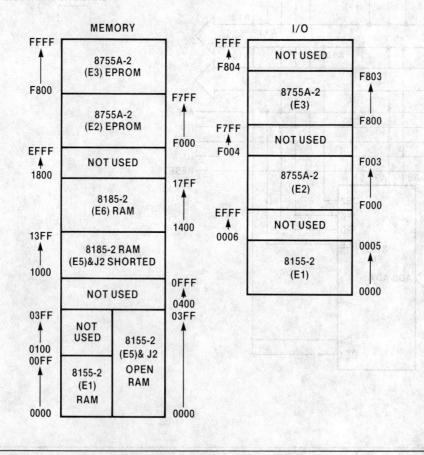

Figure 4-1. iAPX 88 Demo Board Address Map

that eliminate the need for the +12 volt and -12 volt power supplies normally required. The +12 volt power supply was eliminated by connecting the emitter of T1 to +5V. While this produces a signal that is not strictly within the RS232C specification, it works well on interconnections of *less than 10 meters*.

This design also employs a useful trick to eliminate a -12V power supply. Many people have attempted to eliminate this supply by driving the TRANSMIT-DATA line between GROUND and +5V. Because of a circuit switching element (Transistor T2), the low-level signal is always a little higher than ground and hence won't work with many terminals requiring a *negative* voltage for a LOW. This design, however, uses the RECEIVE-DATA line (presumably driven by a true RS232C-compatible terminal) as a source of a negative voltage.

This negative voltage (negative whenever RECEIVE-DATA is low) charges capacitor C1 through diode D1. This circuit has been verified to work when receiving any sequence of characters, except BREAK.

BREAK causes a very long "1" on RECEIVE-DATA; TRANSMIT-DATA eventually exhausts the negative charge on capacitor C1. If desired, a -12 volt supply may be connected to the junction of C1, D1 and R4.

This RS232C interface is driven by software to provide the proper timing for transmitting and receiving characters.

Multiplexed System #2: The Vest Pocket Computer

Combining state-of-the-art microprocessor components results in a usable computer small enough to be carried in a vest pocket (Fig. 4.2).

In only 15 square inches (3"x5"), this system could contain a 2K tiny BASIC operating system, 16K memory for user programs, and an I/O port. The port is designed to interface to a terminal.

The system is designed with an 8088 CPU, 8755A I/O Port with EPROM and 21821 RAMs with 4K byte density each.

The 21821 is a new concept in RAM architecture, interfacing directly on the iAPX 86, 88 or MCS-85 multiplexed bus, responding directly to controls from the processor.

Contained within the 21821 is a complete memory system on a single piece of silicon.

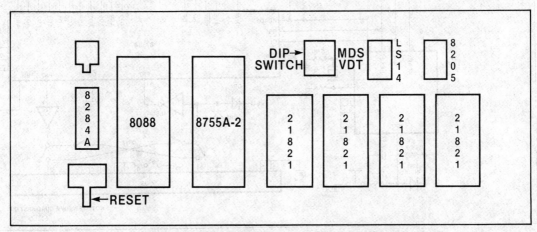

Figure 4-2. Vest Pocket Computer Component Layout

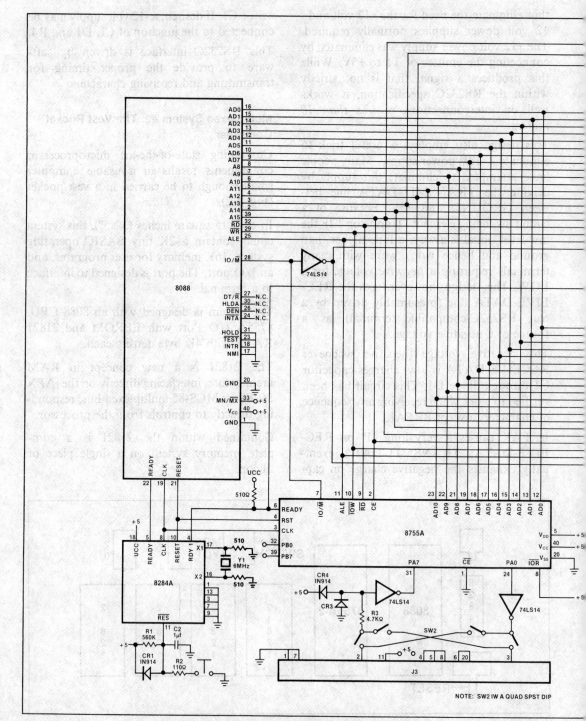

Figure 4-3. Vest Pocket Schematic

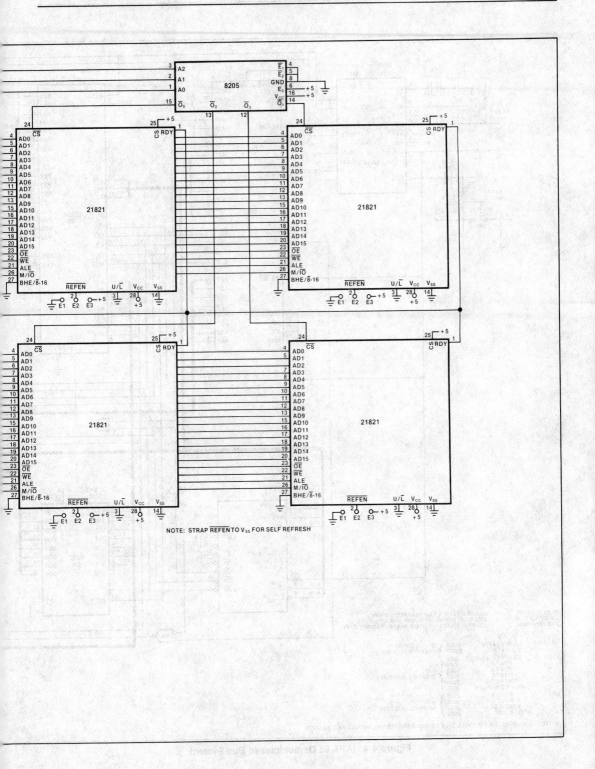

NOTE: STRAP REFEN TO V_{SS} FOR SELF REFRESH

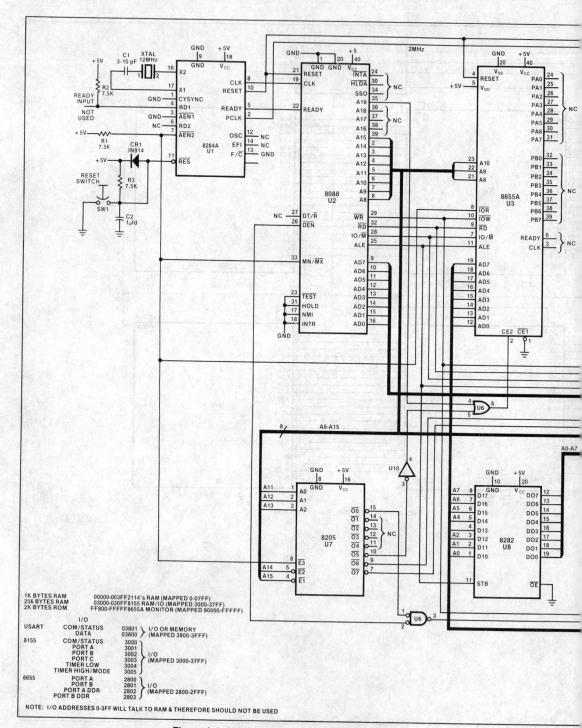

Figure 4-4. iAPX 88 Demultiplexed Bus System

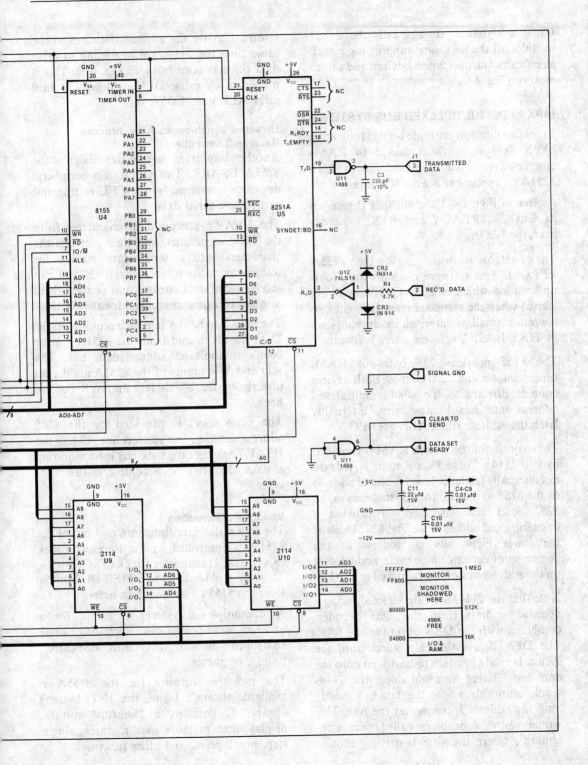

Using a dynamic storage cell, the 21821 includes all the necessary support logic such as refresh control, arbiter, latches, and multiplexers. (Fig. 4-3)

iAPX 88 DEMULTIPLEXED BUS SYSTEM

In this application example we will look at an iAPX 88 system which uses 2114 RAMs connected to a demultiplexed bus, and an 8251A to implement a serial interface.

As seen in Figure 4-4, the 8088 CPU receives its CLOCK, READY and RESET signals from the 8284A.

The control software is in the 8755A EPROM. This software contains the "bootup" routine which tells the CPU how to get started when the system is reset. It might also contain a small monitor, an interpreter such as TINY BASIC, or some game software.

The 8155 provides 256 bytes of RAM, timer/counter and 22 I/O lines. Both devices connect directly to the 8088's multiplexed address/data bus because they internallly latch the address when ALE goes LOW.

The majority of the system RAM is provided by two 2114s. These 1K x 4 static RAMs do not internally latch the lower 8-bits of address as the 8755 and 8155 do. For this reason, an 8282 octal latch is used to provide a demultiplexed address bus. The 8282 looks at the lower eight bits of address at the beginning of each machine cycle, and holds it on the address bus on the falling edge of ALE.

Note that the 2114s are chip selected, using a decoded address from the 8205 decoder, combined with the DEN output of the 8088. The DEN delays the chip select until the system is ready for data to be driven onto the data bus. If this were not done, the 2114s would output data onto the data bus shortly after the address appeared on the bus. This would cause a problem called "bus contention", where the 8088 is driving address

information on the address/data bus at the same time the 2114s are beginning to drive data on that same bus (see Fig. 4-5). This is prevented by using DEN to delay CS until after ALE goes LOW.

Universal Synchronous/Asynchronous Receiver/Transmitter

Another important part of this design is the 8251A USART. The 8251A is a peripheral device programmed by the CPU to transmit and receive serial data.

The USART accepts data characters from the CPU in parallel, and then converts the characters into a serial data stream for transmission. Simultaneously, the 8251A can receive serial data streams and convert them into parallel data characters for the CPU.

The 8088 and 8251A interface is quite simple. Data travels to and from the 8251A via the 8088's multiplexed address/data bus. The $\overline{RD}$ and $\overline{WR}$ inputs of the 8251A are driven directly by the 8088's $\overline{RD}$ and $\overline{WR}$ control lines.

The Chip select is provided by the 8205 address decoder, and address line A0 tells the USART whether the data bus is transmitting a data character or a control/status character.

Baud/Rate Generation

The rate serial data shifts into and out of the 8251A is controlled by the Receiver Clock (RxC) and Transmitter Clock (TxC) inputs. They are provided by the TIMER OUT output from the 8155's 14-bit counter/timer.

A demultiplexed system is useful for a number of applications, including small control or monitoring systems, dedicated testing, or games.

The monitor software for the 8755A is available through Insite, the INTEL users library. It contains a "bootup" routine, display/alter memory and registers, single step, break point, and other functions.

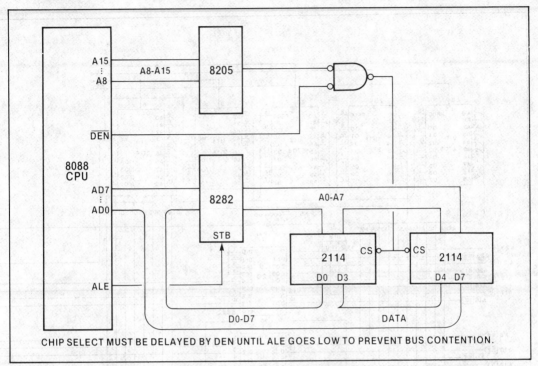

CHIP SELECT MUST BE DELAYED BY DEN UNTIL ALE GOES LOW TO PREVENT BUS CONTENTION.

Figure 4-5. 2114 Chip Select Connection

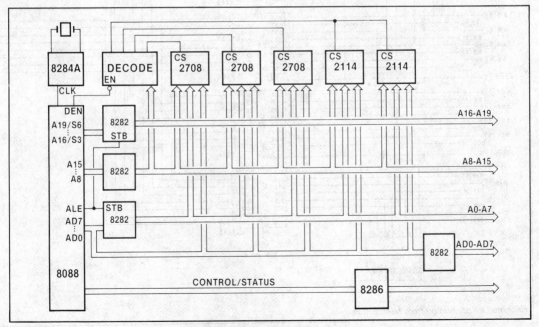

Figure 4-6. iAPX 88 S100 Bus System

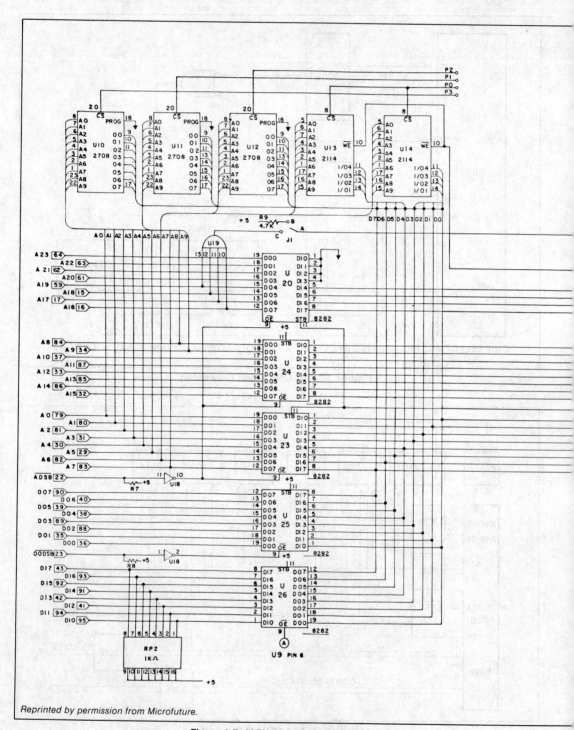

Reprinted by permission from Microfuture.

Figure 4-7. iAPX 88 S100 Schematic

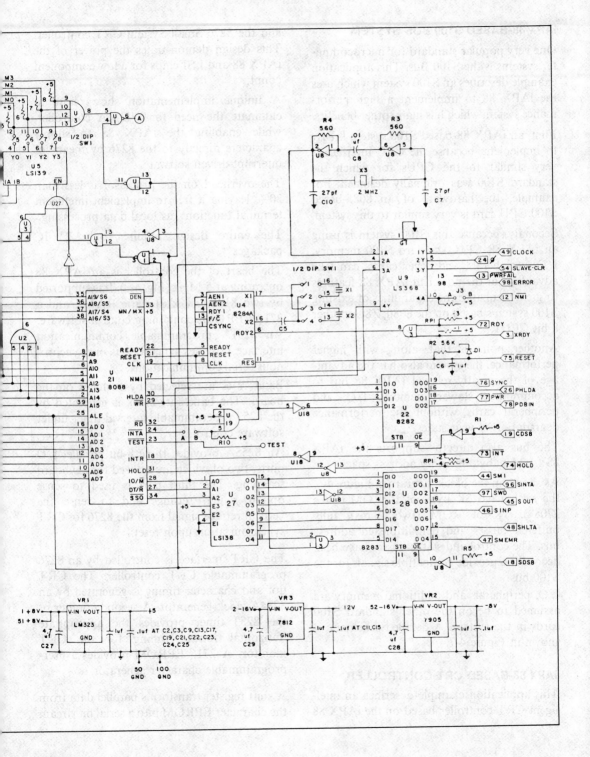

iAPX 88-BASED S100 BUS SYSTEM

One very popular standard for microcomputer systems is the S100 Bus. This application example describes an S100 system which uses the iAPX 88 to implement a high performance system which has many other benefits.

First, an iAPX 88-based S100 system is *easy* to implement, because the CPU interface is very similar to the CPUs for which the standard S100 was originally designed. For example, the hardware of an 8085-based S100 CPU card is very similar to this system.

Secondly, because this S100 system is using an iAPX 88 CPU, standard S100 memory, I/O, peripherals, and other cards, can take advantage of the powerful iAPX 88 features to greatly enhance the capabilities of existing S100 systems based on the 8080, Z80 or other 8-bit CPU's.

Another point is that, along with higher performance, the system also has the advantage of the greatly relaxed iAPX 88 bus to accommodate slower memory, I/O, and peripheral cards without the performance degradation of wait states.

The bus also directly supports the iAPX 88's 1 Megabyte memory address space.

As shown in the block diagram in Figure 4-6, the system has 3K bytes of EPROM (three 2708's), 1K of ROM (two 2114s), fully buffered busses and demultiplexed address bus. The control and status busses have been decoded to provide compatible signals for the S100 bus.

I/O, peripherals and additional memory are assumed to be on the other standard S100 cards in the system. A detailed schematic is shown in Figure 4-7.

iAPX 88-BASED CRT CONTROLLER

This application example describes an intelligent CRT controller based on the iAPX 88 and the 8276 Small System CRT controller. This design demonstrates the power of the iAPX 88 and LSI chips for a low component count.

A unique implementation shows how to eliminate the need for a DMA controller, while enabling the iAPX 88 to supply characters directly to the 8276 by means of interrupt-driven software.

The overhead on the processor is less than 30%, leaving it free to implement intelligent terminal functions, as local data processing.

The entire design requires only 22 IC packages.

The heart of the controller is an iAPX 88 operating at 5 MHz (Fig. 4-8). It is supported by two 8185 (1K x 8) static RAMs, and a 2716 EPROM, containing control software. An 8251A programmable communication interface provides synchronous or asynchronous serial communications.

Baud rates are selected by switches on the board. The baud rate clock is generated by the 8253 programmable interval timer under software control.

An 8255A provides three 8-bit parallel I/O ports, two of which are utilized for keyboard scanning. The third port is used to sense option switch settings and to sense the vertical retrace signal from the 8276 for CRT synchronization upon reset.

The CRT interface is controlled by an 8276 programmable CRT controller. The CRT dot and character timing is generated by an 8284A clock generator. A second counter of the 8253 timer provides the appropriate horizontal retrace timing for the CRT monitor. A 2716 EPROM provides a user-programmable character generator.

A shift register transforms parallel data from the character EPROM into a serial bit stream to illuminate dots on the CRT screen. The 2716 character generator makes it possible to display special symbols for word processing or industrial control applications, or to display characters and words in a foreign language.

Screen Memory Feature

One special feature of this design is the iAPX 88's Load String (LODS) instruction to emulate DMA. This DMA function fills the 8276's row buffers which must receive 80 characters (one row on the CRT screen) every 617 microseconds. This is done using an interrupt routine which saves the registers to be used, points to the first character to be

DMAed, and uses a repeated Load String (REP LODS) to DMA 40 words (80 bytes) to the 8276. The routine then checks to see if it is at the bottom of the screen memory, updates the character pointer in memory, restores the registers, and returns from the interrupt.

DMA Emulation

The LODS instruction actually moves each byte of data from memory to the 8276 in one machine cycle by using a special decoding trick to generate both a read signal to memory and a write signal to the 8276. The address decoding is set up so that the screen memory is at memory locations 30H to 7FFH. This memory is also accessed by memory addresses 1030H through 17FFH.

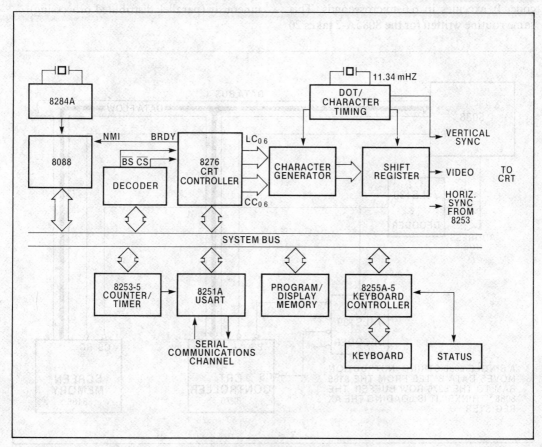

Figure 4-8. CRT Controller Block Diagram

Any memory reads using addresses 1030H-17FFH will simultaneously cause a write to the 8276 row buffers (Fig. 4-9).

In this way, the iAPX 88 emulates DMA by addressing both the 8185s and 8276, directly transferring data from the screen memory to the 8276 row buffers. Other accesses of screen memory, such as inputting a character from the keyboard, are done using addresses between 30H and 7FFH.

Another demonstration of the power of the iAPX 88 is the routine which recognizes escape characters (Fig. 4-10).

Using the iAPX 88's Translate (XLAT) instruction and flexible addressing, this routine takes only 9 lines and 22 bytes of code. It executes in 6.6 microseconds. This same routine written for the 8085A-2 takes 20 lines, 61 bytes, and 31 microseconds. The iAPX 88 uses fewer than half the lines and bytes of code, while executing 4.7 times faster!

iAPX 88 MULTIPROCESSING SYSTEMS

Using multiple processors in medium-to-large systems offers several significant advantages over the centralized approach that relies on a single CPU and extremely fast memory:

1) **System tasks** may be allocated to special-purpose processors whose designs are optimized to perform specific tasks simply and efficiently.

2) **Very high levels of performance** can be attained when processors can execute simultaneously (parallel/distributed processing).

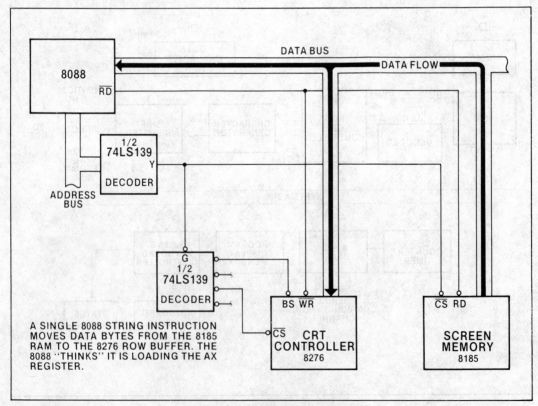

Figure 4-9. 8276 Row Buffer Loading

3) **Reliability** is improved by isolating system functions so a failure or error in one part of the system has a limited effect on the rest of the system.

4) **Modular system design** promotes parallel development of subsystems breaks the application into smaller, more manageable tasks, and helps isolate the effects of system modifications.

The iAPX 88 architecture supports two types of processors: independent processors and coprocessors.

An independent processor executes its own instruction stream. The 8088 CPU and 8089 I/O Processor are examples of independent processors. An 8088 typically executes a program in response to an interrupt. The IOP starts its channels in response to an interrupt-like signal called a channel attention; this signal is typically issued by a CPU.

The iAPX 88 product line architecture also supports processor extensions. The 8087 Numeric Processor Extension is an example. A special interface, designed into the 8088, allows this type of processor to be accomodated.

The processor extension adds additional registers, data types, and instruction resources directly to the system. When one 8087 is configured with one 8089 and an 8088, the system is referred to as iAPX88/21 (Fig. 4-11).

iAPX 88 Multiprocessor Interface
The iAPX 88 architecture simplifies the development of multiple-processor systems by providing facilities for coordinating the interaction of the processors. The iAPX 88 provides built-in solutions to two classic multiprocessing coordination problems: bus arbitration and mutual exclusion.

Bus arbitration may be performed by the bus request/grant logic contained in each of the processors (local bus arbitration), by 8289

bus arbiters (system bus arbitration), or by a combination of the two, when processors have access to multiple shared busses. In all cases, the arbitration mechanism operates invisibly to software.

For mutual exclusion, each processor has a LOCK (bus lock) signal (program activated), to prevent other processors from obtaining a shared system bus.

The IOP may lock the bus during a DMA transfer to ensure both that the transfer completes in the shortest possible time, and that another processor does not access the target of the transfer (e.g., a buffer) while it is begin updated.

Each subsystem can examine and update a memory byte with the bus locked, using a LOCK prefix with the XCHG instruction. This instruction can be used to implement a semaphore mechanism for controlling the access of multiple processors to shared resources. A semaphore is a variable that indicates whether a resource, such as a buffer or a pointer, is "available" or "in use."

One multiprocessing system is shown in Figure 4-12. This iAPX system uses the 8088 CPU to perform data processing activities.

XOR	AX,AX	; clear AX
MOV	BX,ESCTBL	; load table pointer
MOV	AL, USCHR	; read character
CMP	AL,41H	; check for 41H (lowest possible escape character value)
JL	SETUP	; not valid
CMP	AL, 48H	; check for 48H (highest possible escape character value)
JG	SETUP	; not valid
XLAT	**ESCTBL**	; translate to routine address
JMP	(AX)	

Figure 4-10. Escape Character Recognition Code

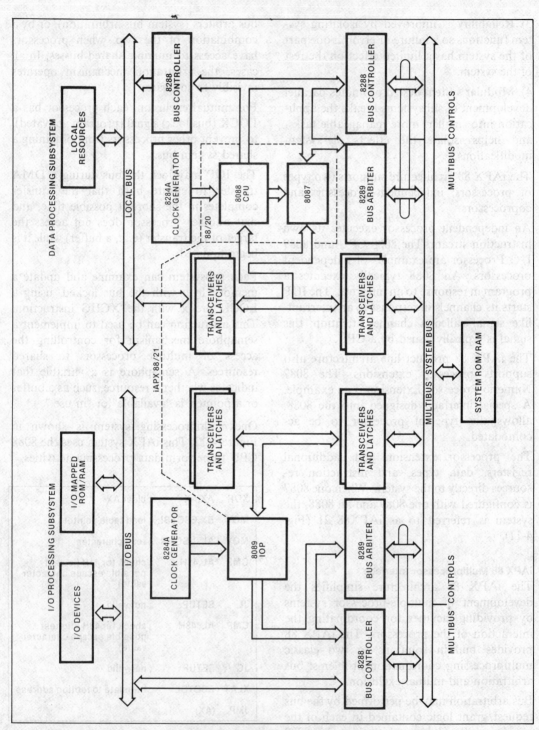

Figure 4-11. iAPX 88 Multiprocessing System

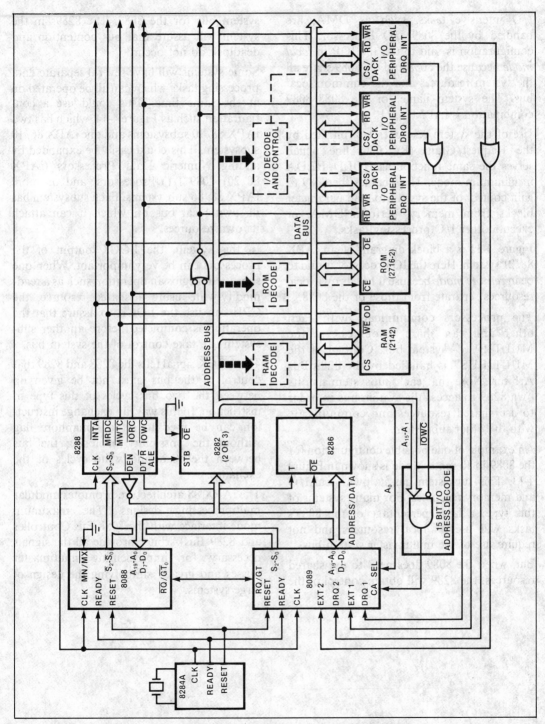

Figure 4-12. Typical iAPX 88 Local Mode Configuration

I/O intensive tasks, such as DMA, are handled by the 8089 I/O Processor. This configuration is said to use the IOP in *local mode* because the 8088 and the 8089 share all the system resources and the common local bus. The system name for the 8088/8089 combination is iAPX 88/11.

Use of the system resources is arbitrated by the Request/Grant (RQ/GT) line which serves the same function as HOLD/HLDA in minimum mode. This enables the 8089 to gain control of the system to read parameter blocks from memory, perform DMA, or execute other I/O processing tasks.

Figure 4-11 is a block diagram of an iAPX 88/21 system. Here the IO processor is said to be in *remote mode* because it has its own local resources separate from those of the 8088.

The processors communicate with each other and can share resources via the MULTIBUS™ system bus. Control of the MULTIBUS™ is handled by the 8289 Bus Arbiter. Note that each subsystem has its own 8289 to access the system bus in order to use shared resources and communicate with the other subsystem.

An example of one possible configuration for the 8089 in Remote Mode is shown in Figure 4-13. This subsystem has its own local I/O and memory resources. For many systems of this type, a large percentage of the 8089's tasks will use its local resources and not require use of the multimaster system bus.

But, when the 8089 does need to use shared resources, the 8289 will obtain control of the

system bus for the 8089. The 8289s in the system will assure that bus contention and deadlock do not occur.

Some systems will have several separate data processing tasks which can all be operated on at the same time. This could use a configuration such as Figure 4-14, which has two iAPX 88/10 subsystems and one iAPX 86/10 subsystem. This could easily be expanded by adding Numeric Data Processors (iAPX 88/20) 8089 I/O Processors, and/or more iAPX 88, 86 subsystems. Each subsystem has its own local bus on which it can attach its own resources.

In this system, the LOCK output of the processors can be very important. When one subsystem begins an operation such as a read-modify-write using a shared resource, the CPU can use the LOCK to assure that the operation is completed before another subsystem can take control of the system bus.

The $\overline{\text{LOCK}}$ signal tells the 8288 and 8289 that control of the bus must not be given up between the two bus cycles of this type of instruction. In this way, an exchange instruction can be used to set a semaphore flag without the possibility of losing the bus between the read and write cycles of the exchange.

The iAPX 88 architecture promotes modular multiprocessing designs. The maximum mode interface with the 8288 Bus Controller and 8289 Bus Arbiter provide all the signals necessary for implementing multimaster busses and greatly simplifying the design of large systems.

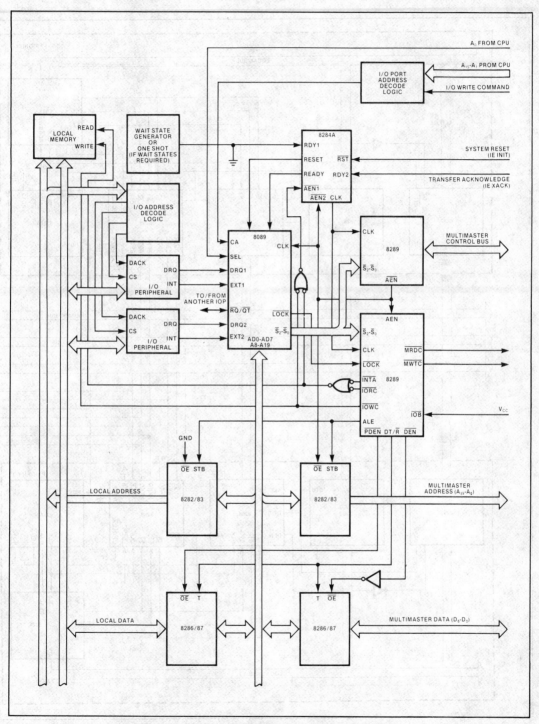

Figure 4-13. Typical 8089 Remote Mode Configuration

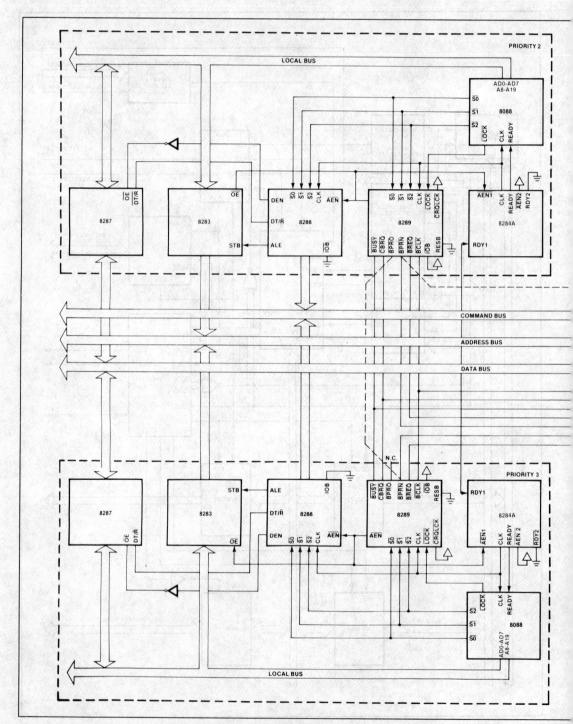

Figure 4-14. iAPX 86,88 Multiprocessing System

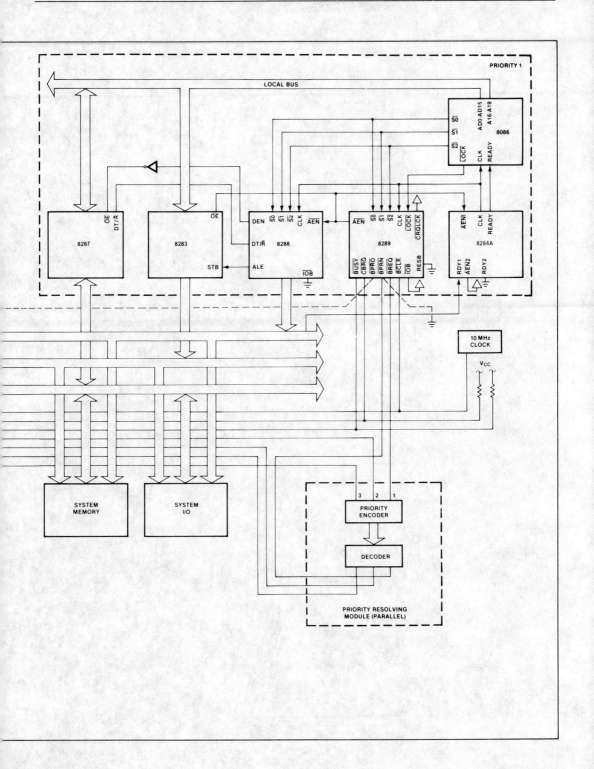

*S*upplement

S

MICROCOMPUTER OVERVIEW

WHAT IS A MICROCOMPUTER?

A Microcomputer is a system of one or more integrated circuit devices using semiconductor technology and digital logic to implement large computer functions on a smaller scale.

Computer miniaturization is a leap-frog technology, with microcomputers getting smaller, faster, and cheaper each year.

There are three main elements in a microcomputer system; each has a special role to play in the overall operation of the computer system. These three elements are shown in Figure 1. They are the *central processing unit* (CPU), the *memory*, and the *input/output* (IO) ports.

The CPU does the actual work of the microcomputer system: numerical processing (additions, subtractions, etc.) logical operations, and timing functions.

The CPU is told what to do by a set of *instructions*, called a *program*, stored in the microcomputer's memory. Data is also kept in the memory and processed according to programmed instructions. The input/output (IO) ports allow the CPU to communicate with the outside world.

The program(s) are specially designed sections of machine code that perform the following, to name a few:

- numeric calculation
- communication with Input/Output devices
- organization and manipulation of data structures
- response to expected and unexpected conditions and program interrupts
- translation of Input/Output data to/from machine-usable format
- coordination, monitoring, and timing of events

While it may appear that the computer does many things simultaneously, the CPU executes just one instruction at a time. Instruction times vary depending on the type of instruction, and the speed of memory or I/O device.

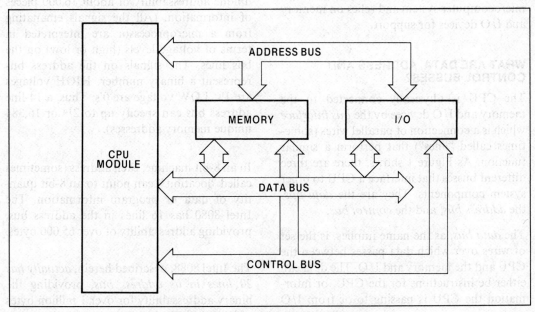

Figure S-1. Microcomputer Block Diagram

The CPU reads in data or control signals through the input ports and sends data or control signals to the outside world through the output ports.

System input/output devices may also be called *peripherals*. Many different types of peripherals exist: some peripheral devices can do limited processing on the data given to them by the CPU.

In a typical microcomputer-based CRT terminal, the input ports are connected to keyboard push buttons while the output ports are connected to the hardware that generates the characters displayed on the CRT screen.

In addition to reading input characters and displaying them on the screen, the CPU may also scroll character lines up the screen and perform special functions such as instructing the displayed characters to blink or to be highlighted.

In this CRT application, as with others, the CPU provides the real intelligence in the microcomputer system and relies on memory and I/O devices for support.

WHAT ARE DATA, ADDRESS AND CONTROL BUSSES?

The CPU is physically connected to the memory and I/O devices by the *bus interface* which is a connection of parallel wires (sometimes called "lines") that perform a similar function. As Figure 1 shows, there are three different busses that interface a CPU to other system components. They are the *data bus,* the *address bus,* and the *control bus.*

The *data bus,* as the name implies, is the set of wires over which data passes between the CPU and the memory and I/O. The data can either be instructions for the CPU, or information the CPU is passing to or from I/O ports.

The CPU uses the *address bus* to select the desired memory or I/O device by providing a unique address that corresponds to one of the many memory or I/O elements in the system.

The *control bus* contains control lines for signals to the memory and I/O devices and specifies whether data is to go into or out of the CPU and exactly when the data is being transferred.

From one microcomputer to another, the number of bus lines may vary. A microcomputer is called an "8-bit machine" if there are eight lines in the data bus and the CPU communicates with memory and I/O using 8-bit bytes. Likewise, a "16-bit machine" has a 16-bit wide data bus.

Also, the number of address bus lines varies from one microcomputer to another. Some smaller machines, like the Intel 8008 have only 14 lines in the address bus, providing unique addressability of about 16,000 pieces of information. (All the signals emanating from a microprocessor are interpreted in terms of voltage levels (high or low) on the bus lines. The signals on the address bus represent a binary number: HIGH voltages are 1's, LOW voltage are 0's. Thus, a 14-line address bus can specify up to 2^{14} or 16,384 unique memory addresses).

In an 8-bit machine, each address (sometimes called "location") can point to an 8-bit quantity of data or program information. The Intel 8080 has 16 lines in the address bus, providing addressability of over 65,000 bytes.

The Intel 8088, described herein, *actually has 20 lines in its address bus,* providing the binary addressability for over 1 million bytes of information.

HOW ARE MACHINE CYCLES, INTERRUPTS, AND DIRECT MEMORY ACCESS RELATED?

Machine Cycles

As the microcomputer program executes, data is transferred to and from memory and I/O devices. Each time the CPU transfers data between itself and one of the other parts of the system, we call this the execution of a *machine cycle* (or *"bus cycle"*). Machine cycles include operations like *instruction fetch, memory read, memory write, read from an input port,* or a *write to an output port.* The timing of these operations is coordinated by the CPU clock signal derived from CPU timing sources from an external crystal or other frequency source.

At the beginning of a machine cycle, the CPU issues a binary code to the address bus to identify the memory location or I/O device to be accessed. Next, the CPU issues an activity command on the control bus. Third, the CPU either receives or transmits data over the data bus.

Following the data transfer, the CPU prepares to issue the next memory or I/O address for the next machine cycle. In this manner, the CPU cycles through the programmed instructions, performing logical arithmetic and I/O operations as required.

The CPU keeps track of the instruction sequence with the *program counter* register containing the binary address of the next instruction in memory.

Normally, the program counter is incremented after a given instruction is executed. The CPU automatically fetches instructions from memory, decodes them, and executes them in sequence, until the program ends, or, until special instructions tell the CPU to execute instructions in other parts of program memory.

Certain situations can interrupt the normal sequential flow of instruction execution. For example, a *wait state* may be imposed in a given machine cycle to provide more time for a memory or I/O device to communicate with the CPU. Wait states are needed when a fast microprocessor needs to communicate with a slow memory. Here's why:

Once the CPU addresses memory, it cannot proceed until the memory responds. While most memories respond faster than required, some cannot supply the addressed byte within the minimum time established by the CPU clock. Therefore, the memory must request a wait state when it receives the CPU signal that a memory read or write operation has commenced. After the memory responds, it signals the CPU to leave the wait state and continue processing.

Another situation that alters sequential instruction execution is an *interrupt*. Interrupts actually improve CPU efficiency. For example, consider a computer that is processing a large volume of data, portions of which are to be output to a printer. The CPU can output to the printer in one machine cycle, but the printer may take many machine cycles to actually print the characters specified by the data byte. So, the CPU must remain idle until the printer can accept the next data byte from the CPU, or, if an interrupt capability is implemented, the CPU can output to the printer and then return to other data processing. When the printer is ready to accept the next data byte, it signals the CPU via special interrupt control line. When the CPU answers the interrupt it suspends main program execution and automatically switches to the instructions that output to the printer, after which, the CPU continues with main program execution where processing was suspended.

Priority interrupt structures are possible where several interrupting devices share the same CPU. If two or more interrupts occur simultaneously, the one with the higher priority is serviced first.

Another feature that improves microprocessor throughput is *direct memory access*, otherwise called *DMA*. In ordinary input/output operations, the CPU itself supervises the entire data transfer as it executes I/O instructions to transfer data from the input device to the CPU and then from the CPU to specified memory location. Similarly, data going from memory to an output device also goes by way of the CPU.

Some peripheral devices transfer information to/from memory faster than the CPU can accomplish the transfer under program control. In this case, using DMA (direct memory access) the CPU allows the peripheral device to hold and control the bus transfer the data directly to/from memory without involving the CPU itself.

When the DMA transfer is done, the peripheral releases the hold request signal. The CPU then resumes processing instructions where it left off.

The DMA allows the high speed data transfers required in many of today's microcomputer systems with hard disk controllers, and CRT terminals, etc.

WHAT'S INSIDE THE CPU?

A typical microprocessor CPU consists of the following three functional units: The *registers, arithmetic/logic unit (ALU)*, and *control circuitry*, described below.

Registers provide temporary storage within the CPU for status codes, memory addresses, and other information useful to the CPU and programmer during program execution. Different microprocessors have different numbers and sizes of registers. In general, 8-bit microprocessors have 8-bit registers and 16-bit microprocessors have 16 bits in each register.

All CPUs contain an *arithmetic logic unit*, often referred to as the *ALU*. The ALU, as its name implies, is the CPU hardware that performs arithmetic and logical operations on binary data. The ALU contains an adder to perform binary arithmetic manipulations on data obtained from memory, the registers or other inputs. Some ALU's perform more complex arithmetic operations such as multiplication and division. ALU's also provide other functions including Boolean logic and data shifting by one or more bit positions. The ALU also contains flag bits that signal the results of arithmetic and logical manipulations such as sign, zero, carry, and parity information. These flag bits frequently determine where the program will continue after the current instruction is executed.

The *control circuitry* coordinates all microprocessor activity. Using clock inputs, the control circuitry maintains the proper sequence of events required for any processing task. The control circuitry decodes the instruction bits and issues control signals to units both internal and external to the CPU to perform the proper processing action. It is the control circuitry that responds to external signals, such as interrupt or wait requests.

As mentioned before, an interrupt request will cause the control circuitry to temporarily interrupt the program in process, and direct the microcomputer to execute a special interrupt service program. A wait request causes the control circuitry to suspend processing of the current instruction until the memory or I/O port is ready with the data.

Addressing Modes

The address that the CPU provides on the address lines selects *one* specific memory or I/O device from all those available. This address can be generated in different ways depending on the operation being performed. For an instruction fetch, the address comes from the CPU program counter register. While executing an instruction, this address can be generated many different ways, called *addressing modes*.

In the simplest addressing mode, the desired data item is contained within the instruction being executed. In a more complex addressing mode the instruction contains the memory address of the data. Or, the instruction may reference a CPU register that contains the memory address of the data.

And finally within some microprocessors, the instruction may instruct the control circuitry to generate a complex address that is the sum of several address components such as multiple registers plus data contained in the instruction itself.

Generally, the most powerful microprocessors are the ones with the widest variety of addressing modes available to the programmer.

When you put it all together: the microcomputer bus structure, the CPU registers, the addressing modes, and the instructions themselves, you have the total microcomputer architecture. The many available microcomputers have many different architectures from which the system designer has to choose in selecting a microcomputer for this application.

*A*ppendix

A

Benchmark Report: Intel® iAPX 88 vs Zilog Z80

Z80 is a registered trademark of Zilog Corporation.

Contents

INTRODUCTION

This benchmark report compares the capabilities of Intel's iAPX 88/10 microprocessor with those of the Zilog Z80. The purpose of the report is to aid the user in his evaluation of the two processors, and to provide him with some of the information he will need in making a knowledgeable decision regarding which processor best satisfies the requirements of his application.

Because system requirements can vary greatly from one application to the next, no one program can adequately display the capabilities of each processor. For this reason, ten programs have been chosen to demonstrate the performance of the iAPX 88/10 and Z80 in several areas. The benchmark programs cover some of the basic tasks which are relevant to many of the applications for which these two processors might be considered. These ten programs demonstrate the processors capabilities in the areas of Data Manipulation, Computation, and Processor Control. Each program was defined in such a way as to be relatively straightforward, while still allowing the processors to use their instruction set efficiently in implementing the program.

The benchmark programs were used to evaluate the iAPX 88/10 and Z80 on the basis of execution speed, ease of programming (number of lines of code) and memory usage. These factors were considered because they are often the key requirements evaluated when a design decision is made. Execution speed is a direct measure of how fast a processor will complete a task. This can be the critical requirement for many real-time control or multi-user systems. Here, cost may not be the primary issue because a less expensive but slower system may be inadequate, regardless of the cost savings. On the other hand, many systems do have critical cost requirements for which it may make sense to sacrifice some execution speed in order to reduce costs. For a memory intensive system, the cost can be reduced significantly by using less memory, or less expensive lower speed memory. For this reason, coding efficiency and memory access time were examined to help evaluate price/performance tradeoffs. Another factor, the ease of programming, is becoming more and more important as the cost of memory decreases and the amount of software in the typical microprocessor application rapidly grows. For many applications, software development costs have become greater than hardware development costs. This means that the total development costs of such a project can be substantially reduced by using the processor which accomplishes the most in the least number of lines of code. To demonstrate performance in this area, the processors have been evaluated on the basis of the number of lines of code required for each program which has been defined as "ease of programming."

The benchmark programs in this report were written for the purpose of comparing the iAPX 88/10 and Z80 microprocessors. They should be used only as a guide in evaluating processor performance and are not an absolute measure of performance for all applications. The programs were written to perform the tasks in a clear and straightforward manner. They do not necessarily show an optimized implementation of the task for either processor. The benchmark programs do, however, provide relevant information and a consistent comparison which may be useful to the designer in choosing the microprocessor which delivers the best solution to the requirements of his design.

PROCESSOR DESCRIPTION

A brief description of some of the key features of the iAPX 88 and Z80 is included here and in Table 1. The topics discussed are Architecture, Memory Timing, Instruction Sets, and Addressing Modes. For more complete descriptions, refer to Intel's 8086 Family Users Manual and Zilog's Z80 Programming Manual or other related literature. Throughout this document iAPX 88 will refer to a 5 MHz system using the 8088 CPU, while Z80A and Z80B will refer to 4 MHz and 6 MHz systems using the Z80 CPU.

Intel iAPX 88

The Intel 8088 (or 88/10) is the host processor of the iAPX 88 microcomputer system. The 88/10 is an N-channel MOS microprocessor which currently has a maximum clock rate of 5 MHz. Internally the 88/10 is a microcoded 16-bit processor which multiplexes a 16-bit internal data bus onto an 8-bit system data bus for external communication. The address space is 1 Megabyte which is segmented to support modular programming. Except for the implementation of the Bus Interface Unit, the 88/10 is identical to the Intel 86/10 microprocessor.

The architecture of the 88/10 is divided into two separate processing units, the Bus Interface Unit (BIU) and the Execution Unit (EU). These two units perform separate functions in parallel to maximize throughput.

The EU contains the 16-bit arithmetic/logic unit (ALU) as well as the general registers and flags of the CPU. It is responsible for executing instructions, and communicates only with the BIU. The BIU performs all bus operations needed by the EU. It contains the segment registers, the instruction pointer, the bus control logic and the instruction queue. Because the BIU operates in parallel with the EU, instruction fetches overlap instruction execution. The result is efficient utilization of the system bus and transparent instruction prefetch.

The 88/10 contains three sets of four 16-bit registers, and nine one-bit flags. The four data group registers, AX, BX, CX and DX, as well as the four pointer and index registers, SP, BP, SI and DI, are all 16-bits wide and can be used as source and destination in most arithmetic and logic operations. All eight of these general registers function as accumulators for many instructions. The data group registers, AX, BX, CX and DX can also be

AFN-01664A

Table 1. Architectural Features

Feature	iAPX 88/10	Z80
Memory Addressability	1 megabyte	64K bytes
General Registers		
Number and Size*	8 × 16 or 8 × 8 and 4 × 16	7 × 8 or 1 × 8 and 3 × 16
Coprocessor Compatibility	Yes	No
Instruction Sizes (bytes)	1,2,3,4,5,6	1,2,3,4
Operand Addressing Modes		
Register	Yes	Yes
Immediate	Yes	Yes
Direct Address	Yes	Yes
Register Indirect	Yes	Yes
Indexed or Based	Yes	Yes
Base + Indexed	Yes	No
Base + Displacement	Yes	Yes
Base + Indexed + Displacement	Yes	No
Auto Increment/Decrement	Yes	Yes
Data Types		
BCD Digits	Yes	Yes
ASCII Digits	Yes	No
Bytes	Yes	Yes
Words	Yes	Yes
Unsigned Integers	Yes	Yes
Signed Integers	Yes	Yes
General Two Operand Operations		
Reg with Reg to Reg	Yes	Yes
Reg with Mem to Reg	Yes	Yes
Reg with Mem to Mem	Yes	No
Reg with Imed to Reg	Yes	Yes
Mem with Imed to Mem	Yes	No
Mem with Mem to Mem	Yes**	Yes**
Interrupts		
NMI	Yes	Yes
Software Interrupts (#)	Yes (256)	Yes (8)
Maskable Hardware Interrupts (#)	Yes (256)	Yes (256)
Memory Access Time	460 ns	250 ns/ 140 ns***

NOTES:

*iAPX 88/10: The AX, BX, CX and DX registers can be used as four 16-bit registers, or as eight 8-bit registers. With the index and pointer registers, this gives eight 16-bit registers, or eight 8-bit and four 16-bit registers.

Z80: Each of the BC, DE, and HL registers can be used as two 8-bit registers or a single 16-bit register. The A register is an eight bit accumulator. The alternate register set can be used for exchanges only (general logic instructions are not supported by the alternate register set).

**For string instructions only.

***250 ns for the Z80A, and 140 ns for the Z80B.

used as eight 8-bit accumulators for byte operations. In addition to their general register functions, the pointer and index registers also serve as address registers. The SI and DI registers function as the source and destination indexes for the string operations. The Stack Pointer register (SP) is used in stack operations, and the BP register is a base pointer for stack relative Based Addressing modes frequently used in high level language programming. The four 16-bit segment registers CS, DS, SS and ES, provide memory segmentation expanding the address space to one megabyte.

The iAPX 88 uses a four clock basic bus cycle. The normal memory access time is 460 nsec. To use memories slower than this, wait states of 200 nsec can be added. Using one wait state produces a memory access time of 660 nsec. Adding one wait state to the iAPX 88 reduces the throughput only approximately 10% because wait states are partially hidden by the queue. For a non-queued machine such as the Z80, the throughput will typically be reduced about 20%.

The iAPX 88/10 instruction set operates on bits, BCD digits, ASCII digits, 8-bit bytes, 16-bit words, and signed or unsigned integers. Many of the two operand instructions allow both operands to reside in registers, or one in a register and one in memory. The order of the operands is interchangeable, and the location of either source operand may serve as the destination for the result. The arithmetic instructions include 8- or 16-bit Add, Subtract, Multiply, Divide and Compare of signed or unsigned integer values. The iAPX 88 instructions are identical to those of the iAPX 86 providing complete software compatibility. Although this report considers only single processor systems, the iAPX 88 has the unique compatibility with the 8087 numeric data processor to extend the data types to include 32-bit integers as well as short (32-bit), long (64-bit), and extended (80-bit) floating point numbers, and decimal numbers of up to 18 digits. Adding an 8087 also adds 68 additional instructions and eight 80-bit registers.

Twenty-four addressing modes are available to directly or indirectly access data and operands. These modes allow from one to four component addressing using combinations of segment, base, and index registers, with optional 8- or 16-bit displacements. The string instructions provide auto increment and auto decrement addressing, memory to memory operations, and have an optional repeat prefix for automatically repeating the string instruction without re-fetching the opcode from memory.

Like the iAPX 86, the iAPX 88 has two modes of operation. In the minimum mode, the iAPX 88 supports the hold/hold acknowledge protocol to enable bus control to be transferred to another bus master such as a DMA controller. In the maximum mode it supports two request/grant lines, each of which can support multiple bus masters for multiprocessor designs using the 8087 Numeric Data Processor and/or the 8089 I/O Processor (iAPX 88/20, iAPX 88/21, iAPX 88/11). This mode also adds support for multiprocessor configurations and Multibus interface.

The iAPX 88 provides nonmaskable software (internal) interrupts and maskable or nonmaskable hardware (external) interrupts. The interrupt structure supports up to 256 different interrupt types using an interrupt vector table located in memory.

Zilog Z80

The Z80 is an eight bit N-channel MOS microprocessor currently available in two versions, the Z80A and Z80B. The maximum clock rates are 4 MHz for the Z80A and 6 MHz for the Z80B. Both speed selections are used in benchmark timing.

The Z80 registers are grouped into the main, alternate and special purpose register sets. The main and alternate register sets are two identical sets of eight-bit registers. Each set consists of eight registers, one accumulator (A), one flag register (F), and six general purpose registers: the B, C, D, E, H, and L. For some operations, the general purpose registers can be concatenated together into sixteen bit register pairs. The user can switch back and forth between the main and alternate register sets using the exchange instructions, but only one set can be active at any one time. One exchange instruction (EX) allows the main accumulator and flags to be exchanged with the alternate accumulator and flags. The other exchange (EXX) switches all of the general purpose registers at once. This is helpful for a single context switch, but makes it difficult to pass data between the main and alternate register sets.

The Z80 has six special purpose registers: IX, IY, IP, SP, R, and I. The IX and IY are sixteen bit index registers which can be added to a displacement to provide indexed addressing. The instruction pointer (IP) and stack pointer (SP) are also sixteen bit registers. The R register is a seven bit counter used for dynamic RAM refresh. The I register is a page register which contains the upper eight address bits for a Mode 2 interrupt.

The Z80 supports one nonmaskable interrupt and has three modes for maskable interrupts. In Mode 0, the Z80 requires the interrupting device to place one instruction on the data bus. (This mode is identical to the way the 8080 handles interrupts.) Mode 1 performs an automatic restart to location 038H. In Mode 2, the interrupting device places an eight bit address on the bus. These eight bits are concatenated with the interrupt page register to point to a location in a memory based table of interrupt vectors.

The basic bus timing of the Z80 consists of an opcode fetch (M1), a memory read (M2), and a memory write (M3). During the M1 cycle, the CPU first fetches and then decodes the instruction opcode. (Because the Z80 does not have a queue there is no overlap of opcode fetch and execution.) The Z80 then outputs a memory refresh address. If no wait states are used, M1 is four clock cycles, while M2 and M3 are each three clock cycles. The M1 zero wait state memory access times are 250 ns and 140 ns for the Z80A and Z80B. These times can be increased by adding wait states. Each wait state adds one clock per memory reference. This adds 250 ns and 165 ns per bus cycle to the Z80A and Z80B to give access times of 500 ns and 305 ns respectively.

The instruction set of the Z80 contains eight major groups: Load and Exchange, Arithmetic, Logical, Rotate and Shift, Bit Manipulation, I/O, CPU and program control, and Block instructions. The processor operates on bits, BCD digits, eight-bit bytes and sixteen-bit words. The Block instructions will search or transfer a block of memory using the DE and HL registers as pointers and the BC register as a counter.

The Z80 provides seven addressing modes to access data operands. It allows the use of eight or sixteen bit immediate addresses, indexing using the IX or IY with an eight bit displacement and register indirect addressing using register pairs.

PERFORMANCE MEASUREMENTS

The processors were compared in four categories of performance measurements. The first two categories measure the execution speed of the iAPX 88/10 and the Z80. The next comparison looks at the ease of use which is the number of lines of code in each program. The last basis for comparison is memory use or coding efficiency.

The first performance measurement tests the processors for maximum execution speed. This is important for many applications where high throughput is a critical factor. To measure this, the processors were run at maximum speed with no wait states. The maximum clock rates are 5 MHz for the iAPX 88/10, 4 MHz for the Z80A and 6 MHz for the Z80B. Table 2 gives the results of this measurement for the iAPX 88/10 and the Z80A. Table 3 gives the results for the iAPX 88/10 and the Z80B.

The next measurement again examines execution speed, but this time memory address access time was also considered. While the processors were again run at their maximum clock rates, they were also required to be compatible with slow memories. The Z80B has a memory access time of 140 ns which often requires the use of expensive speed selected memories. And there are no EPROMs which could be used in this system without wait states. Because of this, many Z80B systems will be required to run with one, or even two wait states, providing memory access times of 305 ns and 470 ns. Many systems using the Z80A also require one wait state which increases the memory access time from 250 ns to 500 ns. The iAPX 88 has a zero wait state memory access time of 460 ns. This is relaxed enough to allow the use of ordinary nonspeed selected memories including most EPROMs. Tables 4 and 5 compare the execution speeds of the processors for systems which have the requirement of a relaxed memory access time. The iAPX 88 is run with no wait states because of its 460 ns zero wait state timing. The Z80A is measured with one wait state providing a 500 ns memory access time. The Z80B is measured for both the one and two wait state cases. These measurements give relative performance for relaxed memory access time.

AFN-01664A

The next method of measuring performance was to count the number of lines of code in each program. These figures (in Table 6) demonstrate the power of the instruction set and the ease with which the programmer can implement the task using that processor. This has been defined as "ease of use," and is becoming increasingly important. Both the cost of programmer time and the amount of software in a typical application are rapidly increasing. This means that a processor which can accomplish more with fewer lines of code can greatly reduce a product's development time and cost.

Table 7 is titled "Bytes of Code." It shows the number of bytes of object code required to encode each program. This coding efficiency is directly translatable into system memory requirements, and therefore, into system cost. Consequently, coding efficiency is very important in cost sensitive applications which have a large amount of software such as a sophisticated operating system or many user programs.

Tables 2 through 7 contain the results of the four categories of performance measurements. The actual times and numbers are given for each program along with the Relative Performance which is the Z80 time or number divided by the iAPX 88 time or number. For each Table the Average Relative Performance was calculated by adding the Relative Performance figures and dividing by the number of programs (10). An "Adjusted Average" Relative Performance was also calculated. This average is calculated without using the highest and lowest Relative Performance figures from that table. This method makes sure that the average is not greatly affected by one figure which may differ widely from the others, such as the Computer Graphics Relative Execution Time in Table 2.

PROGRAM DESCRIPTIONS

The ten benchmark programs were chosen to demonstrate the capabilities of the iAPX 88/10 and the Z80 in the areas of Data Manipulation, Computation, and Processor Control. All iAPX 88 code has been assembled and run.

1. Computer Graphics

The Computer Graphics program scales the X and Y pairs that make up a graphics display. The 16-bit X and Y pairs are offset by constant values (X0 and Y0), then multiplied by a fractional scale factor to obtain the scaled XY pairs. There are 16,384 pairs. This program demonstrates computational capability.

2. 16-Bit Multiply

The 16-Bit Multiply program reads two 16-bit numbers from memory, multiplies them and returns the 32-bit product and the two multiplicands to memory. It demonstrates computational capability.

3. Vector Add

The 16-Bit Vector Add performs an element-by-element add of two twenty element vectors. Vector add demonstrates computation and string processing capabilities.

4. Block Move

The Block Move program reads the block length, source, and destination from memory. The block length was chosen to be 126 bytes. The data is moved from the source to the destination using repeated moves. Block Move demonstrates manipulation of string data.

5. Block Translate

The Block Translate program translates a memory block containing EBCDIC characters to ASCII and stores the ASCII characters in another memory block. The translation is done using an EBCDIC to ASCII translation table, and the block length is 125 bytes. This demonstrates string data manipulation and the use of a lookup table.

6. Character Search

The Character Search program searches a table of known length for a specific character. If that character is found, its address is returned. If it is not found, zero is returned. This program demonstrates data comparison and auto increment addressing.

7. Word Shift

The Word Shift program reads a 16-bit word from memory, and shifts it N places to the right. (N is chosen to be five.) Zeros rotate in on the left. The result is stored in memory. This demonstrates manipulation of 16-bit data.

8. Reentrant Call

The Reentrant Call program passes three parameters to the called procedure. One is pushed from a general register, the other two are pushed from memory. The procedure is called, the state of the processor is pushed onto the stack, and local storage is set up. The procedure body adds the three parameters and places the result in local storage. The procedure is then exited and the state of the processor is restored.

This program demonstrates the processors call and reentrant procedures and its ability to pass variables to a called procedure. Support of these features is essential for procedure oriented structured programming.

9. Bubble Sort

The Bubble Sort program sorts a one dimensional array of sixteen bit integer elements into numerically ascending order using the exchange (bubble) sort algorithm. This program was measured for a ten element array in which the integers are initially in descending order. Bubble Sort demonstrates indexed addressing and data handling.

10. Interrupt Response

This program accepts an interrupt, pushes all the processor registers (except the Stack Pointer) on to the stack, and jumps to a service routine. All registers are restored before returning from the service routine. This program also considers the worst case latency due to finishing the longest instruction. This is because when an interrupt occurs it must wait to be processed until after the completion of the current instruction. The times are measured both with and without this latency. (For each application where interrupt response is critical, the designer should only consider the longest instruction his system will use.)

RESULTS

The benchmark results are presented in Tables 2, 3, 4, 5, 6, and 7. These tables contain performance measurements figures in terms of execution speed, ease of use, and memory usage. For a description of these categories, see the Performance Measurements section.

Tables 2 and 3 show that the iAPX 88 executed nine of the ten programs faster than the Z80A, and that the iAPX 88 was faster than the Z80B for eight of the ten programs. The Computer Graphics program had the largest performance difference. Here the iAPX 88 was

faster than the Z80A and Z80B by relative execution time figures of 14.61 and 9.74. The major reason for this difference is the sixteen bit divide instruction of the iAPX 88. The sixteen bit multiply instruction of the iAPX 88 also gave it a substantial performance advantage in the Sixteen Bit Multiply benchmark. The Z80B (but not the Z80A) was faster for the Block Translate program where the alternate register set and the string move instruction were used effectively. Both the Z80A and Z80B were faster than the iAPX 88 for the Interrupt Response benchmark. (The Z80 could have used the alternate register set for even faster interrupt response, but this would not allow multiple level interrupts.) The two times given for each processor show its execution time with and without latency due to finishing a previous instruction. The relative execution time figures for this program used the average of these numbers. Here the Z80 gained a large advantage on instruction latency time because it does not have the time consuming (but powerful) sixteen bit divide and multiply instructions of the iAPX 88. The hardware interrupt response time of the Z80 is also faster than that of the iAPX 88.

The Average Relative Execution Times from Tables 2 and 3 show that iAPX 88 executed the programs faster than the Z80A and Z80B by ratios of 3.78 to 1 and 2.52 to 1, respectively.

Table 2. Execution Times (iAPX 88 vs Z80A)

Benchmark Programs	Absolute Time*		Relative Execution Time Z80A/iAPX 88
	iAPX 88/10 (5 MHz)	Z80A (4 MHz)	
Computer Graphics	2.32	33.9	14.61
16-Bit Multiply	40.8	354.0	8.68
Vector Add	295.00	480.0	1.63
Block Move	328.00	661.0	2.02
Block Translate	1507.00	1980.0	1.31
Character Search	136.00	220.0	1.62
Word Shift	13.00	48.6	3.60
Bubble Sort	2406.00	4596.0	1.91
Reentrant Call	87.60	140.0	1.60
Interrupt Response**	107/61.5	75.5/69.7	0.86
Average Relative Execution Time***			3.79
Adjusted Average Relative Execution Time†			2.79

NOTES:

*The times are given in microseconds except for the Computer Graphics benchmark where the times are in seconds.

**The times given for the Interrupt Response benchmark show two times. The first the time includes the latency due to finishing the previous instruction. The second time does not include this latency.

The Relative Execution Time and the averages use the average of these two times.

***The Average Relative Execution Time is the sum of the processor's normalized times for all programs divided by the number of programs (10).

†The Adjusted Average Relative Execution Time is the average of the normalized times, excluding the highest and lowest normalized times. This prevents significant shifts in results due to anomalies for one particular benchmark and may be viewed as a better measure of expected relative performance.

AFN-01664A

Table 3. Execution Times (iAPX 88 vs Z80B)

| Benchmark Programs | Absolute Time* | | Relative Execution Time |
	iAPX 88/10 (5 MHz)	Z80B (6 MHz)	Z80B/iAPX 88
Computer Graphics	2.32	22.6	9.74
16-Bit Multiply	40.80	236.0	5.78
Vector Add	295.00	320.0	1.08
Block Move	328.00	441.0	1.34
Block Translate	1507.00	1320.0	0.88
Character Search	136.00	146.0	1.07
Word Shift	13.00	31.1	2.39
Bubble Sort	2406.00	3064.0	1.27
Reentrant Call	87.60	93.3	1.07
Interrupt Response**	107/61.5	50.3/46.5	0.58
Average Relative Execution Time***			2.52
Adjusted Average Relative Execution Time†			1.86

NOTES:

*The times are given in microseconds except for the Computer Graphics benchmark where the times are in seconds.

**The times given for the Interrupt Response benchmark show two times. The first the time includes the latency due to finishing the previous instruction. The second time does not include this latency.

The Relative Execution Time and the averages use the average of these two times.

***The Average Relative Execution Time is the sum of the processor's normalized times for all programs divided by the number of programs (10).

†The Adjusted Average Relative Execution Time is the average of the normalized times, excluding the highest and lowest normalized times.

Tables 4 and 5 give the results for execution time with comparable memory access times. Here, the iAPX 88 was faster than the Z80A for all ten programs, and faster than the Z80B for nine of the ten programs. As explained in the Performance Measurements section, the Z80A was run with one wait state, and the Z80B for both the cases of one and two wait states. The Average Relative Execution Times in Tables 4 and 5 show that the iAPX 88 was faster than the Z80A with one wait state (4.77 to 1), the Z80B with one wait state (3.20 to 1) and the Z80B with two wait states (3.83 to 1).

Table 4. Execution Times with Comparable Memory Access Times (iAPX 88 vs Z80A)

| Benchmark Programs | Absolute Time* | | Relative Execution Time |
	iAPX 88/10 (5 MHz)	Z80A (4 MHz)	Z80/iAPX 88
Computer Graphics	2.32	42.8	18.45
16-Bit Multiply	40.80	452.0	11.08
Vector Add	295.00	598.0	2.03
Block Move	328.00	829.0	2.53
Block Translate	1507.00	2514.0	1.67
Character Search	136.00	272.0	2.00
Word Shift	13.00	59.0	4.54
Bubble Sort	2406.00	5777.0	2.40
Reentrant Call	87.60	181.0	2.06
Interrupt Response**	107/61.5	95.7/88.5	0.90
Average Relative Execution Time***			4.77
Adjusted Average Relative Execution Time***			3.54

NOTES:

*Times for the Z80 include one wait state on memory access. The times are given in microseconds for the Computer Graphics benchmark where the times are in seconds.

**See note 2 of Table 2.

***See Table 3, notes 3 and 4 for description of average calculations.

Table 5. Execution Times with Comparable Memory Access Times (iAPX 88 vs Z80B)

Benchmark Programs	Absolute Time* iAPX 88 (5 MHz)	Z80B**	Z80B***	Relative Execution Time Z80/iAPX 88 Z80B**	Z80B***
Computer Graphics	2.32	28.5	34.5	12.38	14.87
16-Bit Multiply	40.80	302.0	361.0	7.59	8.84
Vector Add	295.00	399.0	477.0	1.35	1.62
Block Move	328.00	552.0	659.0	1.68	2.01
Block Translate	1507.00	1676.0	2032.0	1.11	1.35
Character Search	136.00	181.0	216.0	1.33	1.59
Word Shift	13.00	39.0	48.0	3.02	3.65
Bubble Sort	2406.00	3851.0	4638.0	1.60	1.93
Reentrant Call	87.60	120.0	147.0	1.38	1.69
Interrupt Response†	107/61.5	63.8/59.0	77.3/71.5	0.60	0.73
Average Relative Execution Time††				3.20	3.83
Adjusted Average Relative Execution Time††				2.38	2.84

NOTES:

   *The times are given in microseconds except for the Computer Graphics benchmark where the times are in seconds.

  **These times for the 6 MHz Z80B include one wait state on memory accesses.

 ***These times for the 6 MHz Z80B include two wait states on memory accesses.

   †See note 2 of Table 2.

  ††See Table 3, notes 3 and 4 for description of average calculations.

Table 6 is titled "Ease of Use" and gives the number of lines of code required for each program. The Average Relative Program Length of 2.51 shows that the Z80 required more than twice as many lines of code as the iAPX 88 to accomplish the same tasks. The sixteen bit multiply and divide instructions of the iAPX 88 were the major factors in the 4.73 and 5.00 Relative Program Length figures for the Computer Graphics and Sixteen bit Multiply benchmarks. Some other factors which helped the iAPX 88 in this category are its flexible ad-dressing modes, string instructions and its ease of handling sixteen bit data. The Z80 used fewer lines of code for the Block Move and the Character Search benchmarks. The iAPX 88 Block Move uses word moves. A byte move algorithm could have been used, but with a slight performance degradation (although still faster than the Z80). The program would then have the same number of lines (and bytes) of code used by the Z80 Block Move.

Table 6. Ease of Programming (iAPX 88 vs Z80)

Benchmark Program	Lines of Code iAPX 88/10	Z80	Relative Program Length Z80/iAPX 88
Computer Graphics	15	71	4.73
16-Bit Multiply	4	20	5.00
Vector Add	8	20	2.50
Block Move	7	4	0.57
Block Translate	10	13	1.30
Character Search	8	6	0.75
Word Shift	2	10	5.00
Bubble Sort	17	30	1.76
Reentrant Call	26	47	1.81
Interrupt Response	15	25	1.67
Average Relative Program Length*			2.51
Adjusted Average Relative Program Length*			2.44

NOTE:

*See Table 3, notes 3 and 4 for description of average calculations.

AFN-01664A

Table 7 gives the bytes of object code used to encode the benchmark programs. The Average Relative Code Size number of 1.97 says that the Z80 used nearly twice as much memory to store its programs as the iAPX 88.

Even though the majority of the Z80 opcodes are shorter than iAPX 88 opcodes, the Z80 requires more memory mostly because the iAPX 88 used fewer lines of code as shown in Table 6.

Table 7. Memory Utilization (Bytes) (iAPX 88 vs Z80)

Benchmark Programs	Bytes of Code		Relative Code Size
	iAPX 88/10	Z80	Z80/iAPX 88
Computer Graphics	40	151	3.78
16-Bit Multiply	14	41	2.93
Vector Add	18	30	1.67
Block Move	15	11	0.73
Block Translate	24	26	1.08
Character Search	18	15	0.83
Word Shift	6	21	3.50
Bubble Sort	38	62	1.63
Reentrant Call	48	83	1.73
Interrupt Response	15	28	1.87
Average Relative Code Size*			1.97
Adjusted Average Relative Code Size*			1.91

NOTE:

*See Table 3, notes 3 and 4 for description of average calculations.

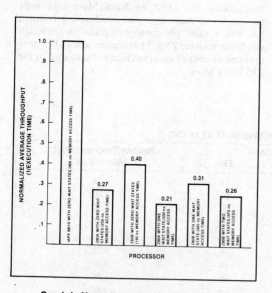

Graph I. Normalized Average Throughput

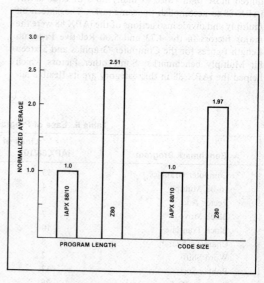

Graph II. Normalized Average: Program Length and Code Size

AFN-01664A

CONCLUSION

The results of this benchmark study show that the iAPX 88/10 significantly outperformed both the Z80A and Z80B for the benchmark programs used. Table 8 shows that the iAPX 88 is faster than both the Z80A and the Z80B, and that the iAPX 88 uses fewer lines of code, less memory and cheaper memory than the Z80.

The iAPX 88 did particularly well in the programs which were word oriented. It was also efficient to program due to the powerful instruction set and flexible addressing modes. Both processors do have useful string instructions and a loop instruction with an automatic counter. The Z80 has faster interrupt response, but was slower and less efficient than the iAPX 88 for nearly all other benchmarks.

In view of these results, it appears that the iAPX 88 is a better choice for applications where high throughput, low development cost and low memory cost are important considerations.

Table 8. Performance Breakdown

Performance Category	Performance Ratio of iAPX 88 to Z80
Execution Speed (Z80A)	iAPX 88/10 is 3.79X faster
Execution Speed (Z80B)	iAPX 88/10 is 2.52X faster
Execution Speed (Z80A)*	iAPX 88/10 is 4.77X faster
Execution Speed (Z80B)**	iAPX 88/10 is 3.20X faster
Execution Speed (Z80B)***	iAPX 88/10 is 3.83X faster
Ease of Programming	iAPX 88/10 is 2.51X more efficient
Coding Efficiency	iAPX 88/10 is 1.97X more efficient

NOTES:

*iAPX 88 vs Z80A with comparable memory (Z80A with 1 wait state).

**iAPX 88 vs Z80B with comparable memory (Z80B with 1 wait state).

***iAPX 88 vs Z80B with comparable memory (Z80B with 2 wait states).

AFN-01664A

APPENDIX

BENCHMARK PROGRAM CODE AND FLOWCHARTS

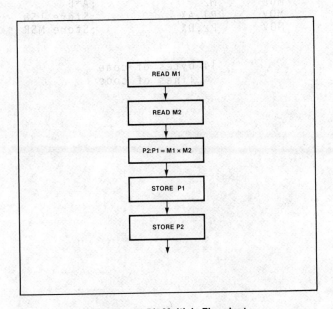

Figure 1. 16-Bit Multiply Flowchart

AFN-01664A

BENCHMARK: 16-Bit Multiply

PROCESSOR: Intel iAPX 88


```
                              ;REGISTER USAGE:
                              ;   AX- ACCUMULATOR
                              ;   DX- ACCUMULATOR
```

Bytes   Cycles

```
  3      18        MOv      AX, M1          ;Read operand
  4     137        MUL      M2              ;A*B
  3      19        MOv      P1,AX           ;Store LSB
  4      19        MOv      P2,DX           ;Store MSB


                    14 bytes of code
                     4 lines of code
```

BENCHMARK: 16-Bit Multiply

PROCESSOR: Z80

```
;Register usage
;       A  - Count
;       DE - Multiplier, Product MSB
;       BC - Multiplicand
;       HL - Product LSB
```

Bytes	Cycles				
4	20		LD	DE,(M1)	;Load multiplier
4	20		LD	BC,(M2)	;Load multiplicand
2	7		LD	A,16	;Load count
3	10		LD	HL,0	;Clear HL
1	11	LP:	ADD	HL,HL	;Shift product LSB left
1	4		EX	HL,DE	;Exchange MSB with LSB
2	7/12		JR	C,MP1	;Jump if carry from LSB
1	11		ADD	HL,HL	;No carry. Shift multiplier left.
3	10		JP	MP2	
1	11	MP1:	ADD	HL,HL	;Carry. Shift multiplier left.
1	6		INC	HL	;Increment multiplier
1	4	MP2:	EX	HL,DE	;
2	7/12		JR	NC,MP3	;Jump if no carry from multiplier
1	11		ADD	HL,BC	;Add multiplicand to product LSB
2	7/12		JR	NC,MP3	;Jump if no carry
1	6		INC	DE	;Increment MSB due to Add carry
1	4	MP3:	DEC	A	;Decrement count
3	10		JP	NZ,LP	;Loop if not zero
4	20		LD	(PRMSB),DE	;Store product
3	16		LD	(PRLSB) HL	

```
41 bytes of code
20 lines of code
```

AFN-01664A

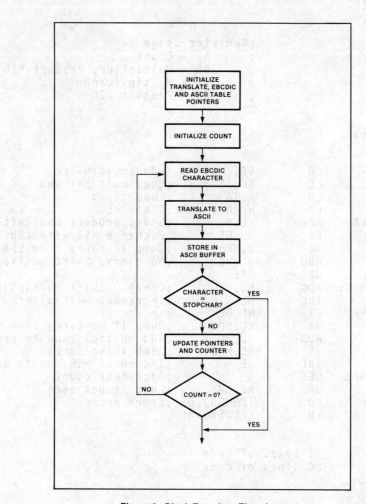

Figure 2. Block Translate Flowchart

AFN-01664A

BENCHMARK: Block Translate

PROCESSOR: Intel iAPX 88

```
; REGISTER USAGE
;   AL - ACCUMULATOR
:   BX - TRANSLATE TABLE POINTER
;   CX - COUNT
;   SI - EBCBUF POINTER
;   DI - ASCIBUF POINTER
```

Bytes   Cycles

```
  4      8          LEA     BX, TABLE         ;Initialize Table Pointer
  4      8          LEA     SI, EBCBUF        ;Initialize EBCDIC Pointer
  4      8          LEA     DI, ASCIBUF       ;Initialize ASCII Pointer
  4     18          MOV     CX, COUNT         ;Initialize COUNT
  1      2          CLD                       ;Clear direction flag

  1     16 NEXT:    LODS    EBCBUF            ;Read EBCDIC character
  1     15          XLAT    TABLE             ;Translate to ASCII
  1     15          STOS    ASCIBUF           ;Store translated byte
  2      3          CMP     AL,EOL            ;Compare with terminator
  2     19/5        LOOPNE  NEXT              ;Loop unless AL=EOL or CX =0

            24 bytes of code
            10 lines of code
```

AFN-01664A

BENCHMARK: Block Translate

PROCESSOR: Z80

```
                    ;Register usage
                    ;   A   - Accumulator
                    ;   BC  - Count
                    ;   DE  - ASCII Buffer
                    ;   DE' - EBCDIC Buffer
                    ;   HL  - Accumulator
                    ;   SP  - Translate table pointer
```

Bytes	Cycles			
3	10		LD	DE',EBCBUF	;Load EBCDIC pointer
1	4		EXX		;Store pointer in DE'
3	10		LD	BC, COUNT	;COUNT = 125
3	10		LD	DE, ASCIBUF	;Load, ASCII pointer
3	10		LD	SP, XTBL	;Load translate table pointer
1	4	LP:	EXX		;Restore EBCDIC pointer
2	7		LDD	A,(DE')	;Load EBCDIC character
1	4		EXX		;Restore pointers
2	7		LD	H,0	;Clear H
1	4		LD	L,A	;Load character into A
1	11		ADD	HL,SP	;Address of ASCII character
2	16		LDI	(DE),(HL)	;Move ASCII character
3	10		JP	PO,LD	;Jump if not done

```
                    26 bytes of code
                    13 lines of code
```

AFN-01664A

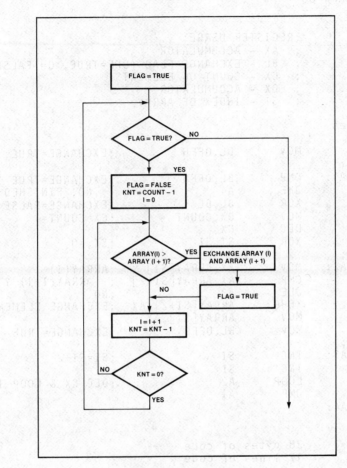

Figure 3. Bubble Sort

AFN-01664A

BENCHMARK: Bubble Sort

PROCESSOR: iAPX 88

```
                 ;REGISTER USAGE:
                 ;   AX - ACCUMULATOR
                 ;   BL - EXCHANGE FLAG (OFF=TRUE, 0= FALSE)
                 ;   CX - COUNT OF ELEMENTS
                 ;   DX - ACCUMULATOR
                 ;   SI - INDEX OF ARRAY

Bytes     Cycles

   2        4           MOV    BL,OFFH           ;EXCHANGE=TRUE
                ;
   3        4   A1:     CMP    BL,OFFH           ;EXCHANGE=TRUE ?
   2       4/16         JNE    A4                ;  NO, FINISHED
   2        3           XOR    BL,BL             ;EXCHANGE=FALSE
   4       14           MOV    CX,COUNT          ;CX=COUNT=1
   1        2           DEC    CX
   2        3           XOR    SI,SI             ;SI,=0
                ;
   3       17   A2:     MOV    AX,ARRAY[SI]      ;ARRAY(I)
   3       18           CMP    AX,ARRAY[SI+2]    ;  ARRAY(I+1) ?
   2       4/16         JLE    A3                ;NO
   3       26           XCHG   ARRAY[SI+2],AX    ;EXCHANGE ELEMENTS
   3       18           MOV    ARRAY[SI],AX
   2        4           MOV    BL,OFFH           ;EXCHANGE=TRUE
                ;
   1        2   A3:     INC    SI                ;SI=SI+2
   1        2           INC    SI
   2       5/17         LOOP   A2                ;DEC CX & LOOP IF CX=0
   2       15           JMP    A1
                A4:


                 38 bytes of code
                 17 lines of code
```

AFN-01664A

BENCHMARK: Bubble Sort

PROCESSOR: Z80

```
                    ;REGISTER USAGE:
                    ;  BC - ACCUMULATOR
                    ;  DE - ACCUMULATOR
                    ;  HL - COUNT
                    ;  HL - ACCUMULATOR
                    ;  IX - ARRAY POINTER
                    ;  DE - TEMPORARY STORAGE

Bytes     Cycles

  2         8        SET     FLAG,A              ;Set FLAG bit
  4        14        LD      IX,PTR              ;Load pointer to array
  3        10        LD      DE,1                ;Load decrement constant

  2         8  LI:   BIT     FLAG,A              ;Test FLAG
  2       7/12       JR      Z,DONE              ;Done if zero
  2         8        RES     FLAG,A              ;Reset FLAG
  3        10        LD      HL,COUNT-1          ;Load COUNT

  1         4  L2:   EXX
  3        19        LD      C,(IX+0)            ;Load data (I)
  3        19        LD      B,(IX+1)
  3        19        LD      L,(IX+2)            ;Load data (I+1)
  3        19        LD      H,(IX+3)
  1         4        LD      E,L                 ;Save date in DE
  1         4        LD      D,H
  1         4        AND     A,A                 ;Clear carry flag
  1        11        SBC     HL,BC               ;Compare data
  2       7/12       JR      NC,NOEX             ;No ex if data(I)  data(I+1)
  3        19        LD      (IX+2)C             ;Exchange
  3        19        LD      (IX+2)B
  3        19        LD      (IX+0)E
  3        19        LD      (IX+1)D
  2         8        SET     FLAG,A              ;Set exchange flag
  1         4  NOEX: EXX
  1         6        INC     IX                  ;Increment Pointer
  1         6        INC     IX
  2         8        AND     A,A                 ;Clear carry flag
  1        11        SBC     HL',DE'             ;Decrement COUNT
  2       7/12       JR      NZ,L2               ;Jump if COUNT not zero
  3        10        JP      L1                  ;Another pass
              DONE:


              62 bytes of code
              30 lines of code
```

AFN-01664A

Benchmark Report: Intel® iAPX 88 vs Motorola MC6809

MC6809 is a registered trademark of Motorola Corporation.

Contents

*Includes code and flowcharts from three benchmark programs. For the code and flowcharts for all benchmark programs contact your local Intel sales office.

†Multibus is a trademark of Intel Corporation.

AFN 01532A

INTRODUCTION

This benchmark report compares the capabilities of Intel's iAPX 88/10 microprocessor with those of the Motorola MC6809. The purpose of the report is to aid the user in his evaluation of the two processors, and to provide him with some of the information he will need in making a knowledgeable decision regarding which processor best satisfies the requirements of his application.

Because the requirements can vary so greatly from one system to the next, no one program can adequately display the capabilities of each processor. For this reason, ten programs have been chosen to demonstrate the performance of the iAPX 88/10 and MC6809 in several areas. The benchmark programs cover some of the basic tasks which are relevant to many of the applications for which these two processors might be considered. These ten programs demonstrate the processors' capabilities in the areas of data manipulation, computation, and processor control. Each program was defined in such a way as to be relatively straightforward, while still allowing the processors to use their instruction set efficiently in implementing the program.

The benchmark programs were used to evaluate the iAPX 88/10 and MC6809 on the basis of execution speed, memory usage, and ease of programming (number of lines of code). These factors were considered because they are often the key requirements evaluated when a design decision is made. Execution speed is a direct measure of how fast a processor will complete a task. This can be the critical requirement for many real-time control or multi-user systems. Here, cost may not be the primary issue because a less expensive but slower system may be inadequate, regardless of the cost savings. On the other hand, many systems do have critical cost requirements for which it may make sense to sacrifice some execution speed in order to reduce costs. For a memory intensive system, the cost can be reduced significantly by using less memory, or cheaper, lower speed memory. For this reason, coding efficiency and memory access time were examined to help evaluate price/performance tradeoffs. Another factor, the ease of programming, is becoming more and more important as the cost of memory decreases and the size of the typical microcomputer application rapidly grows. For many applications, software development costs have become greater than hardware development costs. This means that the total development costs of such a project can be substantially reduced by using the processor which accomplishes the most in the least number of lines of code. To demonstrate performance in this area, the processors have also been evaluated on the basis of the number of lines of code required for each program which has been defined as "ease of programming."

The benchmark programs in this report were written for the purpose of comparing the iAPX 88/10 and MC6809 microprocessors. They should be used only as a guide in evaluating processor performance and are not an absolute measure of performance for all applications. The programs were written to perform the tasks in a clear and straightforward manner. They do not necessarily show an optimized implementation of the task. The benchmark programs do, however, provide relevant information and a consistent comparison which may be useful to the designer in choosing the microprocessor which delivers the best solution to the requirements of his design.

PROCESSOR DESCRIPTION

A brief description of some of the key features of the iAPX 88 and MC6809 is included here and in Table 1.

Table 1. Architectural Features

Feature	iAPX 88/10	MC6809
Memory Addressability	1 megabyte	64K bytes
General Registers		
Number	8 or 8+4*	2 or 1**
Size (bits)	16 or 8,16*	8 or 16**
Instruction Sizes (bytes)	1,2,3,4,5,6	1,2,3,4,5
Operand Addressing Modes		
Register	Yes	Yes
Immediate	Yes	Yes
Direct Address	Yes	Yes
Register Indirect	Yes	Yes
Indexed or Based	Yes	Yes
Base + Indexed	Yes	No
Base + Displacement	Yes	No
Index + Displacement	Yes	Yes
Base + Indexed + Displacement	Yes	No
Indexed Indirect	No	Yes
Auto Increment/Decrement	Yes	Yes
Data Types		
BCD Digits	Yes	Yes
ASCII Digits	Yes	No
Bytes	Yes	Yes
Words	Yes	Yes
Unsigned Integers	Yes	Yes
Signed Integers	Yes	Yes
General Double Operand Operations		
Reg with Reg to Reg	Yes	No
Reg with Mem to Reg	Yes	Yes
Reg with Mem to Mem	Yes	No
Reg with Imed to Reg	Yes	Yes
Mem with Imed to Mem	Yes	No
Mem with Mem to Mem	Yes	No
Interrupts		
NMI	Yes	Yes
Software Interrupts (#)	Yes (256)	Yes (3)
Fast External Interrupts (#)	No	Yes (1)
Multi-Vectored Interrupts (#)	Yes (256)	No

*The AX, BX, CX and DX registers can be used as four 16-bit registers, or as eight 8-bit registers. With the index and pointer registers, this gives eight 16-bit registers, or eight 8-bit and four 16-bit registers.

**The A and B registers can be used as two 8-bit registers or as one 16-bit register.

AFN 01532A

The topics discussed are Architecture, Memory Timing, Instruction Sets, and Addressing Modes. For more complete descriptions, refer to Intel's 8086 Family Users' Manual and Motorola's MC6809 Preliminary Programming Manual or other related literature.

iAPX 88

The Intel 8088 (or 88/10) is the host processor of the iAPX 88 microcomputer system. The 88/10 is an N-channel MOS microprocessor which currently has a maximum clock rate of 5 MHz. Internally the 88/10 is a microcoded 16-bit processor which multiplexes a 16-bit internal data bus onto an 8-bit system data bus for external communication. The address space is one megabyte which is segmented to support modular programming. Except for the implementation of the Bus Interface Unit the 88/10 is identical to the Intel 86/10 microprocessor.

The architecture of the 88/10 is divided into two separate processing units, the Bus Interface Unit (BIU) and the Execution Unit (EU). These two units perform separate functions in parallel to maximize throughput.

The EU contains the 16-bit arithmetic/logic unit (ALU) as well as the general registers and flags of the CPU. It is responsible for executing instructions, and communicates only with the BIU. The BIU performs all bus operations needed by the EU. It contains the segment registers, the instruction pointer, the bus control logic and the instruction queue. Because the BIU operates in parallel with the EU, instruction fetches overlap instruction execution. The result is efficient utilization of the system bus and transparent instruction prefetch.

The 88/10 contains three sets of four 16-bit registers, and nine one-bit flags. The four data group registers, AX, BX, CX and DX, as well as the four pointer and index registers, SP, BP, SI and DI, are all 16-bits wide and can be used as source and destination in most arithmetic and logic operations. All eight of these general registers function as accumulators for many instructions. The data group registers, AX, BX, CX and DX can also be used as eight 8-bit accumulators for byte operations. The pointer and index registers also serve as address registers in addition to their general register functions. The SI and DI registers function as the source and destination pointers for the string operations. The Stack Pointer register (SP) is used in stack operations, and the BP register is a base pointer for stack relative Based Addressing modes frequently used in high level language programming. The four 16-bit segment registers, CS, DS, SS and ES, provide memory segmentation expanding the address space to one megabyte.

The iAPX 88 uses a four-clock basic bus cycle. The normal memory access time is 460 nsec. To use memories slower than this, wait states of 200 nsec can be added. Using one wait state produces a memory access time of 660 nsec.

The iAPX 88/10 instruction set operates on bits, BCD digits, ASCII digits, 8-bit bytes, 16-bit words, and signed or unsigned integers. Many of the two operand instructions allow both operands to reside in registers, or one in a register and one in memory. The order of the operands is interchangeable, and the location of either source operand may serve as the destination for the result. The arithmetic instructions include 8- or 16-bit Add, Subtract, Multiply, Divide and Compare of signed or unsigned integer values. The iAPX 88 instructions are identical to those of the iAPX 86 providing complete software compatibility.

Twenty-four addressing modes are available to directly or indirectly access data and operands. These modes allow from one to four component addressing using combinations of segment, base, and index registers, and/or 8- or 16-bit displacements. The string instructions provide auto increment and auto decrement addressing, memory to memory operations, and have an optional repeat prefix.

The iAPX 88 in the minimum mode supports the hold/hold acknowledge protocol to enable bus control to be transferred to another bus master such as a DMA controller. It can also be configured in the maximum mode with two request/grant lines, each of which can support multiple bus masters for coprocessor designs using the 8087 Numeric Data Processor and/or the 8089 I/O Processor (iAPX 88/20, iAPX 88/21, iAPX 88/11). Even though not considered on these benchmarks, the 8087 (iAPX 88/20) uniquely enhances the iAPX 88/10 (86/10) capabilities with 68 additional instructions, including 64-bit floating point and transcendental functions, eight 80-bit stack oriented registers and seven additional numeric data types.

The iAPX 88 provides nonmaskable software (internal) interrupts and maskable or nonmaskable hardware (external) interrupts. The interrupt structure supports up to 256 different interrupt types using an interrupt vector table located in memory. For more information regarding interrupts see your local Intel office.

MC6809

The Motorola MC6809 is an N-channel random logic MOS microprocessor which is available at 1.0 MHz, 1.5 MHz or 2.0 MHz clock rates. The MC6809 can address up to 64 kbytes of memory. The A and B registers are two 8-bit accumulators which may be concatenated into a single 16-bit accumulator, the D register. There are four pointer registers: X, Y, U and S. All are 16-bits wide and function primarily as base registers for memory addressing. The U and S registers are also used for manipulating the hardware and user stacks. The 16-bit program counter (PC) points to the address of the next instruction, and can also be operated on for control transfer. The 8-bit Direct Page Register (DPR) is used to contain the upper eight address bits for some addressing

AFN 01532A

modes. The processor flags are contained in the 8-bit condition Code Register (CCR).

The basic bus cycle of the MC6809 is a single, 500 nsec clock cycle for the 2.0 MHz version. The normal memory access time is 320 nsec. To accommodate slower memories, 125 nsec wait states can be added. Adding one wait state extends the memory access time to 445 nsec.

Although the instruction set of the MC6809 operates predominantly on 8-bit data, there are a few bit operations, two BCD adjusts, and eight instructions with 16-bit operands. Most two operand instructions require one operand to be in a register, and the other operand to reside in memory, with the result going to the register. Two operand instructions such as Add or Compare cannot be done from register to register. The exceptions to this are the Multiply, Transfer Exchange, and Sign Extend instructions, for which both source operands and the destination operand must be in registers. The arithmetic instructions include 8-bit unsigned integer Multiply and 8- or 16-bit Add, Subtract and Compare. Other 16-bit instructions include Load, Store, Exchange, Transfer, and Sign Extend.

For stack manipulation, a single Push or Pull instruction allows any combination of registers to be placed on or removed from either of the two stacks. There are also 19 branch instructions, in long (16-bit offset) or short (8-bit offset) forms.

The MC6809 supports 13 different addressing modes. Included in these modes are 5 forms of indexed addressing, including indexed Auto Increment and Auto Decrement modes which are useful for string operations. Relative addressing for Branch instructions use one- or two-byte offsets as a pointer to a data location.

The MC6809 provides maskable and nonmaskable hardware interrupts, as well as three software interrupts. There are two maskable hardware interrupts, FIRQ and IRQ. The FIRQ (Fast Interrupt Request) pushes only the Condition Code and Program Counter registers. The IRQ automatically pushes all of the MC6809 registers (except the SP) onto the stack. Each MC6809 interrupt has a fixed vector address, fetching its service routine address from a predefined memory location. For more information regarding hardware and software interrupts see your local Intel office.

PROGRAM DESCRIPTIONS

The ten benchmark programs were chosen to demonstrate the capabilities of the iAPX 88/10 and the MC6809 in the areas of data manipulation, computation, and processor control. The basic algorithms for several of the programs (Block Move, Character Search, Word Shift, Vector Add, and 16-Bit Multiply) are similar to the algorithms of benchmark programs in Motorola's MC6809 Preliminary Programming Manual. All iAPX 88 code has been assembled and run.

1. Computer Graphics

The Computer Graphics program scales the X and Y pairs that make up a graphics display. The 16-bit X and Y pairs are offset by constant values (X0 and Y0), then multiplied by a fractional scale factor to obtain the scaled XY pairs. There are 16,384 pairs. This program demonstrates 16-bit computational capability.

2. 16-Bit Multiply

The 16-Bit Multiply program reads two 16-bit numbers from memory, multiplies them and returns the 32-bit product and the two multiplicands to memory. Multiply demonstrates 16-bit computational capability.

3. Vector Add

The 16-Bit Vector Add performs an element-by-element add of two twenty-element vectors. Vector add demonstrates 16-bit computation and string processing capabilities.

4. Block Move

The Block Move program reads the block length, source, and destination from memory. The block length was chosen to be 126 bytes. The data is moved from the source to the destination using word moves. Block Move demonstrates data manipulation and auto increment addressing.

5. Block Translate

The Block Translate program translates a memory block containing EBCDIC characters to ASCII and stores the ASCII characters in another memory block. The translation is done using an EBCDIC to ASCII translation table, and the block length is 125 bytes. This demonstrates data manipulation, auto increment addressing, and the use of a lookup table.

6. Character Search

The Character Search program searches a table of known length for a specific character. If that character is found, its address is returned. If it is not found, zero is returned. This program demonstrates data comparison and auto increment addressing.

7. Word Shift

The Word Shift program reads a 16-bit word from memory, and shifts it N places to the right. (N is chosen to be five.) Zeros rotate in on the left. The result is stored in memory. This demonstrates manipulation of 16-bit data.

8. Reentrant Call

The Reentrant Call program passes three parameters to the called procedure. One is pushed from a general register, the other two are pushed from memory. The procedure is called, the state of the processor is pushed onto the stack, and local storage is set up. The procedure body adds the three parameters and places the result in local storage. The procedure is then exited and the state of the processor is restored.

This program demonstrates the processor's call and re-entrant procedures and its ability to pass variables to a called procedure. Support of these features is essential for structured programming.

9. Interrupt Response

I. Single-Vectored Interrupt

The Single-Vectored Interrupt pushes all the processor registers (except the Stack Pointer) onto the stack, and jumps to a service routine. All registers are restored before returning. The time also includes the length of time the processor requires to execute the longest instruction before recognizing the interrupt.

II. Multi-Vectored Interrupt

The Multi-Vectored Interrupt stacks only the Instruction Pointer/Program Counter and Flags/Condition Code registers. The processor must determine which of eight possible devices initiated the interrupt request, and jump to the corresponding service routine. The return time is also included.

RESULTS

The results of this study are presented in terms of execution speed, memory usage, and ease of programming. To be relevant to applications where speed is the crucial factor, the processors are first compared at their highest performance, with no wait states. Then for the cases where memory cost is an issue, comparisons are made for execution speed with (nearly) equal memory access times, and for coding efficiency. The processors are also compared on the ease of programming (number of lines of code) which can be an important factor in the development costs of a project.

The zero wait state execution speed of the iAPX 88/10 is compared to that of the MC6809 in Table 2. For each program, the execution time is given in terms of Ab-

solute Time and Normalized Time for each processor. The Normalized Time is the Absolute Time required by the processor for that benchmark divided by the Absolute Time of the iAPX 88/10 for that benchmark. The Average Normalized Time was computed by adding the Normalized Times and dividing by the total number of benchmarks (10). The Adjusted Average Normalized Time is calculated in the same manner as the Average Normalized Time, except that the highest and the lowest numbers were eliminated from this average. This was done because the Average Normalized Time was greatly affected by the Computer Graphics benchmark. This method is used when computing averages for other categories as well.

The execution speed comparison made in Table 2 shows that the iAPX 88/10 performed faster for eight of the ten benchmarks. The MC6809's Average Normalized Time of 3.65 says that it required 265% more time than the iAPX 88/10. The Adjusted Average Normalized Time (1.86), which eliminated the Computer Graphics and Single-Vectored Interrupt benchmarks, shows that the MC6809 is 86% slower, or requires **86% more time**, than the iAPX 88/10 to complete these benchmarks.

For applications where the cost of memory is a critical factor, both the speed of memory, and the amount of memory must be considered. By speed of memory, we are referring to the memory access time, which is a major factor in the price of memory. Because the memory access time of the iAPX 88 is 460 nsec with no wait states, one wait state is added to the MC6809. This gives a 445 nsec memory access time, which is still less than the 460 nsec zero wait state time of the iAPX 88. A comparison of the execution speeds of the two processors for this case is made in Table 3 (Execution Times With "Equal" Memory Access Times), showing that the iAPX 88/10 was again faster than the MC6809 for eight

Table 2. Execution Times (5 MHz 88/10 vs 2 MHz 6809)

Benchmark Programs	Absolute Time		Normalized Time	
	iAPX 88/10	MC6809	iAPX 88/10	MC6809
Computer Graphics	2.32 sec	49.7 sec.	1	21.42
16-Bit Multiply	40.8 us	82.0 us	1	2.01
Vector Add	295.0 us	325.0 us	1	1.10
Block Move	328.0 us	674.0 us	1	2.05
Block Translate	1507.0 us	2687.0 us	1	1.78
Character Search	136.0 us	284.0 us	1	2.09
Word Shift	13.0 us	44.5 us	1	3.42
Reentrant Call	87.6 us	76.5 us	1	0.87
Single-Vectored Interrupt	102.6 us	25.5 us	1	0.27
Multi-Vectored Interrupt	24.6 us	45.5 us	1	1.85
Average Normalized Execution Time*			1	3.69
Adjusted Average Normalized Execution Time**			1	1.90

* Normalized Time is the sum of the processor's normalized times for all programs divided by the number of programs (10).

** Average Normalized Execution Time is the average of the normalized times, excluding the highest and lowest normalized times.

01532A

Table 3. Execution Times with "Equal" Memory Access Times (5 MHz 88/10 vs 2 MHz 6809)

Benchmark Program	Absolute Time		Normalized Time	
	iAPX 88/10	MC6809*	iAPX 88/10	MC6809
Computer Graphics	2.32 sec.	57.1 sec.	1	24.61
16-Bit Multiply	40.8 us	91.9 us	1	2.25
Vector Add	295.0 us	369.0 us	1	1.25
Block Move	328.0 us	763.0 us	1	2.33
Block Translate	1507.0 us	3016.0 us	1	2.00
Character Search	136.0 us	324.0 us	1	2.38
Word Shift	14.4 us	49.1 us	1	3.78
Reentrant Call	87.6 us	84.1 us	1	0.96
Single-Vectored Interrupt	102.6 us	30.1 us	1	0.29
Multi-Vectored Interrupt	24.6 us	55.3 us	1	2.25
Average Normalized Execution Time**			1	4.21
Adjusted Average Normalized Execution Time**			1	2.15

*Times for the MC6809 include one wait state on memory accesses.

**See note, Table 2, for description of average calculations.

of the ten programs. The MC6809's Average Normalized Time of 4.17 greatly reflects (as it did in Table 2) the fact that the iAPX 88/10 outperformed the MC6809 by a large margin (more than 24 to 1) in the Computer Graphics benchmark. The Adjusted Average Normalized Time of 2.10 indicates that, after eliminating the Computer Graphics and Single-Vectored Interrupt, the iAPX 88/10 was more than twice as fast as the MC6809.

Table 4 compares the performance of the iAPX 88 and the MC6809 in terms of memory use, or coding efficiency. The results in this table show that the iAPX 88 used less code for nine of the ten programs. The two programs in which the largest performance differences occurred were the interrupt response benchmarks. The MC6809 won on the Single-Vectored Interrupt, largely due to the use of its IRQ interrupt which automatically stacks all the MC6809's registers. The iAPX 88/10 performed better for the Multi-Vectored Interrupt because its interrupt response requires no extra code to accommodate multiple interrupt vectors. For the other programs, the iAPX 88 provides significant advantages due to its string instructions and its efficient handling of 16-bit quantities. The Adjusted Average Normalized Number of Bytes shows the iAPX 88 with better than a 2 to 1 advantage over the MC6809 in coding efficiency.

Table 4. Memory Utilization (Bytes)

Benchmark Program	Bytes of Code		Normalized Bytes	
	iAPX 88/10	MC6809	iAPX 88/10	MC6809
Computer Graphics	40	180	1	4.50
16-Bit Multiply	14	56	1	4.00
Vector Add	18	21	1	1.17
Block Move	15	26	1	1.73
Block Translate	24	37	1	1.54
Character Search	18	19	1	1.06
Word Shift	6	18	1	3.00
Reentrant Call	48	49	1	1.02
Single-Vectored Interrupt	15	1	1	0.07
Multi-Vectored Interrupt	1	15	1	15.00
Average Normalized Number of Bytes of Code*			1	3.31
Adjusted Average Normalized Number of Bytes of Code*			1	2.25

*See note, Table 2, for description of average calculations.

AFN 01532A

In Table 5 the iAPX 88 and the MC6809 are compared for "Ease of Programming" by counting the number of lines of code required for each benchmark. The iAPX 88 used a smaller number of lines of code than the MC6809 for eight of the ten programs. As in coding efficiency, the greatest differences occurred in the two interrupt response benchmarks, with the MC6809 again having an advantage in the Single-Vectored Interrupt,

and the iAPX 88/10 using fewer instructions in the Multi-Vectored Interrupt. For the other programs, the iAPX 88's use of string instructions, and its ability to handle 8-bit or 16-bit data allowed the algorithms to be implemented in fewer lines of code. The Adjusted Average Normalized Lines of Code was 2.67 showing that the iAPX 88 used less lines of code than the MC6809 by a factor of more than 2.6 to 1.

Table 5. Ease of Programming

Benchmark Program	Lines of Code		Normalized Lines	
	iAPX 88/10	MC6809	iAPX 88/10	MC6809
Computer Graphics	15	87	1	5.80
16-Bit Multiply	4	28	1	7.00
Vector Add	8	8	1	1.00
Block Move	7	14	1	2.00
Block Translate	10	13	1	1.30
Character Search	8	9	1	1.13
Word Shift	2	9	1	4.50
Reentrant Call	26	23	1	0.88
Single-Vectored Interrupt	15	1	1	0.07
Multi-Vectored Interrupt	1	8	1	8.00
Average Normalized Number of Lines of Code*			1	3.17
Adjusted Average Normalized Number of Lines of Code*			1	2.95

*See note, Table 2, for description of average calculations.

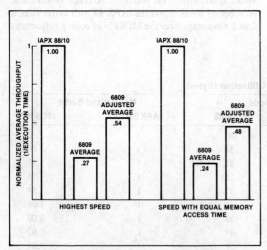

Graph I. Normalized Average Throughput:
5 MHz iAPX 88/10 vs 2 MHz 6809

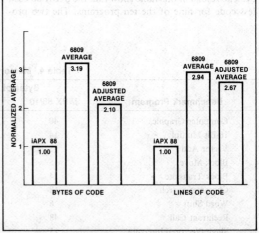

Graph II. Normalized Average Memory Use and Lines
of Code: iAPX 88/10 vs 6809

AFN 01532A

CONCLUSION

The results of this benchmark study show that for the programs used, the Intel iAPX 88/10 significantly outperformed the Motorola MC6809. In absolute execution speed, the iAPX 88/10 proved to be 86% faster than the MC6809 (using the Adjusted Average). When compared at equal memory access times, the iAPX 88/10 outperformed the MC6809 by 110%. On the basis of coding efficiency, the iAPX 88/10 generated less than half as much object code as the MC6809. In the Ease of Programming category, the results showed that the MC6809 required more than 2.6 times the number of lines of code required by the iAPX 88/10. These results are summarized in the table below.

The iAPX 88 is the highest performance 8-bit microprocessor in the market today. The already superior performance of the iAPX 88 will be increased by 60% when the 8 MHz version is available in 1981. This, together with the upgrade path to other object code compatible processor series in the Microsystem 80 product line (iAPX 86, iAPX 188, 186 and iAPX 286, 288), and the unequalled hardware and software support, makes it clear that Intel delivers the best solution to the many applications which require a powerful 8-bit microprocessor.

Table 6. Performance Breakdown

Performance Category	Performance Ratio of iAPX 88 to MC6809
Execution Speed (Fastest)	iAPX 88/10 is 1.86X faster
Execution Speed*	iAPX 88/10 is 2.10X faster
Coding Efficiency	iAPX 88/10 is 1.47X more efficient
Ease of Programming	iAPX 88/10 is 2.67X more efficient

*With equal speed memory

AFN 01532A

APPENDIX I

BENCHMARK PROGRAM CODE AND FLOWCHARTS*

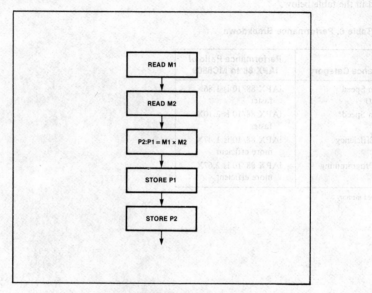

Figure 1. 16-Bit Multiply Flowchart

*This appendix contains the code and flowcharts for three of the benchmark programs (16-Bit Multiply, Block Move, and Character Search). For the code and flowcharts for all benchmark programs contact your local Intel sales office.

AFN 01532A

BENCHMARK: 16-Bit Multiply

PROCESSOR: Intel iAPX 88

```
                              ;REGISTER USAGE:
                              ;  AX- ACCUMULATOR
                              ;  DX- ACCUMULATOR

Bytes  Cycles

  3      18        MOV      AX, M1        ;Read operand
  4      137       MUL      M2            ;A*B
  3      19        MOV      P1,AX         ;Store LSB
  4      19        MOV      P2,DX         ;Store MSB


                              14 bytes of code
                              4 lines of code
```

AFN 01532A

BENCHMARK: 16-Bit Multiply
PROCESSOR: Motorola 6809

```
                        ;REGISTER USAGE:
                        ;      D - ACCUMULATOR
                        ;      X - OPERAND POINTER
                        ;      Y - OPERAND POINTER
                        ;      U - PRODUCT POINTER

Bytes   Cycles

  3       3      LDX    #AA           ;Pointer to multiplicand A(MS Byte)
  4       5      LDY    #BB           ;Pointer to multiplicand B(MS Byte)
  3       3      LDU    #MO           ;Pointer to product

  2       6      CLR    0,U           ;CLR MO
  2       6      CLR    1,U           ;CLR M1
  2       5      LDA    1,X           ;Read LS byte of A (AL)
  2       5      LDB    1,Y           ;Read LS byte of B (BL)
  1      11      MUL                  ;AL*BL
  2       6      STD    2,U           ;Store in M3:M2

  2       4      LDA    0,X           ;Read MS byte of A (AH)
  2       5      LDB    1,Y           ;Read LS byte of B (BL)
  1      11      MUL                  ;AH*BL
  2       7      ADDD   1,U           ;AH*BL + MS byte from AL*BL
  2       6      STD    1,U           ;Store in M2:M1
  2       3      BCC    AB1           ;Skip INC if no carry
  2       6      INC    0,U           ;Add carry to MO

  2       5 AB1  LDA    1,X           ;Read LS byte of A (AL)
  2       4      LDB    0,Y           ;Read LS byte of B (BH)
  1      11      MUL                  ;AL*BH
  2       7      ADDD   1,U           ;AL*BH+ M2:M1
  2       6      STD    1,U           ;Store in M2:M1
  2       3      BCC    AB2           ;Skip INC if no carry
  2       6      INC    0,U           ;Add carry to MO
  2       4 AB2  LDA    0,X           ;Read AH
  2       4      LDB    0,Y           ;Read BH
  1      11      MUL                  ;AH*BH
  2       7      ADDD   0,U           ;AH*BH +M1 + carries
  2       6      STD    0,U           ;Store in M1:MO


                        56 bytes of code
                        28 lines of code
```

AFN 01532A

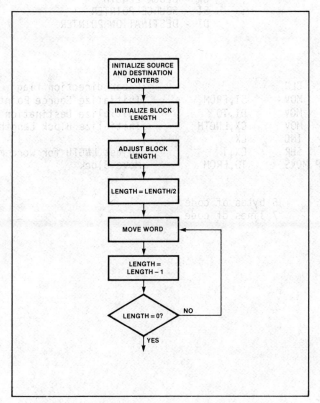

Figure 2. Block Move Flowchart

AFN 01532A

BENCHMARK: Block Move

PROCESSOR: Intel iAPX 88

```
                        ;REGISTER USAGE:
                        ;      CX - BLOCK LENGTH
                        ;      SI - SOURCE POINTER
                        ;      DI - DESTINATION POINTER
```

```
Bytes   Cycles

  1       2            CLD                          ;Clear direction flag
  3       4            MOV       SI,FROM            ;Initialize Source Pointer
  3       4            MOV       DI,TO              ;Initialize Destination Pointer
  3       4            MOV       CX,LNGTH           ;Initialize Block Length
  1       2            INC       CX                 ;
  2       2            SHR       CX,1               ;Adjust LNGTH for word moves
  2     9+25/  REP     MOVS      TO,FROM            ;Move Block


                    15 bytes of code
                     7 lines of code
```

AFN 01532A

BENCHMARK: Block Move

PROCESSOR: Motorola 6809

```
;REGISTER USAGE
;      D - Block Length
;      X - Temporary Storage
;      Y - Source Pointer
;      U - Destination Pointer
```

Bytes Cycles

Bytes	Cycles				
4	4		LDY	#FROM	;Initialize Source Pointer
3	3		LDU	#TO	;Initialize Destination Pointer
3	3		LDD	#LENGTH	:Initialize Block Length
1	2		INCB		
2	3		BNC	SHIFT	;Add one to avoid losing a
1	2		INCA		; byte if LENGTH is odd
1	2	SHIFT	LSRA		;Adjust LENGTH for word
1	2		RORB		; moves
2	8	MOVE	LDX	,Y++	;Read word
2	8		STX	,U++	;Store word
1	2		DECB		;LS Count
2	3		BNE	MOVE	
1	2		DECA		;MS Count
2	3		BNE	MOVE	

```
26 bytes of code
14 lines of code
```

AFN 01532A

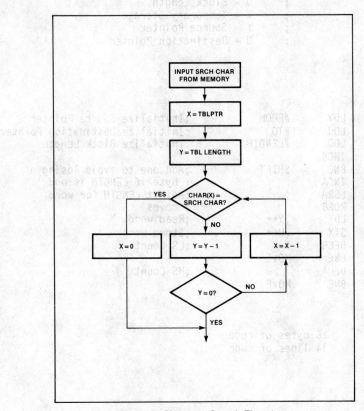

Figure 3. Character Search Flowchart

AFN 01532A

BENCHMARK: Character Search

PROCESSOR: Intel iAPX 88

```
                      ;REGISTER USAGE:
                      ;    AL - ACCUMULATOR
                      ;    CX - COUNT
                      :    DI - TABLE POINTER
```

Bytes   Cycles

```
  4      6           LEA     DI,PTR          ;Initialize Table Pointer
  2      4           MOv     AL,CHAR         ;Search character
  3      4           MOv     CX,40           ;Initialize count
  1      2           CLD                     ;Clear direction flag

  2    9+15/   REPNE SCAS     PTR            ;Search
  2    16/4          JZ      PASTPTR         ;Jump if found
  3      4           MOv     DI,1            ;Not found:DI will return 0
  1      2 PASTPTR:DEC        DI             ;Adjust DI
```

                    18 bytes of code
                     8 lines of code

AFN 01532A

BENCHMARK: Character Search

PROCESSOR: Motorola 6809

```
                         ;REGISTER USAGE:
                         ;    A - ACCUMULATOR
                         ;    B - COUNT
                         :    X - TABLE POINTER
```

Bytes Cycles

```
 3    3           LDX    #PTR       ;Initialize Table Pointer
 2    2           LDA    #CHAR      ;Search character
 2    2           LDB    #40        ;Initialize count

 2    6   AGAIN   CMPA   ,X+        ;Compare, autoincrement
 2    3           BEQ    PASTPTR    ;Jump if found
 1    2           DECB              ;Decrement count
 2    3           BNE    AGAIN      ;Do again unless B=0
 3    3           LDX    #1         ;Not found: X will return 0
 2    5   PASTPTR LEAX   -1,X       ;Adjust X
```

                    19 bytes of code
                     9 lines of code

iAPX 88/10
8-BIT HMOS MICROPROCESSOR
8088/8088-2

- 8-Bit Data Bus Interface

- 16-Bit Internal Architecture

- Direct Addressing Capability to 1 Mbyte of Memory

- Direct Software Compatibility with iAPX 86/10 (8086 CPU)

- 14-Word by 16-Bit Register Set with Symmetrical Operations

- 24 Operand Addressing Modes

- Byte, Word, and Block Operations

- 8-Bit and 16-Bit Signed and Unsigned Arithmetic in Binary or Decimal, Including Multiply and Divide

- Compatible with 8155-2, 8755A-2 and 8185-2 Multiplexed Peripherals

- Two Clock Rates:
  5 MHz for 8088
  8 MHz for 8088-2

- Available in EXPRESS
  - Standard Temperature Range
  - Extended Temperature Range

The Intel® iAPX 88/10 is a new generation, high performance microprocessor implemented in N-channel, depletion load, silicon gate technology (HMOS), and packaged in a 40-pin CerDIP package. The processor has attributes of both 8- and 16-bit microprocessors. It is directly compatible with iAPX 86/10 software and 8080/8085 hardware and peripherals.

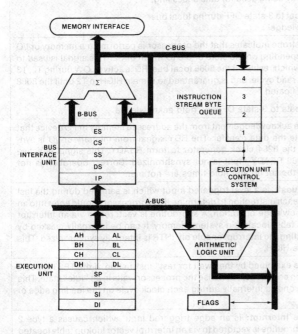

Figure 1. iAPX 88/10 CPU Functional Block Diagram

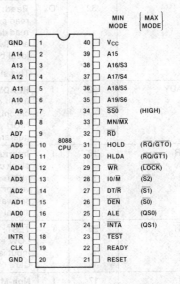

Figure 2. iAPX 88/10 Pin Configuration

AFN-00826D

intel®

Table 1. Pin Description

The following pin function descriptions are for 8088 systems in either minimum or maximum mode. The "local bus" in these descriptions is the direct multiplexed bus interface connection to the 8088 (without regard to additional bus buffers).

Symbol	Pin No.	Type	Name and Function
AD7–AD0	9-16	I/O	**Address Data Bus:** These lines constitute the time multiplexed memory/IO address (T1) and data (T2, T3, Tw, and T4) bus. These lines are active HIGH and float to 3-state OFF during interrupt acknowledge and local bus "hold acknowledge".
A15–A8	2-8, 39	O	**Address Bus:** These lines provide address bits 8 through 15 for the entire bus cycle (T1–T4). These lines do not have to be latched by ALE to remain valid. A15–A8 are active HIGH and float to 3-state OFF during interrupt acknowledge and local bus "hold acknowledge".
A19/S6, A18/S5, A17/S4, A16/S3	34-38	O	**Address/Status:** During T1, these are the four most significant address lines for memory operations. During I/O operations, these lines are LOW. During memory and I/O operations, status information is available on these lines during T2, T3, Tw, and T4. S6 is always low. The status of the interrupt enable flag bit (S5) is updated at the beginning of each clock cycle. S4 and S3 are encoded as shown. *(see table below)* This information indicates which segment register is presently being used for data accessing. These lines float to 3-state OFF during local bus "hold acknowledge".
$\overline{RD}$	32	O	**Read:** Read strobe indicates that the processor is performing a memory or I/O read cycle, depending on the state of the IO/$\overline{M}$ pin or S2. This signal is used to read devices which reside on the 8088 local bus. $\overline{RD}$ is active LOW during T2, T3 and Tw of any read cycle, and is guaranteed to remain HIGH in T2 until the 8088 local bus has floated. This signal floats to 3-state OFF in "hold acknowledge".
READY	22	I	**READY:** is the acknowledgement from the addressed memory or I/O device that it will complete the data transfer. The RDY signal from memory or I/O is synchronized by the 8284 clock generator to form READY. This signal is active HIGH. The 8088 READY input is not synchronized. Correct operation is not guaranteed if the set up and hold times are not met.
INTR	18	I	**Interrupt Request:** is a level triggered input which is sampled during the last clock cycle of each instruction to determine if the processor should enter into an interrupt acknowledge operation. A subroutine is vectored to via an interrupt vector lookup table located in system memory. It can be internally masked by software resetting the interrupt enable bit. INTR is internally synchronized. This signal is active HIGH.
$\overline{TEST}$	23	I	**TEST:** input is examined by the "wait for test" instruction. If the $\overline{TEST}$ input is LOW, execution continues, otherwise the processor waits in an "idle" state. This input is synchronized internally during each clock cycle on the leading edge of CLK.
NMI	17	I	**Non-Maskable Interrupt:** is an edge triggered input which causes a type 2 interrupt. A subroutine is vectored to via an interrupt vector lookup table located in system memory. NMI is not maskable internally by software. A transition from a LOW to HIGH initiates the interrupt at the end of the current instruction. This input is internally synchronized.

Status table within Address/Status row:

S4	S3	CHARACTERISTICS
0 (LOW)	0	Alternate Data
0	1	Stack
1 (HIGH)	0	Code or None
1	1	Data
S6 is 0 (LOW)		

Table 1. Pin Description (Continued)

Symbol	Pin No.	Type	Name and Function
RESET	21	I	**RESET:** causes the processor to immediately terminate its present activity. The signal must be active HIGH for at least four clock cycles. It restarts execution, as described in the instruction set description, when RESET returns LOW. RESET is internally synchronized.
CLK	19	I	**Clock:** provides the basic timing for the processor and bus controller. It is asymmetric with a 33% duty cycle to provide optimized internal timing.
V_{CC}	40		V_{CC}: is the +5V ±10% power supply pin.
GND	1, 20		**GND:** are the ground pins.
MN/$\overline{MX}$	33	I	**Minimum/Maximum:** indicates what mode the processor is to operate in. The two modes are discussed in the following sections.

The following pin function descriptions are for the 8088 minimum mode (i.e., MN/MX = V_{CC}). Only the pin functions which are unique to minimum mode are described; all other pin functions are as described above.

IO/$\overline{M}$	28	O	**Status Line:** is an inverted maximum mode $\overline{S2}$. It is used to distinguish a memory access from an I/O access. IO/$\overline{M}$ becomes valid in the T4 preceding a bus cycle and remains valid until the final T4 of the cycle (I/O=HIGH, M=LOW). IO/$\overline{M}$ floats to 3-state OFF in local bus "hold acknowledge".
$\overline{WR}$	29	O	**Write:** strobe indicates that the processor is performing a write memory or write I/O cycle, depending on the state of the IO/$\overline{M}$ signal. WR is active for T2, T3, and Tw of any write cycle. It is active LOW, and floats to 3-state OFF in local bus "hold acknowledge".
$\overline{INTA}$	24	O	**INTA:** is used as a read strobe for interrupt acknowledge cycles. It is active LOW during T2, T3, and Tw of each interrupt acknowledge cycle.
ALE	25	O	**Address Latch Enable:** is provided by the processor to latch the address into the 8282/8283 address latch. It is a HIGH pulse active during clock low of T1 of any bus cycle. Note that ALE is never floated.
DT/$\overline{R}$	27	O	**Data Transmit/Receive:** is needed in a minimum system that desires to use an 8286/8287 data bus transceiver. It is used to control the direction of data flow through the transceiver. Logically, DT/$\overline{R}$ is equivalent to $\overline{S1}$ in the maximum mode, and its timing is the same as for IO/$\overline{M}$ (T=HIGH, R=LOW). This signal floats to 3-state OFF in local "hold acknowledge".
$\overline{DEN}$	26	O	**Data Enable:** is provided as an output enable for the 8286/8287 in a minimum system which uses the transceiver. $\overline{DEN}$ is active LOW during each memory and I/O access, and for $\overline{INTA}$ cycles. For a read or $\overline{INTA}$ cycle, it is active from the middle of T2 until the middle of T4, while for a write cycle, it is active from the beginning of T2 until the middle of T4. $\overline{DEN}$ floats to 3-state OFF during local bus "hold acknowledge".
HOLD, HLDA	30,31	I, O	**HOLD:** indicates that another master is requesting a local bus "hold". To be acknowledged, HOLD must be active HIGH. The processor receiving the "hold" request will issue HLDA (HIGH) as an acknowledgement, in the middle of a T4 or TI clock cycle. Simultaneous with the issuance of HLDA the processor will float the local bus and control lines. After HOLD is detected as being LOW, the processor lowers HLDA, and when the processor needs to run another cycle, it will again drive the local bus and control lines. Hold is not an asynchronous input. External synchronization should be provided if the system cannot otherwise guarantee the set up time.
$\overline{SSO}$	34	O	**Status line:** is logically equivalent to $\overline{SO}$ in the maximum mode. The combination of $\overline{SSO}$, IO/$\overline{M}$ and DT/$\overline{R}$ allows the system to completely decode the current bus cycle status.

Table in SSO row:

IO/$\overline{M}$	DT/$\overline{R}$	$\overline{SSO}$	CHARACTERISTICS
1 (HIGH)	0	0	Interrupt Acknowledge
1	0	1	Read I/O port
1	1	0	Write I/O port
1	1	1	Halt
0 (LOW)	0	0	Code access
0	0	1	Read memory
0	1	0	Write memory
0	1	1	Passive

AFN-00826D

Table 1. Pin Description (Continued)

The following pin function descriptions are for the 8088, 8228 system in maximum mode (i.e., MN/MX=GND.) Only the pin functions which are unique to maximum mode are described; all other pin functions are as described above.

Symbol	Pin No.	Type	Name and Function
S̄2, S̄1, S̄0	26-28	O	**Status:** is active during clock high of T4, T1, and T2, and is returned to the passive state (1,1,1) during T3 or during Tw when READY is HIGH. This status is used by the 8288 bus controller to generate all memory and I/O access control signals. Any change by S̄2, S̄1, or S̄0 during T4 is used to indicate the beginning of a bus cycle, and the return to the passive state in T3 or Tw is used to indicate the end of a bus cycle. These signals float to 3-state OFF during "hold acknowledge". During the first clock cycle after RESET becomes active, these signals are active HIGH. After this first clock, they float to 3-state OFF.
R̄Q̄/ḠT̄0, R̄Q̄/ḠT̄1	30, 31	I/O	**Request/Grant:** pins are used by other local bus masters to force the processor to release the local bus at the end of the processor's current bus cycle. Each pin is bidirectional with R̄Q̄/ḠT̄0 having higher priority than R̄Q̄/ḠT̄1. R̄Q̄/ḠT̄ has an internal pull-up resistor, so may be left unconnected. The request/grant sequence is as follows (See Figure 8): 1. A pulse of one CLK wide from another local bus master indicates a local bus request ("hold") to the 8088 (pulse 1). 2. During a T4 or TI clock cycle, a pulse one clock wide from the 8088 to the requesting master (pulse 2), indicates that the 8088 has allowed the local bus to float and that it will enter the "hold acknowledge" state at the next CLK. The CPU's bus interface unit is disconnected logically from the local bus during "hold acknowledge". The same rules as for HOLD/HOLDA apply as for when the bus is released. 3. A pulse one CLK wide from the requesting master indicates to the 8088 (pulse 3) that the "hold" request is about to end and that the 8088 can reclaim the local bus at the next CLK. The CPU then enters T4. Each master-master exchange of the local bus is a sequence of three pulses. There must be one idle CLK cycle after each bus exchange. Pulses are active LOW. If the request is made while the CPU is performing a memory cycle, it will release the local bus during T4 of the cycle when all the following conditions are met: 1. Request occurs on or before T2. 2. Current cycle is not the low bit of a word. 3. Current cycle is not the first acknowledge of an interrupt acknowledge sequence. 4. A locked instruction is not currently executing. If the local bus is idle when the request is made the two possible events will follow: 1. Local bus will be released during the next clock. 2. A memory cycle will start within 3 clocks. Now the four rules for a currently active memory cycle apply with condition number 1 already satisfied.

Table within Status row:

S2	S1	S0	CHARACTERISTICS
0 (LOW)	0	0	Interrupt Acknowledge
0	0	1	Read I/O port
0	1	0	Write I/O port
0	1	1	Halt
1 (HIGH)	0	0	Code access
1	0	1	Read memory
1	1	0	Write memory
1	1	1	Passive

Table 1. Pin Description (Continued)

Symbol	Pin No.	Type	Name and Function
$\overline{LOCK}$	29	O	**LOCK:** indicates that other system bus masters are not to gain control of the system bus while $\overline{LOCK}$ is active (LOW). The $\overline{LOCK}$ signal is activated by the "LOCK" prefix instruction and remains active until the completion of the next instruction. This signal is active LOW, and floats to 3-state off in "hold acknowledge".
QS1, QS0	24, 25	O	**Queue Status:** provide status to allow external tracking of the internal 8088 instruction queue. The queue status is valid during the CLK cycle after which the queue operation is performed. | QS1	QS0	CHARACTERISTICS
---	---	---
0 (LOW)	0	No operation
0	1	First byte of opcode from queue
1 (HIGH)	0	Empty the queue
1	1	Subsequent byte from queue	
—	34	O	Pin 34 is always high in the maximum mode.

FUNCTIONAL DESCRIPTION

Memory Organization

The processor provides a 20-bit address to memory which locates the byte being referenced. The memory is organized as a linear array of up to 1 million bytes, addressed as 00000(H) to FFFFF(H). The memory is logically divided into code, data, extra data, and stack segments of up to 64K bytes each, with each segment falling on 16-byte boundaries. (See Figure 3.)

All memory references are made relative to base addresses contained in high speed segment registers. The segment types were chosen based on the addressing needs of programs. The segment register to be selected is automatically chosen according to the rules of the following table. All information in one segment type share the same logical attributes (e.g. code or data). By structuring memory into relocatable areas of similar characteristics and by automatically selecting segment registers, programs are shorter, faster, and more structured.

Word (16-bit) operands can be located on even or odd address boundaries. For address and data operands, the least significant byte of the word is stored in the lower valued address location and the most significant byte in

the next higher address location. The BIU will automatically execute two fetch or write cycles for 16-bit operands.

Certain locations in memory are reserved for specific CPU operations. (See Figure 4.) Locations from addresses FFFF0H through FFFFFH are reserved for operations including a jump to the initial system initialization routine. Following RESET, the CPU will always begin execution at location FFFF0H where the jump must be located. Locations 00000H through 003FFH are reserved for interrupt operations. Four-byte pointers consisting of a 16-bit segment address and a 16-bit offset address direct program flow to one of the 256 possible interrupt service routines. The pointer elements are assumed to have been stored at their respective places in reserved memory prior to the occurrence of interrupts.

Minimum and Maximum Modes

The requirements for supporting minimum and maximum 8088 systems are sufficiently different that they cannot be done efficiently with 40 uniquely defined pins. Consequently, the 8088 is equipped with a strap pin (MN/$\overline{\text{MX}}$) which defines the system configuration. The definition of a certain subset of the pins changes, dependent on the condition of the strap pin. When the MN/$\overline{\text{MX}}$ pin is strapped to GND, the 8088 defines pins 24 through 31 and 34 in maximum mode. When the MN/$\overline{\text{MX}}$ pin is strapped to V_{CC}, the 8088 generates bus control signals itself on pins 24 through 31 and 34.

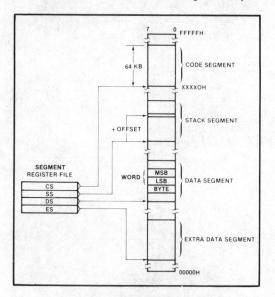

Figure 3. Memory Organization

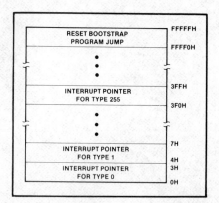

Figure 4. Reserved Memory Locations

Memory Reference Need	Segment Register Used	Segment Selection Rule
Instructions	CODE (CS)	Automatic with all instruction prefetch.
Stack	STACK (SS)	All stack pushes and pops. Memory references relative to BP base register except data references.
Local Data	DATA (DS)	Data references when: relative to stack, destination of string operation, or explicitly overridden.
External (Global) Data	EXTRA (ES)	Destination of string operations: Explicitly selected using a segment override.

AFN-00826D

The minimum mode 8088 can be used with either a multiplexed or demultiplexed bus. The multiplexed bus configuration is compatible with the MCS-85™ multiplexed bus peripherals (8155, 8156, 8355, 8755A, and 8185). This configuration (See Figure 5) provides the user with a minimum chip count system. This architecture provides the 8088 processing power in a highly integrated form.

The demultiplexed mode requires one latch (for 64K addressability) or two latches (for a full megabyte of addressing). A third latch can be used for buffering if the address bus loading requires it. An 8286 or 8287 transceiver can also be used if data bus buffering is required. (See Figure 6.) The 8088 provides $\overline{DEN}$ and DT/$\overline{R}$ to con-

trol the transceiver, and ALE to latch the addresses. This configuration of the minimum mode provides the standard demultiplexed bus structure with heavy bus buffering and relaxed bus timing requirements.

The maximum mode employs the 8288 bus controller. (See Figure 7.) The 8288 decodes status lines $\overline{S0}$, $\overline{S1}$, and $\overline{S2}$, and provides the system with all bus control signals. Moving the bus control to the 8288 provides better source and sink current capability to the control lines, and frees the 8088 pins for extended large system features. Hardware lock, queue status, and two request/grant interfaces are provided by the 8088 in maximum mode. These features allow co-processors in local bus and remote bus configurations.

AFN-00826D

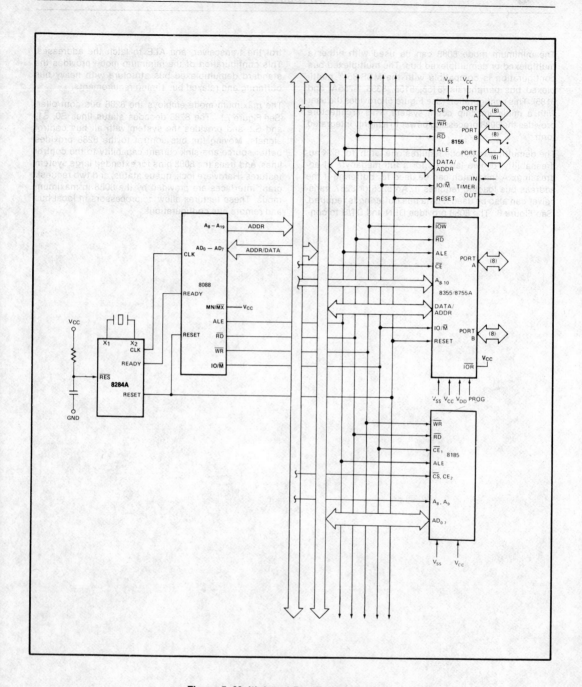

Figure 5. Multiplexed Bus Configuration

AFN-00826D

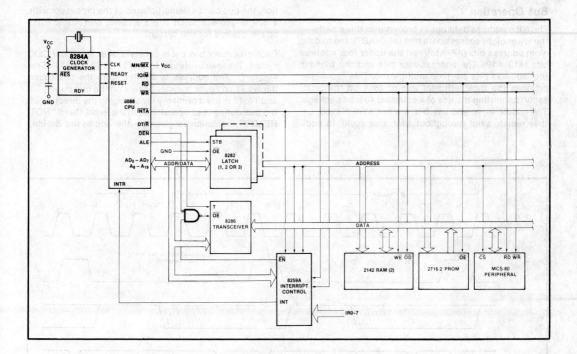

Figure 6. Demultiplexed Bus Configuration

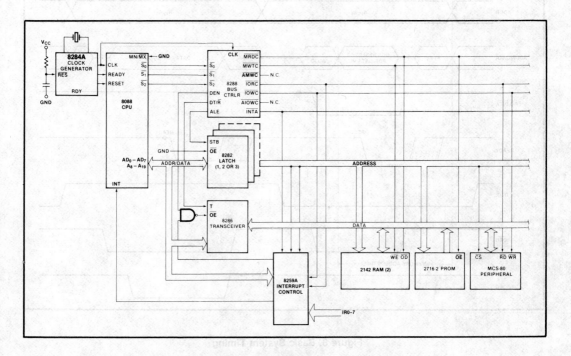

Figure 7. Fully Buffered System Using Bus Controller

AFN-00826D

Bus Operation

The 8088 address/data bus is broken into three parts — the lower eight address/data bits (AD0–AD7), the middle eight address bits (A8–A15), and the upper four address bits (A16–A19). The address/data bits and the highest four address bits are time multiplexed. This technique provides the most efficient use of pins on the processor, permitting the use of a standard 40 lead package. The middle eight address bits are not multiplexed, i.e. they remain valid throughout each bus cycle. In addi-

tion, the bus can be demultiplexed at the processor with a single address latch if a standard, non-multiplexed bus is desired for the system.

Each processor bus cycle consists of at least four CLK cycles. These are referred to as T1, T2, T3, and T4. (See Figure 8). The address is emitted from the processor during T1 and data transfer occurs on the bus during T3 and T4. T2 is used primarily for changing the direction of the bus during read operations. In the event that a "NOT READY" indication is given by the addressed device,

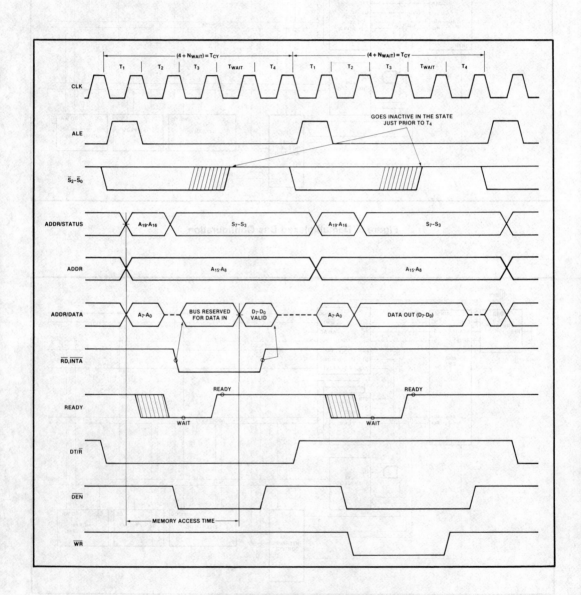

Figure 8. Basic System Timing

46

"wait" states (Tw) are inserted between T3 and T4. Each inserted "wait" state is of the same duration as a CLK cycle. Periods can occur between 8088 driven bus cycles. These are referred to as "idle" states (Ti), or inactive CLK cycles. The processor uses these cycles for internal housekeeping.

During T1 of any bus cycle, the ALE (address latch enable) signal is emitted (by either the processor or the 8288 bus controller, depending on the MN/$\overline{\text{MX}}$ strap). At the trailing edge of this pulse, a valid address and certain status information for the cycle may be latched.

Status bits $\overline{\text{S0}}$, $\overline{\text{S1}}$, and $\overline{\text{S2}}$ are used by the bus controller, in maximum mode, to identify the type of bus transaction according to the following table:

$\overline{S}_2$	$\overline{S}_1$	$\overline{S}_0$	CHARACTERISTICS
0 (LOW)	0	0	Interrupt Acknowledge
0	0	1	Read I/O
0	1	0	Write I/O
0	1	1	Halt
1 (HIGH)	0	0	Instruction Fetch
1	0	1	Read Data from Memory
1	1	0	Write Data to Memory
1	1	1	Passive (no bus cycle)

Status bits S3 through S6 are multiplexed with high order address bits and are therefore valid during T2 through T4. S3 and S4 indicate which segment register was used for this bus cycle in forming the address according to the following table:

S_4	S_3	CHARACTERISTICS
0 (LOW)	0	Alternate Data (extra segment)
0	1	Stack
1 (HIGH)	0	Code or None
1	1	Data

S5 is a reflection of the PSW interrupt enable bit. S6 is always equal to 0.

I/O Addressing

In the 8088, I/O operations can address up to a maximum of 64K I/O registers. The I/O address appears in the same format as the memory address on bus lines A15-A0. The address lines A19-A16 are zero in I/O operations. The variable I/O instructions, which use register DX as a pointer, have full address capability, while the direct I/O instructions directly address one or two of the 256 I/O byte locations in page 0 of the I/O address space. I/O ports are addressed in the same manner as memory locations.

Designers familiar with the 8085 or upgrading an 8085 design should note that the 8085 addresses I/O with an 8-bit address on both halves of the 16-bit address bus. The 8088 uses a full 16-bit address on its lower 16 address lines.

EXTERNAL INTERFACE

Processor Reset and Initialization

Processor initialization or start up is accomplished with activation (HIGH) of the RESET pin. The 8088 RESET is required to be HIGH for greater than four clock cycles. The 8088 will terminate operations on the high-going edge of RESET and will remain dormant as long as RESET is HIGH. The low-going transition of RESET triggers an internal reset sequence for approximately 7 clock cycles. After this interval the 8088 operates normally, beginning with the instruction in absolute location FFFF0H. (See Figure 4.) The RESET input is internally synchronized to the processor clock. At initialization, the HIGH to LOW transition of RESET must occur no sooner than 50 μs after power up, to allow complete initialization of the 8088.

If INTR is asserted sooner than nine clock cycles after the end of RESET, the processor may execute one instruction before responding to the interrupt.

All 3-state outputs float to 3-state OFF during RESET. Status is active in the idle state for the first clock after RESET becomes active and then floats to 3-state OFF.

Interrupt Operations

Interrupt operations fall into two classes: software or hardware initiated. The software initiated interrupts and software aspects of hardware interrupts are specified in the instruction set description in the iAPX 88 book or the iAPX 86,88 User's Manual. Hardware interrupts can be classified as nonmaskable or maskable.

Interrupts result in a transfer of control to a new program location. A 256 element table containing address pointers to the interrupt service program locations resides in absolute locations 0 through 3FFH (see Figure 4), which are reserved for this purpose. Each element in the table is 4 bytes in size and corresponds to an interrupt "type." An interrupting device supplies an 8-bit type number, during the interrupt acknowledge sequence, which is used to vector through the appropriate element to the new interrupt service program location.

Non-Maskable Interrupt (NMI)

The processor provides a single non-maskable interrupt (NMI) pin which has higher priority than the maskable interrupt request (INTR) pin. A typical use would be to activate a power failure routine. The NMI is edge-triggered on a LOW to HIGH transition. The activation of this pin causes a type 2 interrupt.

NMI is required to have a duration in the HIGH state of greater than two clock cycles, but is not required to be synchronized to the clock. Any higher going transition of NMI is latched on-chip and will be serviced at the end of the current instruction or between whole moves (2 bytes in the case of word moves) of a block type instruction. Worst case response to NMI would be for multiply, divide, and variable shift instructions. There is no specification on the occurrence of the low-going edge; it may occur

AFN-00826D

before, during, or after the servicing of NMI. Another high-going edge triggers another response if it occurs after the start of the NMI procedure. The signal must be free of logical spikes in general and be free of bounces on the low-going edge to avoid triggering extraneous responses.

Maskable Interrupt (INTR)

The 8088 provides a single interrupt request input (INTR) which can be masked internally by software with the resetting of the interrupt enable (IF) flag bit. The interrupt request signal is level triggered. It is internally synchronized during each clock cycle on the high-going edge of CLK. To be responded to, INTR must be present (HIGH) during the clock period preceding the end of the current instruction or the end of a whole move for a block type instruction. During interrupt response sequence, further interrupts are disabled. The enable bit is reset as part of the response to any interrupt (INTR, NMI, software interrupt, or single step), although the FLAGS register which is automatically pushed onto the stack reflects the state of the processor prior to the interrupt. Until the old FLAGS register is restored, the enable bit will be zero unless specifically set by an instruction.

During the response sequence (See Figure 9), the processor executes two successive (back to back) interrupt acknowledge cycles. The 8088 emits the LOCK signal (maximum mode only) from T2 of the first bus cycle until T2 of the second. A local bus "hold" request will not be honored until the end of the second bus cycle. In the second bus cycle, a byte is fetched from the external interrupt system (e.g., 8259A PIC) which identifies the source (type) of the interrupt. This byte is multiplied by four and used as a pointer into the interrupt vector lookup table. An INTR signal left HIGH will be continually responded to within the limitations of the enable bit

and sample period. The interrupt return instruction includes a flags pop which returns the status of the original interrupt enable bit when it restores the flags.

HALT

When a software HALT instruction is executed, the processor indicates that it is entering the HALT state in one of two ways, depending upon which mode is strapped. In minimum mode, the processor issues ALE, delayed by one clock cycle, to allow the system to latch the halt status. Halt status is available on IO/$\overline{M}$, DT/$\overline{R}$, and $\overline{SSO}$. In maximum mode, the processor issues appropriate HALT status on $\overline{S2}$, $\overline{S1}$, and $\overline{S0}$, and the 8288 bus controller issues one ALE. The 8088 will not leave the HALT state when a local bus hold is entered while in HALT. In this case, the processor reissues the HALT indicator at the end of the local bus hold. An interrupt request or RESET will force the 8088 out of the HALT state.

Read/Modify/Write (Semaphore) Operations via LOCK

The LOCK status information is provided by the processor when consecutive bus cycles are required during the execution of an instruction. This allows the processor to perform read/modify/write operations on memory (via the "exchange register with memory" instruction), without another system bus master receiving intervening memory cycles. This is useful in multiprocessor system configurations to accomplish "test and set lock" operations. The $\overline{LOCK}$ signal is activated (LOW) in the clock cycle following decoding of the LOCK prefix instruction. It is deactivated at the end of the last bus cycle of the instruction following the LOCK prefix. While $\overline{LOCK}$ is active, a request on a $\overline{RQ}/\overline{GT}$ pin will be recorded, and then honored at the end of the LOCK.

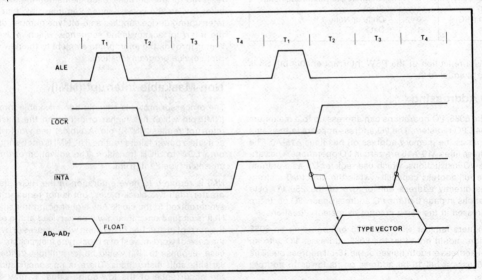

Figure 9. Interrupt Acknowledge Sequence

AFN-00826D

External Synchronization via TEST

As an alternative to interrupts, the 8088 provides a single software-testable input pin (TEST). This input is utilized by executing a WAIT instruction. The single WAIT instruction is repeatedly executed until the TEST input goes active (LOW). The execution of WAIT does not consume bus cycles once the queue is full.

If a local bus request occurs during WAIT execution, the 8088 3-states all output drivers. If interrupts are enabled, the 8088 will recognize interrupts and process them. The WAIT instruction is then refetched, and reexecuted.

Basic System Timing

In minimum mode, the MN/MX pin is strapped to V_{CC} and the processor emits bus control signals compatible with the 8085 bus structure. In maximum mode, the MN/MX pin is strapped to GND and the processor emits coded status information which the 8288 bus controller uses to generate MULTIBUS compatible bus control signals.

System Timing — Minimum System

(See Figure 8.)

The read cycle begins in T1 with the assertion of the address latch enable (ALE) signal. The trailing (low going) edge of this signal is used to latch the address information, which is valid on the address/data bus (AD0–AD7) at this time, into the 8282/8283 latch. Address lines A8 through A15 do not need to be latched because they remain valid throughout the bus cycle. From T1 to T4 the IO/M signal indicates a memory or I/O operation. At T2 the address is removed from the address/data bus and the bus goes to a high impedance state. The read control signal is also asserted at T2. The read (RD) signal causes the addressed device to enable its data bus drivers to the local bus. Some time later, valid data will be available on the bus and the addressed device will drive the READY line HIGH. When the processor returns the read signal to a HIGH level, the addressed device will again 3-state its bus drivers. If a transceiver (8286/8287) is required to buffer the 8088 local bus, signals DT/R and DEN are provided by the 8088.

A write cycle also begins with the assertion of ALE and the emission of the address. The IO/M signal is again asserted to indicate a memory or I/O write operation. In T2, immediately following the address emission, the processor emits the data to be written into the addressed location. This data remains valid until at least the middle of T4. During T2, T3, and T_W, the processor asserts the write control signal. The write (WR) signal becomes active at the beginning of T2, as opposed to the read, which is delayed somewhat into T2 to provide time for the bus to float.

The basic difference between the interrupt acknowledge cycle and a read cycle is that the interrupt acknowledge (INTA) signal is asserted in place of the read (RD) signal and the address bus is floated. (See Figure 9.) In the second of two successive INTA cycles,

a byte of information is read from the data bus, as supplied by the interrupt system logic (i.e. 8259A priority interrupt controller). This byte identifies the source (type) of the interrupt. It is multiplied by four and used as a pointer into the interrupt vector lookup table, as described earlier.

Bus Timing — Medium Complexity Systems

(See Figure 10.)

For medium complexity systems, the MN/MX pin is connected to GND and the 8288 bus controller is added to the system, as well as an 8282/8283 latch for latching the system address, and an 8286/8287 transceiver to allow for bus loading greater than the 8088 is capable of handling. Signals ALE, DEN, and DT/R are generated by the 8288 instead of the processor in this configuration, although their timing remains relatively the same. The 8088 status outputs (S2, S1, and S0) provide type of cycle information and become 8288 inputs. This bus cycle information specifies read (code, data, or I/O), write (data or I/O), interrupt acknowledge, or software halt. The 8288 thus issues control signals specifying memory read or write, I/O read or write, or interrupt acknowledge. The 8288 provides two types of write strobes, normal and advanced, to be applied as required. The normal write strobes have data valid at the leading edge of write. The advanced write strobes have the same timing as read strobes, and hence, data is not valid at the leading edge of write. The 8286/8287 transceiver receives the usual T and OE inputs from the 8288's DT/R and DEN outputs.

The pointer into the interrupt vector table, which is passed during the second INTA cycle, can derive from an 8259A located on either the local bus or the system bus. If the master 8289A priority interrupt controller is positioned on the local bus, a TTL gate is required to disable the 8286/8287 transceiver when reading from the master 8259A during the interrupt acknowledge sequence and software "poll".

The 8088 Compared to the 8086

The 8088 CPU is an 8-bit processor designed around the 8086 internal structure. Most internal functions of the 8088 are identical to the equivalent 8086 functions. The 8088 handles the external bus the same way the 8086 does with the distinction of handling only 8 bits at a time. Sixteen-bit operands are fetched or written in two consecutive bus cycles. Both processors will appear identical to the software engineer, with the exception of execution time. The internal register structure is identical and all instructions have the same end result. The differences between the 8088 and 8086 are outlined below. The engineer who is unfamiliar with the 8086 is referred to the iAPX 86, 88 User's Manual, Chapters 2 and 4, for function description and instruction set information. Internally, there are three differences between the 8088 and the 8086. All changes are related to the 8-bit bus interface.

- The queue length is 4 bytes in the 8088, whereas the 8086 queue contains 6 bytes, or three words. The queue was shortened to prevent overuse of the bus by the BIU when prefetching instructions. This was required because of the additional time necessary to fetch instructions 8 bits at a time.

- To further optimize the queue, the prefetching algorithm was changed. The 8088 BIU will fetch a new instruction to load into the queue each time there is a 1 byte hole (space available) in the queue. The 8086 waits until a 2-byte space is available.

- The internal execution time of the instruction set is affected by the 8-bit interface. All 16-bit fetches and writes from/to memory take an additional four clock cycles. The CPU is also limited by the speed of instruction fetches. This latter problem only occurs when a series of simple operations occur. When the more sophisticated instructions of the 8088 are being used, the queue has time to fill and the execution proceeds as fast as the execution unit will allow.

The 8088 and 8086 are completely software compatible by virtue of their identical execution units. Software that is system dependent may not be completely transferable, but software that is not system dependent will operate equally as well on an 8088 or an 8086.

The hardware interface of the 8088 contains the major differences between the two CPUs. The pin assignments are nearly identical, however, with the following functional changes:

- A8–A15 — These pins are only address outputs on the 8088. These address lines are latched internally and remain valid throughout a bus cycle in a manner similar to the 8085 upper address lines.

- $\overline{BHE}$ has no meaning on the 8088 and has been eliminated.

- $\overline{SSO}$ provides the $\overline{SO}$ status information in the minimum mode. This output occurs on pin 34 in minimum mode only. DT/$\overline{R}$, IO/$\overline{M}$, and $\overline{SSO}$ provide the complete bus status in minimum mode.

- IO/$\overline{M}$ has been inverted to be compatible with the MCS-85 bus structure.

- ALE is delayed by one clock cycle in the minimum mode when entering HALT, to allow the status to be latched with ALE.

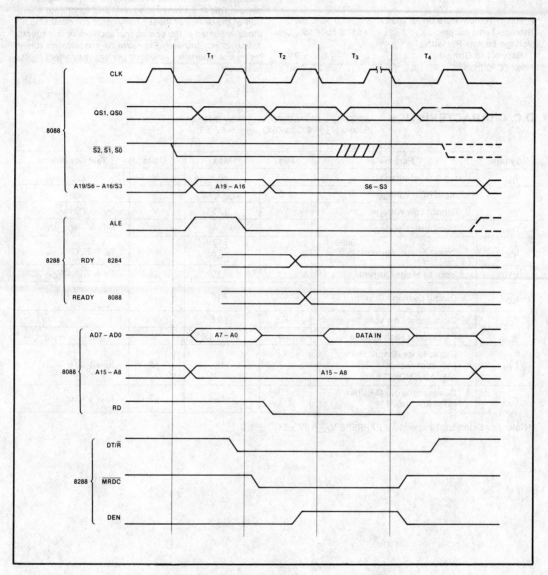

Figure 10. Medium Complexity System Timing

ABSOLUTE MAXIMUM RATINGS*

Ambient Temperature Under Bias.........0°C to 70°C
Storage Temperature............. – 65°C to + 150°C
Voltage on Any Pin with
   Respect to Ground.................. – 1.0 to + 7V
Power Dissipation .... 2.5 Watt

*NOTICE: Stresses above those listed under "Absolute Maximum Ratings" may cause permanent damage to the device. This is a stress rating only and functional operation of the device at these or any other conditions above those indicated in the operational sections of this specification is not implied. Exposure to absolute maximum rating conditions for extended periods may affect device reliability.

D.C. CHARACTERISTICS

(8088: T_A = 0°C to 70°C, V_{CC} = 5V ±10%) *
(8088-2: T_A = 0°C to 70°C, V_{CC} = 5V ±5%)

Symbol	Parameter	Min.	Max.	Units	Test Conditions
V_{IL}	Input Low Voltage	−0.5	+0.8	V	
V_{IH}	Input High Voltage	2.0	V_{CC} +0.5	V	
V_{OL}	Output Low Voltage		0.45	V	I_{OL} = 2.0 mA
V_{OH}	Output High Voltage	2.4		V	I_{OH} = −400 μA
I_{CC}	Power Supply Current: 8088 / 8088-2 / P8088		340 350 250	mA	T_A = 25°C
I_{LI}	Input Leakage Current		±10	μA	0V ≤ V_{IN} ≤ V_{CC}
I_{LO}	Output Leakage Current		±10	μA	0.45V ≤ V_{OUT} ≤ V_{CC}
V_{CL}	Clock Input Low Voltage	−0.5	+0.6	V	
V_{CH}	Clock Input High Voltage	3.9	V_{CC} +1.0	V	
C_{IN}	Capacitance if Input Buffer (All input except AD_0-AD_7, RQ/GT		15	pF	fc = 1 MHz
C_{IO}	Capacitance of I/O Buffer (AD_0-AD_7, RQ/GT)		15	pF	fc = 1 MHz

*Note: For Extended Temperature EXPRESS V_{CC} = 5V ± 5%

A.C. CHARACTERISTICS
(8088: T_A = 0°C to 70°C, V_{CC} = 5V ±10%)*
(8088-2: T_A = 0°C to 70°C, V_{CC} = 5V ±5%)

MINIMUM COMPLEXITY SYSTEM TIMING REQUIREMENTS

Symbol	Parameter	8088		8088-2		Units	Test Conditions
		Min.	Max.	Min.	Max.		
TCLCL	CLK Cycle Period	200	500	125	500	ns	
TCLCH	CLK Low Time	118		68		ns	
TCHCL	CLK High Time	69		44		ns	
TCH1CH2	CLK Rise Time		10		10	ns	From 1.0V to 3.5V
TCL2CL1	CLK Fall Time		10		10	ns	From 3.5V to 1.0V
TDVCL	Data in Setup Time	30		20		ns	
TCLDX	Data in Hold Time	10		10		ns	
TR1VCL	RDY Setup Time into 8284 (See Notes 1, 2)	35		35		ns	
TCLR1X	RDY Hold Time into 8284 (See Notes 1, 2)	0		0		ns	
TRYHCH	READY Setup Time into 8088	118		68		ns	
TCHRYX	READY Hold Time into 8088	30		20		ns	
TRYLCL	READY Inactive to CLK (See Note 3)	−8		−8		ns	
THVCH	HOLD Setup Time	35		20		ns	
TINVCH	INTR, NMI, TEST Setup Time (See Note 2)	30		15		ns	
TILIH	Input Rise Time (Except CLK)		20		20	ns	From 0.8V to 2.0V
TIHIL	Input Fall Time (Except CLK)		12		12	ns	From 2.0V to 0.8V

*Note: For Extended Temperature EXPRESS V_{CC} = 5V ± 5%

AFN-00826D

A.C. CHARACTERISTICS (Continued)

TIMING RESPONSES

Symbol	Parameter	8088 Min.	8088 Max.	8088-2 Min.	8088-2 Max.	Units	Test Conditions
TCLAV	Address Valid Delay	10	110	10	60	ns	
TCLAX	Address Hold Time	10		10		ns	
TCLAZ	Address Float Delay	TCLAX	80	TCLAX	50	ns	
TLHLL	ALE Width	TCLCH−20		TCLCH−10		ns	
TCLLH	ALE Active Delay		80		50	ns	
TCHLL	ALE Inactive Delay		85		55	ns	
TLLAX	Address Hold Time to ALE Inactive	TCHCL−10		TCHCL−10		ns	
TCLDV	Data Valid Delay	10	110	10	60	ns	C_L = 20-100 pF for all 8088 Outputs in addition to internal loads
TCHDX	Data Hold Time	10		10		ns	
TWHDX	Data Hold Time After $\overline{WR}$	TCLCH−30		TCLCH−30		ns	
TCVCTV	Control Active Delay 1	10	110	10	70	ns	
TCHCTV	Control Active Delay 2	10	110	10	60	ns	
TCVCTX	Control Inactive Delay	10	110	10	70	ns	
TAZRL	Address Float to READ Active	0		0		ns	
TCLRL	$\overline{RD}$ Active Delay	10	165	10	100	ns	
TCLRH	$\overline{RD}$ Inactive Delay	10	150	10	80	ns	
TRHAV	$\overline{RD}$ Inactive to Next Address Active	TCLCL−45		TCLCL−40		ns	
TCLHAV	HLDA Valid Delay	10	160	10	100	ns	
TRLRH	$\overline{RD}$ Width	2TCLCL−75		2TCLCL−50		ns	
TWLWH	$\overline{WR}$ Width	2TCLCL−60		2TCLCL−40		ns	
TAVAL	Address Valid to ALE Low	TCLCH−60		TCLCH−40		ns	
TOLOH	Output Rise Time		20		20	ns	From 0.8V to 2.0V
TOHOL	Output Fall Time		12		12	ns	From 2.0V to 0.8V

A.C. TESTING INPUT, OUTPUT WAVEFORM

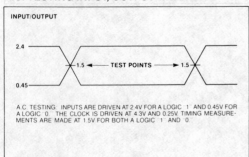

A.C. TESTING: INPUTS ARE DRIVEN AT 2.4V FOR A LOGIC "1" AND 0.45V FOR A LOGIC "0". THE CLOCK IS DRIVEN AT 4.3V AND 0.25V. TIMING MEASURE-MENTS ARE MADE AT 1.5V FOR BOTH A LOGIC "1" AND "0".

A.C. TESTING LOAD CIRCUIT

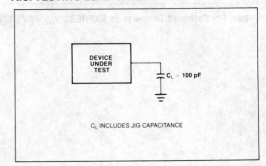

C_L INCLUDES JIG CAPACITANCE

AFN-00826D

WAVEFORMS

BUS TIMING—MINIMUM MODE SYSTEM

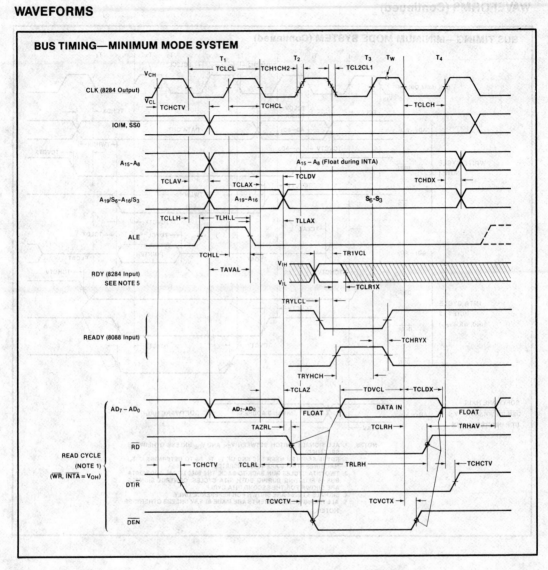

WAVEFORMS (Continued)

BUS TIMING—MINIMUM MODE SYSTEM (Continued)

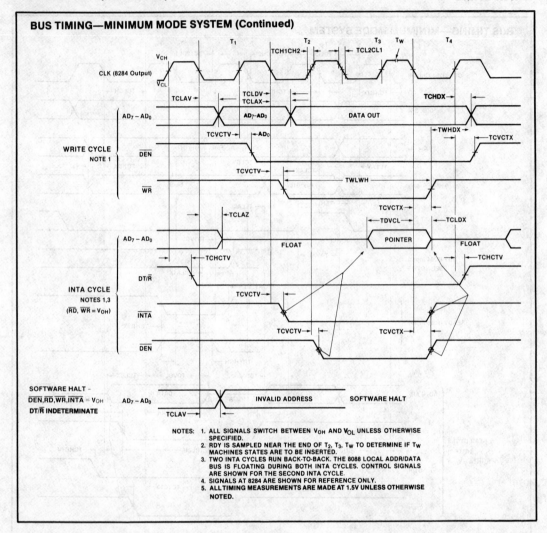

NOTES: 1. ALL SIGNALS SWITCH BETWEEN V_{OH} AND V_{OL} UNLESS OTHERWISE SPECIFIED.
2. RDY IS SAMPLED NEAR THE END OF T_2, T_3, T_W TO DETERMINE IF T_W MACHINES STATES ARE TO BE INSERTED.
3. TWO INTA CYCLES RUN BACK-TO-BACK. THE 8088 LOCAL ADDR/DATA BUS IS FLOATING DURING BOTH INTA CYCLES. CONTROL SIGNALS ARE SHOWN FOR THE SECOND INTA CYCLE.
4. SIGNALS AT 8284 ARE SHOWN FOR REFERENCE ONLY.
5. ALL TIMING MEASUREMENTS ARE MADE AT 1.5V UNLESS OTHERWISE NOTED.

AFN-00826D

A.C. CHARACTERISTICS

MAX MODE SYSTEM (USING 8288 BUS CONTROLLER)
TIMING REQUIREMENTS

Symbol	Parameter	8088		8088-2		Units	Test Conditions
		Min.	Max.	Min.	Max.		
TCLCL	CLK Cycle Period	200	500	125	500	ns	
TCLCH	CLK Low Time	118		68		ns	
TCHCL	CLK High Time	69		44		ns	
TCH1CH2	CLK Rise Time		10		10	ns	From 1.0V to 3.5V
TCL2CL1	CLK Fall Time		10		10	ns	From 3.5V to 1.0V
TDVCL	Data In Setup Time	30		20		ns	
TCLDX	Data In Hold Time	10		10		ns	
TR1VCL	RDY Setup Time into 8284 (See Notes 1, 2)	35		35		ns	
TCLR1X	RDY Hold Time into 8284 (See Notes 1, 2)	0		0		ns	
TRYHCH	READY Setup Time into 8088	118		68		ns	
TCHRYX	READY Hold Time into 8088	30		20		ns	
TRYLCL	READY Inactive to CLK (See Note 4)	−8		−8		ns	
TINVCH	Setup Time for Recognition (INTR, NMI, TEST) (See Note 2)	30		15		ns	
TGVCH	RQ/GT Setup Time	30		15		ns	
TCHGX	RQ Hold Time into 8086	40		30		ns	
TILIH	Input Rise Time (Except CLK)		20		20	ns	From 0.8V to 2.0V
TIHIL	Input Fall Time (Except CLK)		12		12	ns	From 2.0V to 0.8V

NOTES:
1. Signal at 8284 or 8288 shown for reference only.
2. Setup requirement for asynchronous signal only to guarantee recognition at next CLK.
3. Applies only to T2 state (8 ns into T3 state).
4. Applies only to T2 state (8 ns into T3 state).

AFN-00826D

A.C. CHARACTERISTICS
TIMING RESPONSES

Symbol	Parameter	8088		8088-2		Units	Test Conditions
		Min.	Max.	Min.	Max.		
TCLML	Command Active Delay (See Note 1)	10	35	10	35	ns	
TCLMH	Command Inactive Delay (See Note 1)	10	35	10	35	ns	
TRYHSH	READY Active to Status Passive (See Note 3)		110		65	ns	
TCHSV	Status Active Delay	10	110	10	60	ns	
TCLSH	Status Inactive Delay	10	130	10	70	ns	
TCLAV	Address Valid Delay	10	110	10	60	ns	
TCLAX	Address Hold Time	10		10		ns	
TCLAZ	Address Float Delay	TCLAX	80	TCLAX	50	ns	
TSVLH	Status Valid to ALE High (See Note 1)		15		15	ns	
TSVMCH	Status Valid to MCE High (See Note 1)		15		15	ns	
TCLLH	CLK Low to ALE Valid (See Note 1)		15		15	ns	
TCLMCH	CLK Low to MCE High (See Note 1)		15		15	ns	
TCHLL	ALE Inactive Delay (See Note 1)		15		15	ns	
TCLMCL	MCE Inactive Delay (See Note 1)		15		15	ns	C_L = 20-100 pF for all 8088 Outputs in addition to internal loads
TCLDV	Data Valid Delay	10	110	10	60	ns	
TCHDX	Data Hold Time	10		10		ns	
TCVNV	Control Active Delay (See Note 1)	5	45	5	45	ns	
TCVNX	Control Inactive Delay (See Note 1)	10	45	10	45	ns	
TAZRL	Address Float to Read Active	0		0		ns	
TCLRL	RD Active Delay	10	165	10	100	ns	
TCLRH	RD Inactive Delay	10	150	10	80	ns	
TRHAV	RD Inactive to Next Address Active	TCLCL−45		TCLCL−40		ns	
TCHDTL	Direction Control Active Delay (See Note 1)		50		50	ns	
TCHDTH	Direction Control Inactive Delay (See Note 1)		30		30	ns	
TCLGL	GT Active Delay		85		50	ns	
TCLGH	GT Inactive Delay		85		50	ns	
TRLRH	RD Width	2TCLCL−75		2TCLCL−50		ns	
TOLOH	Output Rise Time		20		20	ns	From 0.8V to 2.0V
TOHOL	Output Fall Time		12		12	ns	From 2.0V to 0.8V

AFN-00826D

WAVEFORMS

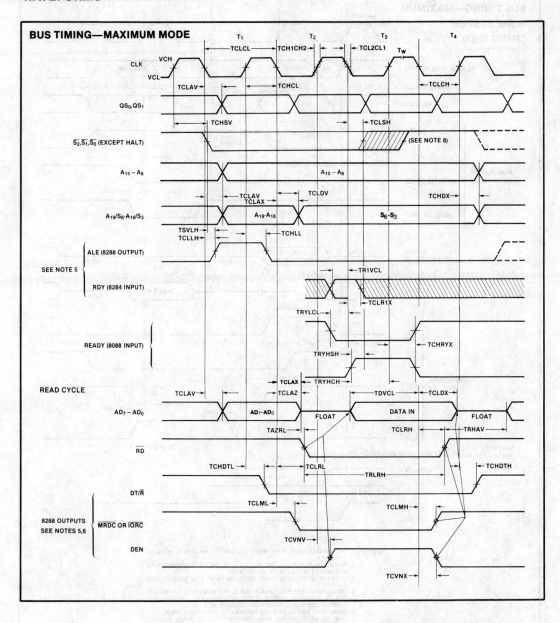

BUS TIMING—MAXIMUM MODE

AFN-00826D

WAVEFORMS (Continued)

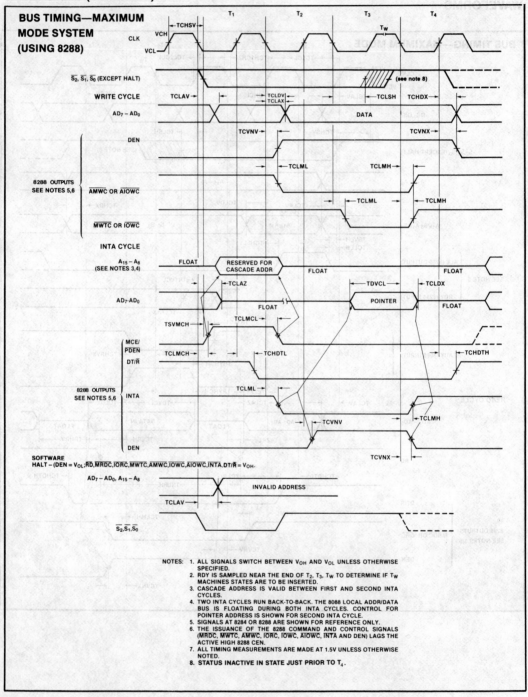

BUS TIMING—MAXIMUM MODE SYSTEM (USING 8288)

NOTES:
1. ALL SIGNALS SWITCH BETWEEN V_{OH} AND V_{OL} UNLESS OTHERWISE SPECIFIED.
2. RDY IS SAMPLED NEAR THE END OF T_2, T_3, T_W TO DETERMINE IF T_W MACHINES STATES ARE TO BE INSERTED.
3. CASCADE ADDRESS IS VALID BETWEEN FIRST AND SECOND INTA CYCLES.
4. TWO INTA CYCLES RUN BACK-TO-BACK. THE 8088 LOCAL ADDR/DATA BUS IS FLOATING DURING BOTH INTA CYCLES. CONTROL FOR POINTER ADDRESS IS SHOWN FOR SECOND INTA CYCLE.
5. SIGNALS AT 8284 OR 8288 ARE SHOWN FOR REFERENCE ONLY.
6. THE ISSUANCE OF THE 8288 COMMAND AND CONTROL SIGNALS (MRDC, MWTC, AMWC, IORC, IOWC, AIOWC, INTA AND DEN) LAGS THE ACTIVE HIGH 8288 CEN.
7. ALL TIMING MEASUREMENTS ARE MADE AT 1.5V UNLESS OTHERWISE NOTED.
8. STATUS INACTIVE IN STATE JUST PRIOR TO T_4.

AFN-00826D

WAVEFORMS (Continued)

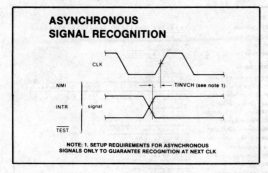

ASYNCHRONOUS SIGNAL RECOGNITION

NOTE: 1. SETUP REQUIREMENTS FOR ASYNCHRONOUS SIGNALS ONLY TO GUARANTEE RECOGNITION AT NEXT CLK

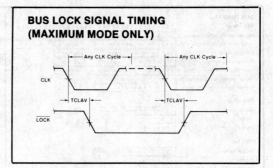

BUS LOCK SIGNAL TIMING (MAXIMUM MODE ONLY)

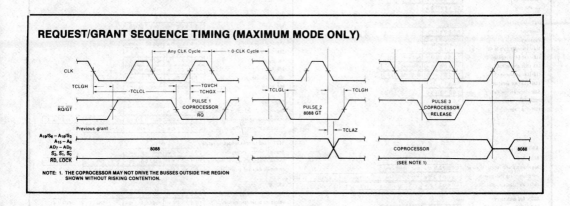

REQUEST/GRANT SEQUENCE TIMING (MAXIMUM MODE ONLY)

NOTE: 1. THE COPROCESSOR MAY NOT DRIVE THE BUSSES OUTSIDE THE REGION SHOWN WITHOUT RISKING CONTENTION.

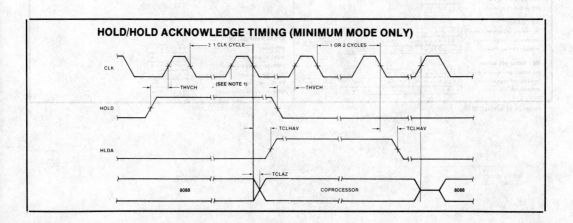

HOLD/HOLD ACKNOWLEDGE TIMING (MINIMUM MODE ONLY)

AFN-00826D

iAPX 86/10, 88/10
INSTRUCTION SET SUMMARY

DATA TRANSFER

MOV = Move:

	7 6 5 4 3 2 1 0	7 6 5 4 3 2 1 0	7 6 5 4 3 2 1 0	7 6 5 4 3 2 1 0
Register/memory to/from register	1 0 0 0 1 0 d w	mod reg r/m		
Immediate to register/memory	1 1 0 0 0 1 1 w	mod 0 0 0 r/m	data	data if w 1
Immediate to register	1 0 1 1 w reg	data	data if w 1	
Memory to accumulator	1 0 1 0 0 0 0 w	addr-low	addr-high	
Accumulator to memory	1 0 1 0 0 0 1 w	addr-low	addr-high	
Register/memory to segment register	1 0 0 0 1 1 1 0	mod 0 reg r/m		
Segment register to register/memory	1 0 0 0 1 1 0 0	mod 0 reg r/m		

PUSH = Push:

Register/memory	1 1 1 1 1 1 1 1	mod 1 1 0 r/m
Register	0 1 0 1 0 reg	
Segment register	0 0 0 reg 1 1 0	

POP = Pop:

Register/memory	1 0 0 0 1 1 1 1	mod 0 0 0 r/m
Register	0 1 0 1 1 reg	
Segment register	0 0 0 reg 1 1 1	

XCHG = Exchange:

Register/memory with register	1 0 0 0 0 1 1 w	mod reg r/m
Register with accumulator	1 0 0 1 0 reg	

IN = Input from:

Fixed port	1 1 1 0 0 1 0 w	port
Variable port	1 1 1 0 1 1 0 w	

OUT = Output to:

Fixed port	1 1 1 0 0 1 1 w	port
Variable port	1 1 1 0 1 1 1 w	
XLAT=Translate byte to AL	1 1 0 1 0 1 1 1	
LEA=Load EA to register	1 0 0 0 1 1 0 1	mod reg r/m
LDS=Load pointer to DS	1 1 0 0 0 1 0 1	mod reg r/m
LES=Load pointer to ES	1 1 0 0 0 1 0 0	mod reg r/m
LAHF=Load AH with flags	1 0 0 1 1 1 1 1	
SAHF=Store AH into flags	1 0 0 1 1 1 1 0	
PUSHF=Push flags	1 0 0 1 1 1 0 0	
POPF=Pop flags	1 0 0 1 1 1 0 1	

ARITHMETIC

ADD = Add:

Reg/memory with register to either	0 0 0 0 0 0 d w	mod reg r/m		
Immediate to register/memory	1 0 0 0 0 0 s w	mod 0 0 0 r/m	data	data if s w 01
Immediate to accumulator	0 0 0 0 0 1 0 w	data	data if w 1	

ADC = Add with carry:

Reg/memory with register to either	0 0 0 1 0 0 d w	mod reg r/m		
Immediate to register/memory	1 0 0 0 0 0 s w	mod 0 1 0 r/m	data	data if s w 01
Immediate to accumulator	0 0 0 1 0 1 0 w	data	data if w 1	

INC = Increment:

Register/memory	1 1 1 1 1 1 1 w	mod 0 0 0 r/m
Register	0 1 0 0 0 reg	
AAA=ASCII adjust for add	0 0 1 1 0 1 1 1	
DAA=Decimal adjust for add	0 0 1 0 0 1 1 1	

SUB = Subtract:

Reg/memory and register to either	0 0 1 0 1 0 d w	mod reg r/m		
Immediate from register/memory	1 0 0 0 0 0 s w	mod 1 0 1 r/m	data	data if s w 01
Immediate from accumulator	0 0 1 0 1 1 0 w	data	data if w 1	

SBB = Subtract with borrow:

Reg/memory and register to either	0 0 0 1 1 0 d w	mod reg r/m		
Immediate from register/memory	1 0 0 0 0 0 s w	mod 0 1 1 r/m	data	data if s w 01
Immediate from accumulator	0 0 0 1 1 1 0 w	data	data if w 1	

DEC = Decrement:

	7 6 5 4 3 2 1 0	7 6 5 4 3 2 1 0	7 6 5 4 3 2 1 0	7 6 5 4 3 2 1 0
Register/memory	1 1 1 1 1 1 1 w	mod 0 0 1 r/m		
Register	0 1 0 0 1 reg			
NEG Change sign	1 1 1 1 0 1 1 w	mod 0 1 1 r/m		

CMP = Compare:

Register/memory and register	0 0 1 1 1 0 d w	mod reg r/m		
Immediate with register/memory	1 0 0 0 0 0 s w	mod 1 1 1 r/m	data	data if s w 01
Immediate with accumulator	0 0 1 1 1 1 0 w	data	data if w 1	
AAS ASCII adjust for subtract	0 0 1 1 1 1 1 1			
DAS Decimal adjust for subtract	0 0 1 0 1 1 1 1			
MUL Multiply (unsigned)	1 1 1 1 0 1 1 w	mod 1 0 0 r/m		
IMUL Integer multiply (signed)	1 1 1 1 0 1 1 w	mod 1 0 1 r/m		
AAM ASCII adjust for multiply	1 1 0 1 0 1 0 0	0 0 0 0 1 0 1 0		
DIV Divide (unsigned)	1 1 1 1 0 1 1 w	mod 1 1 0 r/m		
IDIV Integer divide (signed)	1 1 1 1 0 1 1 w	mod 1 1 1 r/m		
AAD ASCII adjust for divide	1 1 0 1 0 1 0 1	0 0 0 0 1 0 1 0		
CBW Convert byte to word	1 0 0 1 1 0 0 0			
CWD Convert word to double word	1 0 0 1 1 0 0 1			

LOGIC

NOT Invert	1 1 1 1 0 1 1 w	mod 0 1 0 r/m
SHL/SAL Shift logical/arithmetic left	1 1 0 1 0 0 v w	mod 1 0 0 r/m
SHR Shift logical right	1 1 0 1 0 0 v w	mod 1 0 1 r/m
SAR Shift arithmetic right	1 1 0 1 0 0 v w	mod 1 1 1 r/m
ROL Rotate left	1 1 0 1 0 0 v w	mod 0 0 0 r/m
ROR Rotate right	1 1 0 1 0 0 v w	mod 0 0 1 r/m
RCL Rotate through carry flag left	1 1 0 1 0 0 v w	mod 0 1 0 r/m
RCR Rotate through carry right	1 1 0 1 0 0 v w	mod 0 1 1 r/m

AND = And:

Reg/memory and register to either	0 0 1 0 0 0 d w	mod reg r/m		
Immediate to register/memory	1 0 0 0 0 0 0 w	mod 1 0 0 r/m	data	data if w 1
Immediate to accumulator	0 0 1 0 0 1 0 w	data	data if w 1	

TEST = And function to flags, no result:

Register/memory and register	1 0 0 0 0 1 0 w	mod reg r/m		
Immediate data and register/memory	1 1 1 1 0 1 1 w	mod 0 0 0 r/m	data	data if w 1
Immediate data and accumulator	1 0 1 0 1 0 0 w	data	data if w 1	

OR = Or:

Reg/memory and register to either	0 0 0 0 1 0 d w	mod reg r/m		
Immediate to register/memory	1 0 0 0 0 0 0 w	mod 0 0 1 r/m	data	data if w 1
Immediate to accumulator	0 0 0 0 1 1 0 w	data	data if w 1	

XOR = Exclusive or:

Reg/memory and register to either	0 0 1 1 0 0 d w	mod reg r/m		
Immediate to register/memory	1 0 0 0 0 0 0 w	mod 1 1 0 r/m	data	data if w 1
Immediate to accumulator	0 0 1 1 0 1 0 w	data	data if w 1	

STRING MANIPULATION

REP=Repeat	1 1 1 1 0 0 1 z
MOVS=Move byte/word	1 0 1 0 0 1 0 w
CMPS=Compare byte/word	1 0 1 0 0 1 1 w
SCAS=Scan byte/word	1 0 1 0 1 1 1 w
LODS=Load byte/wd to AL/AX	1 0 1 0 1 1 0 w
STOS=Stor byte/wd from AL/A	1 0 1 0 1 0 1 w

Mnemonics ©Intel, 1978

AFN-00826D

INSTRUCTION SET SUMMARY (Continued)

CONTROL TRANSFER

CALL = Call:

	7 6 5 4 3 2 1 0	7 6 5 4 3 2 1 0	7 6 5 4 3 2 1 0
Direct within segment	1 1 1 0 1 0 0 0	disp-low	disp-high
Indirect within segment	1 1 1 1 1 1 1 1	mod 0 1 0 r/m	
Direct intersegment	1 0 0 1 1 0 1 0	offset-low	offset-high
		seg-low	seg-high
Indirect intersegment	1 1 1 1 1 1 1 1	mod 0 1 1 r/m	

JMP = Unconditional Jump:

	7 6 5 4 3 2 1 0	7 6 5 4 3 2 1 0	7 6 5 4 3 2 1 0
Direct within segment	1 1 1 0 1 0 0 1	disp-low	disp-high
Direct within segment-short	1 1 1 0 1 0 1 1	disp	
Indirect within segment	1 1 1 1 1 1 1 1	mod 1 0 0 r/m	
Direct intersegment	1 1 1 0 1 0 1 0	offset-low	offset-high
		seg-low	seg-high
Indirect intersegment	1 1 1 1 1 1 1 1	mod 1 0 1 r/m	

RET = Return from CALL:

	7 6 5 4 3 2 1 0	7 6 5 4 3 2 1 0	7 6 5 4 3 2 1 0
Within segment	1 1 0 0 0 0 1 1		
Within seg. adding immed to SP	1 1 0 0 0 0 1 0	data-low	data-high
Intersegment	1 1 0 0 1 0 1 1		
Intersegment, adding immediate to SP	1 1 0 0 1 0 1 0	data-low	data-high
JE/JZ=Jump on equal/zero	0 1 1 1 0 1 0 0	disp	
JL/JNGE=Jump on less/not greater or equal	0 1 1 1 1 1 0 0	disp	
JLE/JNG=Jump on less or equal/not greater	0 1 1 1 1 1 1 0	disp	
JB/JNAE=Jump on below/not above or equal	0 1 1 1 0 0 1 0	disp	
JBE/JNA=Jump on below or equal/not above	0 1 1 1 0 1 1 0	disp	
JP/JPE=Jump on parity/parity even	0 1 1 1 1 0 1 0	disp	
JO=Jump on overflow	0 1 1 1 0 0 0 0	disp	
JS=Jump on sign	0 1 1 1 1 0 0 0	disp	
JNE/JNZ=Jump on not equal/not zero	0 1 1 1 0 1 0 1	disp	
JNL/JGE=Jump on not less/greater or equal	0 1 1 1 1 1 0 1	disp	
JNLE/JG=Jump on not less or equal/greater	0 1 1 1 1 1 1 1	disp	

	7 6 5 4 3 2 1 0	7 6 5 4 3 2 1 0
JNB/JAE Jump on not below/above or equal	0 1 1 1 0 0 1 1	disp
JNBE/JA Jump on not below or equal/above	0 1 1 1 0 1 1 1	disp
JNP/JPO Jump on not par/par odd	0 1 1 1 1 0 1 1	disp
JNO Jump on not overflow	0 1 1 1 0 0 0 1	disp
JNS Jump on not sign	0 1 1 1 1 0 0 1	disp
LOOP Loop CX times	1 1 1 0 0 0 1 0	disp
LOOPZ/LOOPE Loop while zero/equal	1 1 1 0 0 0 0 1	disp
LOOPNZ/LOOPNE Loop while not zero/equal	1 1 1 0 0 0 0 0	disp
JCXZ Jump on CX zero	1 1 1 0 0 0 1 1	disp

INT Interrupt

	7 6 5 4 3 2 1 0	7 6 5 4 3 2 1 0
Type specified	1 1 0 0 1 1 0 1	type
Type 3	1 1 0 0 1 1 0 0	
INTO Interrupt on overflow	1 1 0 0 1 1 1 0	
IRET Interrupt return	1 1 0 0 1 1 1 1	

PROCESSOR CONTROL

	7 6 5 4 3 2 1 0	7 6 5 4 3 2 1 0
CLC Clear carry	1 1 1 1 1 0 0 0	
CMC Complement carry	1 1 1 1 0 1 0 1	
STC Set carry	1 1 1 1 1 0 0 1	
CLD Clear direction	1 1 1 1 1 1 0 0	
STD Set direction	1 1 1 1 1 1 0 1	
CLI Clear interrupt	1 1 1 1 1 0 1 0	
STI Set interrupt	1 1 1 1 1 0 1 1	
HLT Halt	1 1 1 1 0 1 0 0	
WAIT Wait	1 0 0 1 1 0 1 1	
ESC Escape (to external device)	1 1 0 1 1 x x x	mod x x x r/m
LOCK Bus lock prefix	1 1 1 1 0 0 0 0	

Footnotes:

AL = 8-bit accumulator
AX = 16-bit accumulator
CX = Count register
DS = Data segment
ES = Extra segment
Above/below refers to unsigned value.
Greater = more positive;
Less = less positive (more negative) signed values
if d = 1 then "to" reg; if d = 0 then "from" reg
if w = 1 then word instruction; if w = 0 then byte instruction

if mod = 11 then r/m is treated as a REG field
if mod = 00 then DISP = 0*, disp-low and disp-high are absent
if mod = 01 then DISP = disp-low sign-extended to 16-bits, disp-high is absent
if mod = 10 then DISP = disp-high: disp-low
if r/m = 000 then EA = (BX) + (SI) + DISP
if r/m = 001 then EA = (BX) + (DI) + DISP
if r/m = 010 then EA = (BP) + (SI) + DISP
if r/m = 011 then EA = (BP) + (DI) + DISP
if r/m = 100 then EA = (SI) + DISP
if r/m = 101 then EA = (DI) + DISP
if r/m = 110 then EA = (BP) + DISP*
if r/m = 111 then EA = (BX) + DISP
DISP follows 2nd byte of instruction (before data if required)

*except if mod = 00 and r/m = 110 then EA = disp-high: disp-low.

if s:w = 01 then 16 bits of immediate data form the operand.
if s:w = 11 then an immediate data byte is sign extended to
form the 16-bit operand.
if v = 0 then "count" = 1; if v = 1 then "count" in (CL)
x = don't care
z is used for string primitives for comparison with ZF FLAG.

SEGMENT OVERRIDE PREFIX

0 0 1 reg 1 1 0

REG is assigned according to the following table:

16-Bit (w = 1)		8-Bit (w = 0)		Segment	
000	AX	000	AL	00	ES
001	CX	001	CL	01	CS
010	DX	010	DL	10	SS
011	BX	011	BL	11	DS
100	SP	100	AH		
101	BP	101	CH		
110	SI	110	DH		
111	DI	111	BH		

Instructions which reference the flag register file as a 16-bit object use the symbol FLAGS to represent the file:

FLAGS = X:X:X:X:(OF):(DF):(IF):(TF):(SF):(ZF):X:(AF):X:(PF):X:(CF)

Mnemonics © Intel, 1978

AFN-00

8284A
CLOCK GENERATOR AND DRIVER FOR
iAPX 86, 88 PROCESSORS

- Generates the System clock for the iAPX 86, 88 Processors

- Uses a Crystal or a TTL Signal for Frequency Source

- Provides Local READY and Multibus™ READY Synchronization

- 18-Pin Package

- Single +5V Power Supply

- Generates System Reset Output from Schmitt Trigger Input

- Capable of Clock Synchronization with Other 8284As

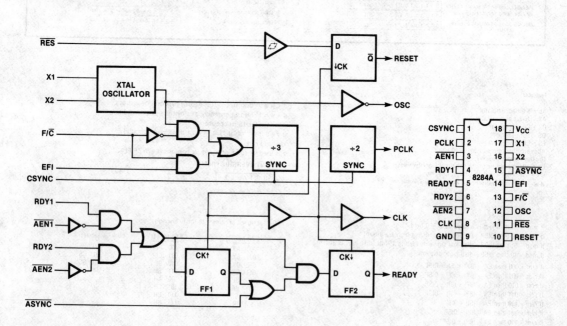

Figure 1. 8284A Block Diagram

Figure 2.
8284A Pin Configuration

Table 1. Pin Description

Symbol	Type	Name and Function
AEN1, AEN2	I	**Address Enable:** AEN is an active LOW signal. AEN serves to qualify its respective Bus Ready Signal (RDY1 or RDY2). AEN1 validates RDY1 while AEN2 validates RDY2. Two AEN signal inputs are useful in system configurations which permit the processor to access two Multi-Master System Busses. In non Multi-Master configurations the AEN signal inputs are tied true (LOW).
RDY1, RDY2	I	**Bus Ready:** (Transfer Complete). RDY is an active HIGH signal which is an indication from a device located on the system data bus that data has been received, or is available. RDY1 is qualified by AEN1 while RDY2 is qualified by AEN2.
ASYNC	I	**Ready Synchronization Select:** ASYNC is an input which defines the synchronization mode of the READY logic. When ASYNC is low, two stages of READY synchronization are provided. When ASYNC is left open or HIGH a single stage of READY synchronization is provided.
READY	O	**Ready:** READY is an active HIGH signal which is the synchronized RDY signal input. READY is cleared after the guaranteed hold time to the processor has been met.
X1, X2	I	**Crystal In:** X1 and X2 are the pins to which a crystal is attached. The crystal frequency is 3 times the desired processor clock frequency.
F/C̄	I	**Frequency/Crystal Select:** F/C̄ is a strapping option. When strapped LOW, F/C̄ permits the processor's clock to be generated by the crystal. When F/C̄ is strapped HIGH, CLK is generated from the EFI input.
EFI	I	**External Frequency:** When F/C̄ is strapped HIGH, CLK is generated from the input frequency appearing on this pin. The input signal is a square wave 3 times the frequency of the desired CLK output.

Symbol	Type	Name and Function
CLK	O	**Processor Clock:** CLK is the clock output used by the processor and all devices which directly connect to the processor's local bus (i.e., the bipolar support chips and other MOS devices). CLK has an output frequency which is ⅓ of the crystal or EFI input frequency and a ⅓ duty cycle. An output HIGH of 4.5 volts (V_{CC}= 5V) is provided on this pin to drive MOS devices.
PCLK	O	**Peripheral Clock:** PCLK is a TTL level peripheral clock signal whose output frequency is ½ that of CLK and has a 50% duty cycle.
OSC	O	**Oscillator Output:** OSC is the TTL level output of the internal oscillator circuitry. Its frequency is equal to that of the crystal.
RES	I	**Reset In:** RES is an active LOW signal which is used to generate RESET. The 8284A provides a Schmitt trigger input so that an RC connection can be used to establish the power-up reset of proper duration.
RESET	O	**Reset:** RESET is an active HIGH signal which is used to reset the 8086 family processors. Its timing characteristics are determined by RES.
CSYNC	I	**Clock Synchronization:** CSYNC is an active HIGH signal which allows multiple 8284As to be synchronized to provide clocks that are in phase. When CSYNC is HIGH the internal counters are reset. When CSYNC goes LOW the internal counters are allowed to resume counting. CSYNC needs to be externally synchronized to EFI. When using the internal oscillator CSYNC should be hardwired to ground.
GND		**Ground.**
V_{CC}		**Power:** +5V supply.

FUNCTIONAL DESCRIPTION

General

The 8284A is a single chip clock generator/driver for the iAPX 86, 88 processors. The chip contains a crystal-controlled oscillator, a divide-by-three counter, complete MULTIBUS™ "Ready" synchronization and reset logic. Refer to Figure 1 for Block Diagram and Figure 2 for Pin Configuration.

Oscillator

The oscillator circuit of the 8284A is designed primarily for use with an external series resonant, fundamental mode, crystal from which the basic operating frequency is derived.

The crystal frequency should be selected at three times the required CPU clock. X1 and X2 are the two crystal input crystal connections. For the most stable operation of the oscillator (OSC) output circuit, two series resistors ($R_1 = R_2 = 510 \, \Omega$) as shown in the waveform figures are recommended. The output of the oscillator is buffered and brought out on OSC so that other system timing signals can be derived from this stable, crystal-controlled source.

For systems which have a V_{CC} ramp time $\geq$ 1V/ms and/or have inherent board capacitance between X1 or X2, exceeding 10pF (not including 8284A pin capacitance), the configuration in Figures 4 and 6 is recommended. This circuit provides optimum stability for the oscillator in such extreme conditions. It is advisable to limit stray capacitances to less than 10pF on X1 and X2 to minimize deviation from operating at the fundamental frequency.

AFN-01472B

Clock Generator

The clock generator consists of a synchronous divide-by-three counter with a special clear input that inhibits the counting. This clear input (CSYNC) allows the output clock to be synchronized with an external event (such as another 8284A clock). It is necessary to synchronize the CSYNC input to the EFI clock external to the 8284A. This is accomplished with two Schottky flip-flops. The counter output is a 33% duty cycle clock at one-third the input frequency.

The F/$\overline{C}$ input is a strapping pin that selects either the crystal oscillator or the EFI input as the clock for the ÷3 counter. If the EFI input is selected as the clock source, the oscillator section can be used independently for another clock source. Output is taken from OSC.

Clock Outputs

The CLK output is a 33% duty cycle MOS clock driver designed to drive the iAPX 86, 88 processors directly. PCLK is a TTL level peripheral clock signal whose output frequency is ½ that of CLK. PCLK has a 50% duty cycle.

Reset Logic

The reset logic provides a Schmitt trigger input ($\overline{RES}$) and a synchronizing flip-flop to generate the reset timing. The reset signal is synchronized to the falling edge of CLK. A simple RC network can be used to provide power-on reset by utilizing this function of the 8284A.

READY Synchronization

Two READY inputs (RDY1, RDY2) are provided to accommodate two Multi-Master system busses. Each input has a qualifier ($\overline{AEN1}$ and $\overline{AEN2}$, respectively). The $\overline{AEN}$ signals validate their respective RDY signals. If a Multi-

Master system is not being used the $\overline{AEN}$ pin should be tied LOW.

Synchronization is required for all asynchronous active-going edges of either RDY input to guarantee that the RDY setup and hold times are met. Inactive-going edges of RDY in normally ready systems do not require synchronization but must satisfy RDY setup and hold as a matter of proper system design.

The $\overline{ASYNC}$ input defines two modes of READY synchronization operation.

When $\overline{ASYNC}$ is LOW, two stages of synchronization are provided for active READY input signals. Positive-going asynchronous READY inputs will first be synchronized to flip-flop one at the rising edge of CLK and then synchronized to flip-flop two at the next falling edge of CLK, after which time the READY output will go active (HIGH). Negative-going asynchronous READY inputs will be synchronized directly to flip-flop two at the falling edge of CLK, after which time the READY output will go inactive. This mode of operation is intended for use by asynchronous (normally not ready) devices in the system which cannot be guaranteed by design to meet the required RDY setup timing, T_{R1VCL}, on each bus cycle.

When $\overline{ASYNC}$ is high or left open, the first READY flip-flop is bypassed in the READY synchronization logic. READY inputs are synchronized by flip-flop two on the falling edge of CLK before they are presented to the processor. This mode is available for synchronous devices that can be guaranteed to meet the required RDY setup time.

$\overline{ASYNC}$ can be changed on every bus cycle to select the appropriate mode of synchronization for each device in the system.

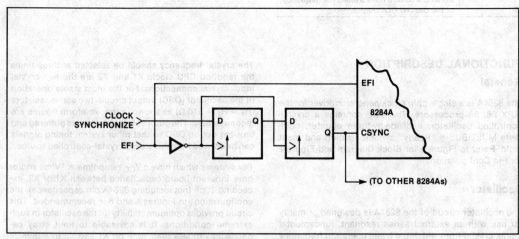

Figure 3. CSYNC Synchronization

AFN-01472B

ABSOLUTE MAXIMUM RATINGS*

Temperature Under Bias . . . . .0°C to 70°C
Storage Temperature . . . . −65°C to +150°C
All Output and Supply Voltages . . . . −0.5V to +7V
All Input Voltages . . . . −1.0V to +5.5V
Power Dissipation . . . . 1 Watt

*NOTICE: Stresses above those listed under "Absolute Maximum Ratings" may cause permanent damage to the device. This is a stress rating only and functional operation of the device at these or any other conditions above those indicated in the operational sections of this specification is not implied. Exposure to absolute maximum rating conditions for extended periods may affect device reliability.

D.C. CHARACTERISTICS ($T_A = 0°C$ to $70°C$, $V_{CC} = 5V \pm 10\%$)

Symbol	Parameter	Min.	Max.	Units	Test Conditions
I_F	Forward Input Current ($\overline{ASYNC}$)		−1.3	mA	$V_F = 0.45V$
	Other Inputs		−0.5	mA	$V_F = 0.45V$
I_R	Reverse Input Current ($\overline{ASYNC}$)		50	μA	$V_R = V_{CC}$
	Other Inputs		50	μA	$V_R = 5.25V$
V_C	Input Forward Clamp Voltage		−1.0	V	$I_C = −5mA$
I_{CC}	Power Supply Current		162	mA	
V_{IL}	Input LOW Voltage		0.8	V	
V_{IH}	Input HIGH Voltage	2.0		V	
V_{IHR}	Reset Input HIGH Voltage	2.6		V	
V_{OL}	Output LOW Voltage		0.45	V	5 mA
V_{OH}	Output HIGH Voltage CLK	4		V	−1 mA
	Other Outputs	2.4		V	−1 mA
$V_{IHR} − V_{ILR}$	$\overline{RES}$ Input Hysteresis	0.25		V	

A.C. CHARACTERISTICS ($T_A = 0°C$ to $70°C$, $V_{CC} = 5V \pm 10\%$)

TIMING REQUIREMENTS

Symbol	Parameter	Min.	Max.	Units	Test Conditions
t_{EHEL}	External Frequency HIGH Time	13		ns	90% – 90% V_{IN}
t_{ELEH}	External Frequency LOW Time	13		ns	10% – 10% V_{IN}
t_{ELEL}	EFI Period	$t_{EHEL} + t_{ELEH} + \delta$		ns	(Note 1)
	XTAL Frequency	12	30	MHz	
t_{R1VCL}	RDY1, RDY2 Active Setup to CLK	35		ns	$\overline{ASYNC}$ = HIGH
t_{R1VCH}	RDY1, RDY2 Active Setup to CLK	35		ns	$\overline{ASYNC}$ = LOW
t_{R1VCL}	RDY1, RDY2 Inactive Setup to CLK	35		ns	
t_{CLR1X}	RDY1, RDY2 Hold to CLK	0		ns	
t_{AYVCL}	$\overline{ASYNC}$ Setup to CLK	50		ns	
t_{CLAYX}	$\overline{ASYNC}$ Hold to CLK	0		ns	
t_{A1VR1V}	$\overline{AEN1}$, $\overline{AEN2}$ Setup to RDY1, RDY2	15		ns	
t_{CLA1X}	$\overline{AEN1}$, $\overline{AEN2}$ Hold to CLK	0		ns	
t_{YHEH}	CSYNC Setup to EFI	20		ns	
t_{EHYL}	CSYNC Hold to EFI	20		ns	
t_{YHYL}	CSYNC Width	$2 \cdot t_{ELEL}$		ns	
t_{I1HCL}	$\overline{RES}$ Setup to CLK	65		ns	(Note 2)
t_{CLI1H}	$\overline{RES}$ Hold to CLK	20		ns	(Note 2)
t_{ILIH}	Input Rise Time		20	ns	From 0.8V to 2.0V
t_{ILIL}	Input Fall Time		12	ns	From 2.0V to 0.8V

AFN-01472B

A.C. CHARACTERISTICS (Continued)
TIMING RESPONSES

Symbol	Parameter	Min.	Max.	Units	Test Conditions
t_{CLCL}	CLK Cycle Period	100		ns	
t_{CHCL}	CLK HIGH Time	($\frac{1}{3}$ t_{CLCL})+2 for CLK Freq. ≤ 8 MHz ($\frac{1}{3}$ t_{CLCL})+6 for CLK Freq.=10 MHz		ns	Fig. 7 & Fig. 8
t_{CLCH}	CLK LOW Time	($\frac{2}{3}$ t_{CLCL})−15 for CLK Freq.≤8 MHz ($\frac{2}{3}$ t_{CLCL})−14 for CLK Freq.=10 MHz		ns	Fig. 7 & Fig. 8
t_{CH1CH2} t_{CL2CL1}	CLK Rise or Fall Time		10	ns	1.0V to 3.5V
t_{PHPL}	PCLK HIGH Time	t_{CLCL}−20		ns	
t_{PLPH}	PCLK LOW Time	t_{CLCL}−20		ns	
t_{RYLCL}	Ready Inactive to CLK (See Note 4)	−8		ns	Fig. 9 & Fig. 10
t_{RYHCH}	Ready Active to CLK (See Note 3)	($\frac{2}{3}$ t_{CLCL})−15 for CLK Freq.≤8 MHz ($\frac{2}{3}$ t_{CLCL})−14 for CLK Freq.=10 MHz		ns	Fig. 9 & Fig. 10
t_{CLIL}	CLK to Reset Delay		40	ns	
t_{CLPH}	CLK to PCLK HIGH DELAY		22	ns	
t_{CLPL}	CLK to PCLK LOW Delay		22	ns	
t_{OLCH}	OSC to CLK HIGH Delay	−5	22	ns	
t_{OLCL}	OSC to CLK LOW Delay	2	35	ns	
t_{OLOH}	Output Rise Time (except CLK)		20	ns	From 0.8V to 2.0V
t_{OHOL}	Output Fall Time (except CLK)		12	ns	From 2.0V to 0.8V

NOTES:
1. $δ$ = EFI rise (5 ns max) + EFI fall (5 ns max).
2. Setup and hold necessary only to guarantee recognition at next clock.
3. Applies only to T3 and TW states.
4. Applies only to T2 states.

A.C. TESTING INPUT, OUTPUT WAVEFORM

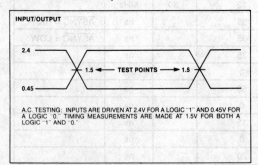

INPUT/OUTPUT

2.4

1.5 ◄── TEST POINTS ──► 1.5

0.45

A.C. TESTING: INPUTS ARE DRIVEN AT 2.4V FOR A LOGIC "1" AND 0.45V FOR A LOGIC "0." TIMING MEASUREMENTS ARE MADE AT 1.5V FOR BOTH A LOGIC "1" AND "0."

A.C. TESTING LOAD CIRCUIT

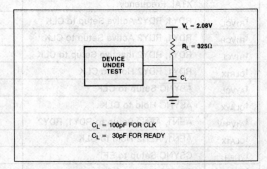

V_L = 2.08V

R_L = 325Ω

DEVICE UNDER TEST

C_L

C_L = 100pF FOR CLK
C_L = 30pF FOR READY

AFN-01472B

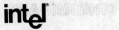

WAVEFORMS

CLOCKS AND RESET SIGNALS

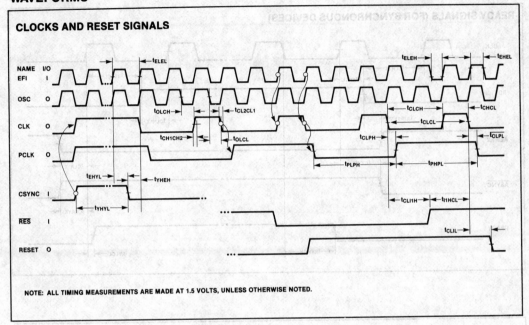

NOTE: ALL TIMING MEASUREMENTS ARE MADE AT 1.5 VOLTS, UNLESS OTHERWISE NOTED.

READY SIGNALS (FOR ASYNCHRONOUS DEVICES)

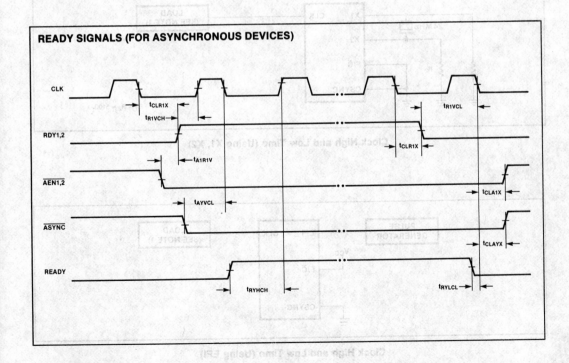

AFN-01472B

8284A   PRELIMINARY

WAVEFORMS (Continued)

READY SIGNALS (FOR SYNCHRONOUS DEVICES)

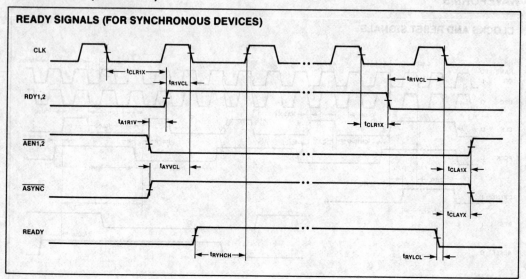

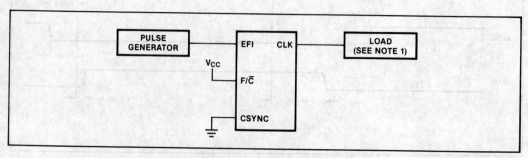

Clock High and Low Time (Using X1, X2)

$R_1 = R_2 = 510\Omega.$

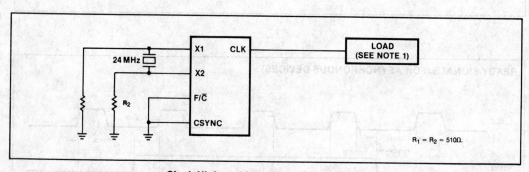

Clock High and Low Time (Using EFI)

70

AFN-01472B

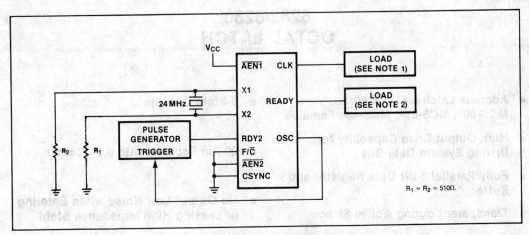

Ready to Clock (Using X1, X2)

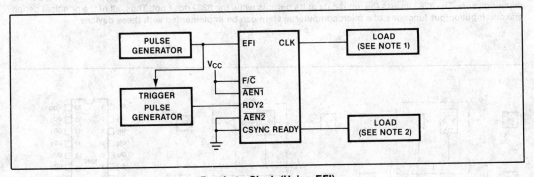

Ready to Clock (Using EFI)

NOTES:
1. C_L = 100 pF
2. C_L = 30 pF

AFN-01472B

8282/8283
OCTAL LATCH

- **Address Latch for iAPX 86, 88, MCS-80®, MCS-85®, MCS-48® Families**

- **High Output Drive Capability for Driving System Data Bus**

- **Fully Parallel 8-Bit Data Register and Buffer**

- **Transparent during Active Strobe**

- **3-State Outputs**

- **20-Pin Package with 0.3" Center**

- **No Output Low Noise when Entering or Leaving High Impedance State**

The 8282 and 8283 are 8-bit bipolar latches with 3-state output buffers. They can be used to implement latches, buffers or multiplexers. The 8283 inverts the input data at its outputs while the 8282 does not. Thus, all of the principal peripheral and input/output functions of a microcomputer system can be implemented with these devices.

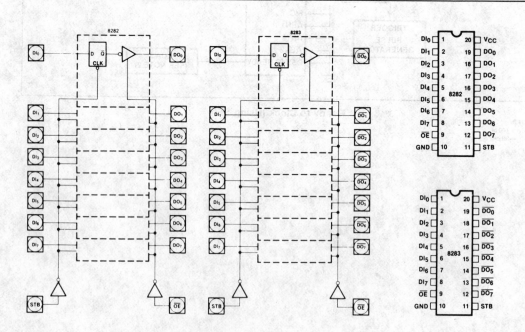

Figure 1. Logic Diagrams

Figure 2. Pin Configurations

Table 1. Pin Description

Pin	Description
STB	STROBE (Input). STB is an input control pulse used to strobe data at the data input pins (A_0-A_7) into the data latches. This signal is active HIGH to admit input data. The data is latched at the HIGH to LOW transition of STB.
$\overline{OE}$	OUTPUT ENABLE (Input). $\overline{OE}$ is an input control signal which when active LOW enables the contents of the data latches onto the data output pin (B_0-B_7). OE being inactive HIGH forces the output buffers to their high impedance state.
DI_0-DI_7	DATA INPUT PINS (Input). Data presented at these pins satisfying setup time requirements when STB is strobed and latched into the data input latches.
DO_0-DO_7 (8282) $\overline{DO_0}$-$\overline{DO_7}$ (8283)	DATA OUTPUT PINS (Output). When $\overline{OE}$ is true, the data in the data latches is presented as inverted (8283) or non-inverted (8282) data onto the data output pins.

FUNCTIONAL DESCRIPTION

The 8282 and 8283 octal latches are 8-bit latches with 3-state output buffers. Data having satisfied the setup time requirements is latched into the data latches by strobing the STB line HIGH to LOW. Holding the STB line in its active HIGH state makes the latches appear transparent. Data is presented to the data output pins by activating the $\overline{OE}$ input line. When $\overline{OE}$ is inactive HIGH the output buffers are in their high impedance state. Enabling or disabling the output buffers will not cause negative-going transients to appear on the data output bus.

AFN-00727C

ABSOLUTE MAXIMUM RATINGS*

Temperature Under Bias.................0°C to 70°C
Storage Temperature............. −65°C to +150°C
All Output and Supply Voltages........ −0.5V to +7V
All Input Voltages.................. −1.0V to +5.5V
Power Dissipation..........................1 Watt

*NOTICE: Stresses above those listed under "Absolute Maximum Ratings" may cause permanent damage to the device. This is a stress rating only and functional operation of the device at these or any other conditions above those indicated in the operational sections of this specification is not implied. Exposure to absolute maximum rating conditions for extended periods may affect device reliability.

D.C. CHARACTERISTICS ($V_{CC} = 5V \pm 10\%$, $T_A = 0°C$ to $70°C$)

Symbol	Parameter	Min.	Max.	Units	Test Conditions
V_C	Input Clamp Voltage		−1	V	$I_C = -5$ mA
I_{CC}	Power Supply Current		160	mA	
I_F	Forward Input Current		−0.2	mA	$V_F = 0.45V$
I_R	Reverse Input Current		50	µA	$V_R = 5.25V$
V_{OL}	Output Low Voltage		.45	V	$I_{OL} = 32$ mA
V_{OH}	Output High Voltage	2.4		V	$I_{OH} = -5$ mA
I_{OFF}	Output Off Current		± 50	µA	$V_{OFF} = 0.45$ to $5.25V$
V_{IL}	Input Low Voltage		0.8	V	$V_{CC} = 5.0V$ See Note 1
V_{IH}	Input High Voltage	2.0		V	$V_{CC} = 5.0V$ See Note 1
C_{IN}	Input Capacitance		12	pF	$F = 1$ MHz $V_{BIAS} = 2.5V$, $V_{CC} = 5V$ $T_A = 25°C$

NOTE:
1. Output Loading $I_{OL} = 32$ mA, $I_{OH} = -5$ mA, $C_L = 300$ pF.

A.C. CHARACTERISTICS ($V_{CC} = 5V \pm 10\%$, $T_A = 0°C$ to $70°C$)
Loading: Outputs — $I_{OL} = 32$ mA, $I_{OH} = -5$ mA, $C_L = 300$ pF)

Symbol	Parameter	Min.	Max.	Units	Test Conditions
TIVOV	Input to Output Delay —Inverting —Non-Inverting	5 5	22 30	ns ns	(See Note 1)
TSHOV	STB to Output Delay —Inverting —Non-Inverting	10 10	40 45	ns ns	
TEHOZ	Output Disable Time	5	18	ns	
TELOV	Output Enable Time	10	30	ns	
TIVSL	Input to STB Setup Time	0		ns	
TSLIX	Input to STB Hold Time	25		ns	
TSHSL	STB High Time	15		ns	
TILIH, TOLOH	Input, Output Rise Time		20	ns	From 0.8V to 2.0V
TIHIL, TOHOL	Input, Output Fall Time		12	ns	From 2.0V to 0.8V

NOTE:
1. See waveforms and test load circuit on following page.

AFN-00727C

A.C. TESTING INPUT, OUTPUT WAVEFORM

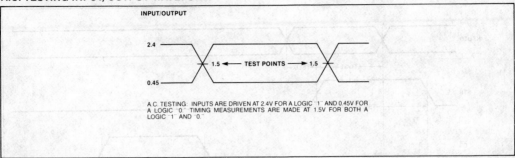

INPUT/OUTPUT

2.4

1.5 ◄── TEST POINTS ──► 1.5

0.45

A.C. TESTING: INPUTS ARE DRIVEN AT 2.4V FOR A LOGIC "1" AND 0.45V FOR A LOGIC "0". TIMING MEASUREMENTS ARE MADE AT 1.5V FOR BOTH A LOGIC "1" AND "0."

OUTPUT TEST LOAD CIRCUITS

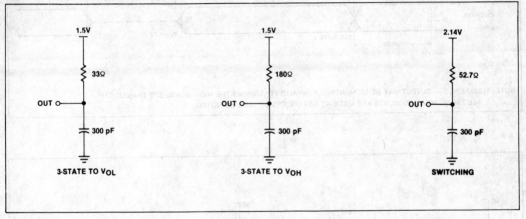

1.5V

33Ω

OUT

300 pF

3-STATE TO V$_{OL}$

1.5V

180Ω

OUT

300 pF

3-STATE TO V$_{OH}$

2.14V

52.7Ω

OUT

300 pF

SWITCHING

AFN-00727C

WAVEFORMS

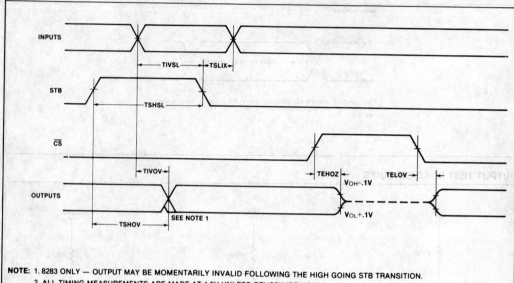

INPUTS

TIVSL — TSLIX

STB

TSHSL

$\overline{CS}$

TIVOV — TEHOZ — TELOV

V_{OH}-.1V

OUTPUTS

SEE NOTE 1

V_{OL}+.1V

TSHOV

NOTE: 1. 8283 ONLY — OUTPUT MAY BE MOMENTARILY INVALID FOLLOWING THE HIGH GOING STB TRANSITION.
2. ALL TIMING MEASUREMENTS ARE MADE AT 1.5V UNLESS OTHERWISE NOTED.

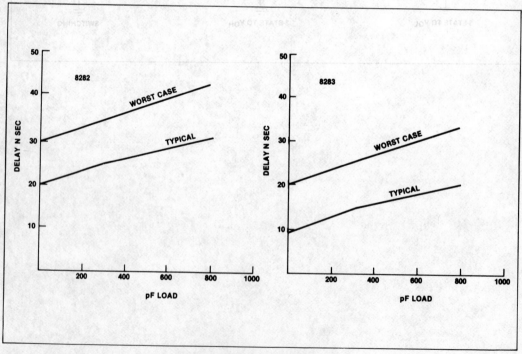

Output Delay vs. Capacitance

AFN-00727C

8286/8287
OCTAL BUS TRANSCEIVER

- **Data Bus Buffer Driver for iAPX 86,88, MCS-80™, MCS-85™, and MCS-48™ Families**

- **High Output Drive Capability for Driving System Data Bus**

- **Fully Parallel 8-Bit Transceivers**

- **3-State Outputs**

- **20-Pin Package with 0.3" Center**

- **No Output Low Noise when Entering or Leaving High Impedance State**

The 8286 and 8287 are 8-bit bipolar transceivers with 3-state outputs. The 8287 inverts the input data at its outputs while the 8286 does not. Thus, a wide variety of applications for buffering in microcomputer systems can be met.

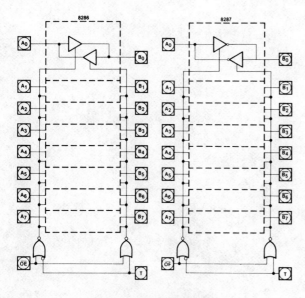

Figure 1. Logic Diagrams

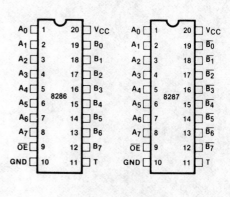

Figure 2. Pin Configurations

Table 1. Pin Description

Symbol	Type	Name and Function
T	I	**Transmit:** T is an input control signal used to control the direction of the transceivers. When HIGH, it configures the transceiver's B_0–B_7 as outputs with A_0–A_7 as inputs. T LOW configures A_0–A_7 as the outputs with B_0–B_7 serving as the inputs.
$\overline{OE}$	I	**Output Enable:** $\overline{OE}$ is an input control signal used to enable the appropriate output driver (as selected by T) onto its respective bus. This signal is active LOW.
A_0–A_7	I/O	**Local Bus Data Pins:** These pins serve to either present data to or accept data from the processor's local bus depending upon the state of the T pin.
B_0–B_7(8286) $\overline{B_0}$–$\overline{B_7}$(8287)	I/O	**System Bus Data Pins:** These pins serve to either present data to or accept data from the system bus depending upon the state of the T pin.

FUNCTIONAL DESCRIPTION

The 8286 and 8287 transceivers are 8-bit transceivers with high impedance outputs. With T active HIGH and $\overline{OE}$ active LOW, data at the A_0–A_7 pins is driven onto the B_0–B_7 pins. With T inactive LOW and $\overline{OE}$ active LOW, data at the B_0–B_7 pins is driven onto the A_0–A_7 pins. No output low glitching will occur whenever the transceivers are entering or leaving the high impedance state.

AFN-01506B

---

intel

8286/8287

TEST LOAD CIRCUITS

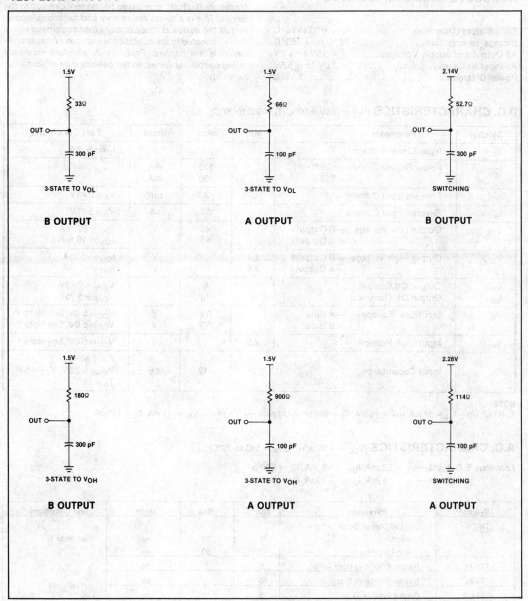

B OUTPUT — 3-STATE TO V_{OL} (1.5V, 33Ω, 300 pF)

A OUTPUT — 3-STATE TO V_{OL} (1.5V, 66Ω, 100 pF)

B OUTPUT — SWITCHING (2.14V, 52.7Ω, 300 pF)

B OUTPUT — 3-STATE TO V_{OH} (1.5V, 180Ω, 300 pF)

A OUTPUT — 3-STATE TO V_{OH} (1.5V, 900Ω, 100 pF)

A OUTPUT — SWITCHING (2.28V, 114Ω, 100 pF)

79

AFN-01506B

ABSOLUTE MAXIMUM RATINGS*

Temperature Under Bias . . . . 0°C to 70°C
Storage Temperature . . . . − 65°C to + 150°C
All Output and Supply Voltages . . . . − 0.5V to + 7V
All Input Voltages . . . . − 1.0V to + 5.5V
Power Dissipation . . . . 1 Watt

NOTICE: Stresses above those listed under "Absolute Maximum Ratings" may cause permanent damage to the device. This is a stress rating only and functional operation of the device at these or any other conditions above those indicated in the operational sections of this specification is not implied. Exposure to absolute maximum rating conditions for extended periods may affect device reliability.

D.C. CHARACTERISTICS (V_{CC} = +5V ±10%, T_A = 0°C to 70°C)

Symbol	Parameter	Min	Max	Units	Test Conditions
V_C	Input Clamp Voltage		−1	V	I_C = −5 mA
I_{CC}	Power Supply Current—8287		130	mA	
	—8286		160	mA	
I_F	Forward Input Current		−0.2	mA	V_F = 0.45V
I_R	Reverse Input Current		50	μA	V_R = 5.25V
V_{OL}	Output Low Voltage —B Outputs		.45	V	I_{OL} = 32 mA
	—A Outputs		.45	V	I_{OL} = 16 mA
V_{OH}	Output High Voltage —B Outputs	2.4		V	I_{OH} = −5 mA
	—A Outputs	2.4		V	I_{OH} = −1 mA
I_{OFF}	Output Off Current		I_F		V_{OFF} = 0.45V
I_{OFF}	Output Off Current		I_R		V_{OFF} = 5.25V
V_{IL}	Input Low Voltage —A Side		0.8	V	V_{CC} = 5.0V, See Note 1
	—B Side		0.9	V	V_{CC} = 5.0V, See Note 1
V_{IH}	Input High Voltage	2.0		V	V_{CC} = 5.0V, See Note 1
C_{IN}	Input Capacitance		12	pF	F = 1 MHz V_{BIAS} = 2.5V, V_{CC} = 5V T_A = 25°C

NOTE:
1. B Outputs—I_{OL} = 32 mA, I_{OH} = −5 mA, C_L = 300 pF; A Outputs—I_{OL} = 16 mA, I_{OH} = −1 mA, C_L = 100 pF.

A.C. CHARACTERISTICS (V_{CC} = +5V ±10%, T_A = 0°C to 70°C)

Loading: B Outputs—I_{OL} = 32 mA, I_{OH} = −5 mA, C_L = 300 pF
A Outputs—I_{OL} = 16 mA, I_{OH} = −1 mA, C_L = 100 pF

Symbol	Parameter	Min	Max	Units	Test Conditions
TIVOV	Input to Output Delay				
	Inverting	5	22	ns	(See Note 1)
	Non-Inverting	5	30	ns	
TEHTV	Transmit/Receive Hold Time	5		ns	
TTVEL	Transmit/Receive Setup	10		ns	
TEHOZ	Output Disable Time	5	18	ns	
TELOV	Output Enable Time	10	30	ns	
TILIH, TOLOH	Input, Output Rise Time		20	ns	From 0.8 V to 2.0V
TIHIL, TOHOL	Input, Output Fall Time		12	ns	From 2.0V to 8.0V

NOTE:
1. See waveforms and test load circuit on following page.

AFN-01506B

WAVEFORMS

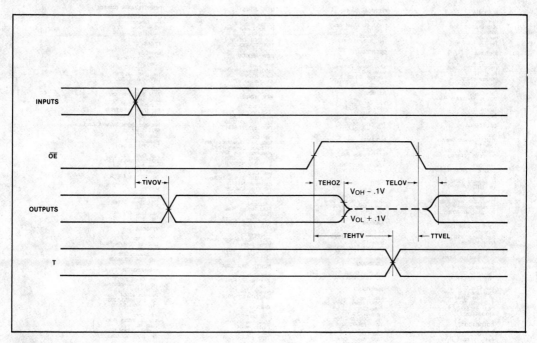

NOTE:

1. All timing measurements are made at 1.5V unless otherwise noted.

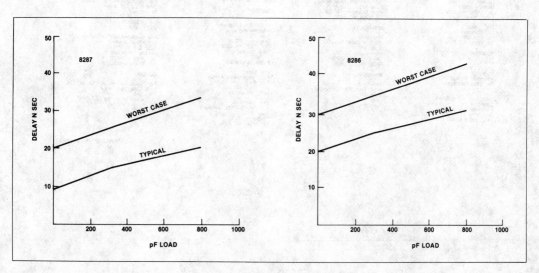

Output Delay versus Capacitance

81

intel

DOMESTIC SALES OFFICES

ALABAMA

Intel Corp.
5015 Bradford Drive
Suite 2
Huntsville 35805
Tel: (205) 830-4010

ARIZONA

Intel Corp.
11225 N. 28th Drive
Suite 214D
Phoenix 85029
Tel: (602) 869-4980

Intel Corp.
1161 N. El Dorado Place
Suite 301
Tucson 85715
Tel: (602) 299-6815

CALIFORNIA

Intel Corp.
21515 Vanowen Street
Suite 116
Canoga Park 91303
Tel: (818) 704-8500

Intel Corp.
2250 E. Imperial Highway
Suite 218
El Segundo 90245
Tel: (213) 640-6040

Intel Corp.
1510 Arden Way, Suite 101
Sacramento 95815
Tel: (916) 920-8096

Intel Corp.
4350 Executive Drive
Suite 150
San Diego 92111
(619) 452-5880

Intel Corp.*
2000 East 4th Street
Suite 100
Santa Ana 92705
Tel: (714) 835-9642
TWX: 910-595-1114

Intel Corp.*
1350 Shorebird Way
Mt. View 94043
Tel: (415) 968-8086
TWX: 910-339-9279
910-338-0255

COLORADO

Intel Corp.
4445 Northpark Drive
Suite 100
Colorado Springs 80907
Tel: (303) 594-6622

Intel Corp.*
650 S. Cherry Street
Suite 720
Denver 80222
Tel: (303) 321-8086
TWX: 910-931-2289

CONNECTICUT

Intel Corp.
26 Mill Plain Road
Danbury 06810
Tel: (203) 748-3130
TWX: 710-456-1199

EMC Corp.
222 Summer Street
Stamford 06901
Tel: (203) 327-2934

FLORIDA

Intel Corp.
242 N. Westmonte Drive
Suite 105
Altamonte Springs 32714
Tel: (305) 869-5588

Intel Corp.
1500 N.W. 62nd Street
Suite 104
Ft. Lauderdale 33309
Tel: (305) 771-0600
TWX: 510-956-9407

FLORIDA (Cont'd)

Intel Corp.
11300 4th Street South
Suite 170
St. Petersburg 33702
Tel: (813) 577-2413

GEORGIA

Intel Corp.
3280 Pointe Parkway
Suite 200
Norcross 30092
Tel: (404) 449-0541

ILLINOIS

Intel Corp.*
2550 Golf Road
Suite 815
Rolling Meadows 60008
Tel: (312) 981-7200
TWX: 910-651-5881

INDIANA

Intel Corp.
8777 Purdue Road
Suite 125
Indianapolis 46268
Tel: (317) 875-0623

IOWA

Intel Corp.
St. Andrews Building
1930 St. Andrews Drive N.E.
Cedar Rapids 52402
Tel: (319) 393-5510

KANSAS

Intel Corp.
8400 W. 110th Street
Suite 170
Overland Park 66210
Tel: (913) 642-8080

LOUISIANA

Industrial Digital Systems Corp.
Tel: (504) 899-1654

MARYLAND

Intel Corp.*
7321 Parkway Drive South
Suite C
Hanover 21076
Tel: (301) 796-7500
TWX: 710-862-1944

Intel Corp.
7833 Walker Drive
Greenbelt 20770
Tel: (301) 441-1020

MASSACHUSETTS

Intel Corp.*
27 Industrial Avenue
Chelmsford 01824
Tel: (617) 256-1800
TWX: 710-343-6333

MICHIGAN

Intel Corp.
7071 Orchard Lake Road
Suite 100
West Bloomfield 48033
Tel: (313) 851-8096

MINNESOTA

Intel Corp.
3500 W. 80th Street
Suite 360
Bloomington 55431
Tel: (612) 835-6722
TWX: 910-576-2867

MISSOURI

Intel Corp.
4203 Earth City Expressway
Suite 131
Earth City 63045
Tel: (314) 291-1990

NEW JERSEY

Intel Corp.*
Raritan Plaza III
Raritan Center
Edison 08837
Tel: (201) 225-3000
TWX: 710-480-6238

NEW MEXICO

Intel Corp.
8500 Menual Boulevard N.E.
Suite B 295
Albuquerque 87112
Tel: (505) 292-8086

NEW YORK

Intel Corp.*
300 Vanderbilt Motor Parkway
Hauppauge 11788
Tel: (516) 231-3300
TWX: 510-227-6236

Intel Corp.
Suite 2B Hollowbrook Park
15 Myers Corners Road
Wappinger Falls 12590
Tel: (914) 297-6161
TWX: 510-248-0060

Intel Corp.*
211 White Spruce Boulevard
Rochester 14623
Tel: (716) 424-1050
TWX: 510-253-7391

T-Squared
6443 Ridings Road
Syracuse 13206
Tel: (315) 463-8592
TWX: 710-541-0554

T-Squared
7353 Pittsford-Victor Road
Victor 14564
Tel: (716) 924-9101
TWX: 510-254-8542

NORTH CAROLINA

Intel Corp.
2700 Wycliff Road
Suite 102
Raleigh 27607
Tel: (919) 781-8022

OHIO

Intel Corp.*
6500 Poe Avenue
Dayton 45414
Tel: (513) 890-5350
TWX: 810-450-2528

Intel Corp.*
Chagrin-Brainard Bldg., No. 300
28001 Chagrin Boulevard
Cleveland 44122
Tel: (216) 464-2736
TWX: 810-427-9298

OKLAHOMA

Intel Corp.
4157 S. Harvard Avenue
Suite 123
Tulsa 74135
Tel: (918) 749-8688

OREGON

Intel Corp.
10700 S.W. Beaverton
Hillsdale Highway
Suite 22
Beaverton 97005
Tel: (503) 641-8086
TWX: 910-467-8741

PENNSYLVANIA

Intel Corp.*
455 Pennsylvania Avenue
Fort Washington 19034
Tel: (215) 641-1000
TWX: 510-661-2077

Intel Corp.*
400 Penn Center Boulevard
Suite 610
Pittsburgh 15235
Tel: (412) 823-4970

PENNSYLVANIA (Cont'd)

Q.E.D. Electronics
139 Terwood Road
Willow Grove 19090
Tel: (215) 657-5600

TEXAS

Intel Corp.*
12300 Ford Road
Suite 380
Dallas 75234
Tel: (214) 241-8087
TWX: 910-860-5617

Intel Corp.*
7322 S.W. Freeway
Suite 1490
Houston 77074
Tel: (713) 988-8086
TWX: 910-881-2490

Industrial Digital Systems Corp.
5925 Sovereign
Suite 101
Houston 77036
Tel: (713)988-9421

Intel Corp.
313 E. Anderson Lane
Suite 314
Austin 78752
Tel: (512) 454-3628

UTAH

Intel Corp.
5201 Green Street
Suite 290
Salt Lake City 84123
Tel: (801) 263-8051

VIRGINIA

Intel Corp.
1603 Santa Rosa Road
Suite 109
Richmond 23288
Tel: (804) 282-5568

WASHINGTON

Intel Corp.
110 110th Avenue N.E.
Suite 510
Bellevue 98004
Tel: (206) 453-8086
TWX: 910-443-3002

Intel Corp.
408 N. Mullan Road
Suite 102
Spokane 99206
Tel: (509) 928-8086

WISCONSIN

Intel Corp.
450 N. Sunnyslope Road
Suite 130
Chancellory Park I
Brookfield 53005
Tel: (414) 784-8087

CANADA

ONTARIO

Intel Semiconductor of Canada, Ltd.
Suite 202, Bell Mews
39 Highway 7
Nepean K2H 8R2
Tel: (613) 829-9714
TELEX: 053-4115

Intel Semiconductor of Canada, Ltd.
190 Attwell Drive
Suite 500
Rexdale M9W 6H8
Tel: (416) 675-2105
TELEX: 06983574

QUEBEC

Intel Semiconductor of Canada, Ltd.
3860 Cote Vertu Rd.
Suite 210
St. Laurent H4R 1V4
Tel: (514) 334-0560
TELEX: 05-824172

*Field Application Location

EUROPEAN SALES OFFICES

BELGIUM

Intel Corporation S.A.
Parc Seny
Rue du Moulin a Papier 51
Boite 1
B-1160 Brussels
Tel: (02)661 07 11
TELEX: 24814

DENMARK

Intel Denmark A/S*
Glentevej 61 - 3rd Floor
DK-2400 Copenhagen
Tel: (01) 19 80 33
TELEX: 19567

FINLAND

Intel Finlan JY
Hameentie 103
SF - 00550 Helsinki 55
Tel: 0/716 955
TELEX: 123 332

FRANCE

Intel Corporation, S.A.R.L.*
5 Place de la Balance
Silic 223
94528 Rungis Cedex
Tel: (01) 687 22 21
TELEX: 270475

FRANCE (Cont'd)

Intel Corporation, S.A.R.L.
Immeuble BBC
4 Quai des Etroits
69005 Lyon
Tel: (7) 842 40 89
TELEX: 305153

WEST GERMANY

Intel Semiconductor GmbH*
Seidlstrasse 27
D-8000 Munchen 2
Tel: (89) 53891
TELEX: 05-23177 INTL D

Intel Semiconductor GmbH*
Mainzer Strasse 75
D-6200 Wiesbaden 1
Tel: (6121) 70 08 74
TELEX: 04186183 INTW D

Intel Semiconductor GmbH
Brueckstrasse 61
7012 Fellbach
Stuttgart
Tel: (711) 58 00 82
TELEX: 7254826 INTS D

Intel Semiconductor GmbH*
Hohenzollern Strasse 5*
3000 Hannover 1
Tel: (511) 34 40 81
TELEX: 923625 INTH D

ISRAEL

Intel Semiconductor Ltd.*
P.O. Box 1659
Haifa
Tel: 4/524 261
TELEX: 46511

ITALY

Intel Corporation Italia Spa*
Milanofiori, Palazzo E
20094 Assago (Milano)
Tel: (02) 824 00 06
TELEX: 315183 INTMIL

NETHERLANDS

Intel Semiconductor Nederland B.V.*
Alexanderpoort Building
Marten Meesweg 93
3068 Rotterdam
Tel: (10) 21 23 77
TELEX: 22283

NORWAY

Intel Norway A/S
P.O. Box 92
Hvamveien 4
N-2013
Skjetten
Tel: (2) 742 420
TELEX: 18018

SPAIN

Intel Iberia
Calle Zurbaran 28
Madrid 04
Tel: (34) 1410 40 04
TELEX: 46880

SWEDEN

Intel Sweden A.B.*
Dalvagen 24
S-17136 Solna
Tel: (08) 734 01 00
TELEX: 12261

SWITZERLAND

Intel Semiconductor A.G.*
Talackerstrasse 17
8152 Glattbrugg postfach
CH-8065 Zurich
Tel: (01) 829 29 77
TELEX: 57989 ICH CH

UNITED KINGDOM

Intel Corporation (U.K.) Ltd.*
Pipers Way
Swindon, Wiltshire SN3 1RJ
Tel: (0793) 488 388
TELEX: 444447 INT SWN

*Field Application Location

EUROPEAN DISTRIBUTORS/REPRESENTATIVES

AUSTRIA

Bacher Elektronische Geraete GmbH
Rotemuehlgasse 26
A 1120 Vienna
Tel: (222) 83 56 46
TELEX: 11532 BASAT A

BELGIUM

Inelco Belgium S.A.
Ave. des Croix de Guerre 94
B1120 Brussels
Tel: (02) 216 01 60
TELEX: 25441

DENMARK

ITT MultiKomponent A/S
Naverland 29
DK-2600 Gloskrup
Tel: (02) 45 66 45
TX: 33355

FINLAND

Oy Fintronic AB
Melkonkatu 24 A
SF-00210
Helsinki 21
Tel: (0) 692 60 22
TELEX: 124 224 Ftron SF

FRANCE

Generim
Z.I. de Courtaboeuf
Avenue de la Baltique
91943 Les Ulis Cedex-B.P.88
Tel: (1) 907 78 78
TELEX: F691700

Jermyn S.A.
16, Avenue Jean-Jaures
94600 Choisy-Le-Roi
Tel: (1) 853 12 00
TELEX: 260967

Metrologie
La Tour d' Asnieres
4, Avenue Laurent Cely
92606-Asnieres
Tel: (1) 790 62 40
TELEX: 611-448

Tekelec Airtronic
Cite des Bruyeres
Rue Carle Vernet B.P. 2
92310 Sevres
Tel: (1) 534 75 35
TELEX: 204552

WEST GERMANY

Electronic 2000 Vertriebs A.G.
Stahlgruberring 12
D-8000 Munich 82
Tel: (89) 42 00 10
TELEX 522561 EIEC D

Jermyn GmbH
Postfach 1180
Schulstrasse 84
D-6277 Bad Camberg
Tel: (06434) 231
TELEX: 484426 JERM D

CES Computer Electronics Systems
GmbH
Gutenbergstrasse 4
2359 Henstedt-Ulzburg
Tel: (04193) 4026
TELEX: 2180260

Metrologie GmbH
Hansastrasse 15
8000 Munich 21
Tel: (89) 57 30 84
TELEX: D 5213189

Proelectron Vertriebs GmbH
Max Planck Strasse 1-3
6072 Dreieich bei Frankfurt
Tel: (6103) 33564
TELEX: 417983

IRELAND

Micro Marketing
Glenageary Office Park
Glenageary
Co. Dublin
Tel: (1) 85 62 88
TELEX: 31584

ISRAEL

Eastronics Ltd.
11 Rozanis Street
P.O. Box 39300
Tel Aviv 61390
Tel: (3) 47 51 51
TELEX: 33638

ITALY

Eledra 3S S.P.A.
Viale Elvezia, 18
I 20154 Milano
Tel: (2) 34 97 51
TELEX: 332332

Intesi
Milanofiori Pal. E/5
20090 Assago
Milano
Tel: (02) 82470
TELEX: 311351

NETHERLANDS

Koning & Hartman
Koperwerf 30
P.O. Box 43220
2544 EN's Gravenhage
Tel: 31 (70) 210.101
TELEX: 31528

NORWAY

Nordisk Elektronic (Norge) A/S
Postoffice Box 122
Smedsvingen 4
1364 Hvalstad
Tel: (2) 846 210
TELEX: 17546

PORTUGAL

Ditram
Componentes E Electronica LDA
Av. Miguel Bombarda, 133
P1000 Lisboa
Tel: (19) 545 313
TELEX: 14182 Brieks-P

SPAIN

Interface S.A.
Av. Pompeu Fabra 12
08024 Barcelona
Tel: (3) 219 80 11
TELEX: 51508

ITT SESA
Miguel Angel 21, 6 Piso
Madrid 10
Tel: (34) 14 1954 00
TELEX: 27461

SWEDEN

AB Gosta Backstrom
Box 12009
Alstroemergatan 22
S-10221 Stockholm 12
Tel: (8) 541 080
TELEX: 10135

Nordisk Electronik AB
Box 27301
Sandhamnsgatan 71
S-10254 Stockholm
Tel: (8) 635 040
TELEX: 10547

Telko AB
Gardsfogdevagen 1
Box 186
S-161 26 Bromma
Tel: (8) 98 08 20
TELEX: 11941

SWITZERLAND

Industrade AG
Herlistrasse 31
CH-8304 Wallisellen
Tel: (01) 830 50 40
TELEX: 56788 INDEL CH

UNITED KINGDOM

Bytech Ltd.
Unit 57
London Road
Earley, Reading
Berkshire
Tel: (0734) 61031
TELEX: 848215

Comway Microsystems Ltd.
Market Street
UK-Bracknell, Berkshire
Tel: 44 (344) 55333
TELEX: 847201

Jermyn Industries
Vestry Estate
Sevenoaks, Kent
Tel: (0732) 450144
TELEX: 95142

M.E.D.L.
East Lane Road
North Wembley
Middlesex HA9 7PP
Tel: (190) 49307
TELEX: 28817

Rapid Recall, Ltd.
Rapid House/Denmark St
High Wycombe
Berks, England HP11 2ER
Tel: (0494) 26 271
TELEX: 837931

YUGOSLAVIA

H. R. Microelectronics Enterprises
P.O. Box 5604
San Jose, California 95150
Tel: 408/978-8000
TELEX: 278-559

INTERNATIONAL SALES OFFICES

AUSTRALIA

Intel Australia Pty. Ltd.*
(Mailing Address)
P.O. Box 571
North Sydney NSW, 2065

(Shipping Address)
Spectrum Building
200 Pacific Highway
Level 6
Crows Nest, NSW, 2065
TELEX: 790-20097
FAX: 011-61-2-957-2744

HONG KONG

Intel Semiconductor Ltd.*
1701-3 Connaught Centre
1 Connaught Road
Tel: 011-852-5-215-311
TWX: 60410 ITLHK

JAPAN

Intel Japan K.K.
5-6 Tokodai, Toyosato-machi
Tsukuba-gun, Ibaraki-ken 300-26
Tel: 029747-8511
TELEX: 03656-160

Intel Japan K.K.*
2-1-15 Naka-machi
Atsugi, Kanagawa 243
Tel: 0462-23-3511

Intel Japan K.K.*
2-51-2 Kojima-cho
Chofu, Tokyo 182
Tel: 0424-88-3151

Intel Japan K.K.*
2-69 Hon-cho
Kumagaya, Saitama 360
Tel: 0485-24-6871

Intel Japan K.K.*
2-4-1 Terauchi
Toyonaka, Osaka 560
Tel: 06-863-1091

JAPAN (Cont'd)

Intel Japan K.K.
1-5-1 Marunouchi
Chiyoda-ku, Tokyo 100
Tel: 03-201-3621

Intel Japan K.K.*
1-23-9 Shinmachi
Setagaya-ku, Tokyo 154
Tel: 03-426-2231

Intel Japan K.K.*
Mitsui-Seimei Musashi-Kosugi Bldg.
915 Shinmaruko, Nakahara-ku
Kawasaki-Shi, Kanagawa 211
Tel: 044-733-7011

Intel Japan K.K.
1-1 Shibahon-cho
Mishima-shi
Shizuoka-Ken 411
Tel: 0559-72-4121

KOREA

Intel Semiconductor Asia Ltd.
Singsong Bldg. 8th Floor #906
25-4 Yoido-Dong, Youngdeungpo-Ku
Seoul 150
Tel: 011-82-2-784-8186 or 8286
TELEX: K29312 INTELKO

SINGAPORE

Intel Semiconductor Ltd.
101 Thomson Road
21-06 Goldhill Square
Singapore 1130
Tel: 011-65-2507811
TWX: RS 39921
CABLE: INTELSGP

*Field Application Location

INTERNATIONAL DISTRIBUTORS/REPRESENTATIVES

ARGENTINA

VLC S.R.L.
Sarmiento 1630, 1 Piso
1042 Buenos Aires
Tel: 011-54-1-35-1201/9242
TELEX: 17575 EDARG

Agent:
Scimex International Corporation
15 Park Row, Room #1730
New York, New York 10038
Tel: (212) 406-3052
Attn: Gaston Briones

AUSTRALIA

Total Electronics
(Mailing Address)
Private Bag 250
Burwood, Victoria 3125

(Shipping Address)
9 Harker Street
Burwood
Victoria 3125
Tel: 011-61-3-288-4044
TELEX: AA 31261

Total Electronics
P.O. Box 139
Artarmon, N.S.W. 2064
Tel: 011-61-02-438-1855
TELEX: 26297

BRAZIL

Icotron S.A.
05110 Av. Mutinga 3650-6 Andar
Pirituba Sao Paulo
Tel: 011-55-11-833-2572
TELEX: 1122274 ICOTBR

CHILE

DIN
(Mailing Address)
Av. VIC. MacKenna 204
Casilla 6055
Santiago
Tel: 011-56-2-277-564
TELEX: 352-0003

(Shipping Address)
A102 Greenville Center
3801 Kennett Pike
Wilmington, Delaware 19807

HONG KONG

Novel Precision Machinery Co., Ltd.
Flat D 20 Kingsford Ind. Bldg.
Phase 1 26 Kwai Hei Street NT
Tel: 011-852-5-0-223222
TWX: 39114 JINMI HX

Schmidt & Co. Ltd.
18/F. Great Eagle Centre
Wanchai
Tel: 011-852-5-833-0222
TWX: 74766 SCHMC HK

INDIA

Micronic Devices
65 ARUN Complex
D V G Road
Basavan Gudi
Bangalore 560004
Tel: 011-91-812-600-631
TELEX: 011-5947 MDEV

Micronic Devices
104/109C Nirmal Industrial Estate
Sion (E)
Bombay 400022
Tel: 011-91-22-48-61-70
TELEX: 011-71447 MDEV IN

Micronic Devices
R-694 New Rajinder Nager
New Delhi 110060

Ramlak International, Inc. (Agent)
465 S. Mathilda Avenue
Suite 302
Sunnyvale, CA 94086
Tel: (408) 733-8767

S & S Corporation
(Mailing Address)
P.O. Box 1185
Mauldin, South Carolina 29657

(Shipping Address)
308 Green Drive
Liberty, South Carolina 29657

JAPAN

Asahi Electronics Co. Ltd.
KMM Bldg. Room 407
2-14-1 Asano, Kokurakita-Ku
Kitakyushu City 802
Tel: (093) 511-6471
TELEX: AECKY 7126-16

JAPAN (Cont'd)

Hamilton-Avnet Electronics Japan Ltd.
YU and YOU Bldg. 1-5-7 Horidome-Cho
Nihonbashi Chuo-Ku, Tokyo 103
Tel: (03) 662-9911
TELEX: 2523774

Ryoyo Electric Corporation
Konwa Bldg.
1-12-22, Tsukiji
Chuo-Ku, Tokyo 104
Tel: (03) 543-7711/541-7311

Tokyo Electron Ltd.
Shinjuku Nomura Bldg.
26-2 Nishi-Shinjuku 1-Chome
Shinjuku-Ku, Tokyo 160
Tel: (03) 343-4411
TELEX: 232-2220 LABTEL J

KOREA

J-TEK Corporation
2nd Floor, Government Pension Bldg.
24-3, Yoido-Dong
Youngdungpo-Ku
Seoul 150
Tel: 011-82-2-782-8039
TELEX: KODIGIT K25299

Koram Digital USA (Agent)
14066 East Firestone Boulevard
Sante Fe Springs, CA 90670
Tel: (714) 739-2204
TWX: 194715 KORAM DIGIT LSA

NEW ZEALAND

McLean Information Technology Ltd.
459 Kyber Pass Road, Newmarket,
P.O. Box 9464, Newmarket
Auckland 1, New Zealand
Tel: 011-64-9-501-219, 501-801, 587-037
TELEX: NZ21570 THERMAL

PAKISTAN

Computer Applications Ltd.
7D Gizri Boulevard
Defense
Karachi-46
Tel: 011-92-21-530-306/7
TELEX: 24434 GAFAR PK

PAKISTAN (Cont'd)

Horizon Training Co., Inc. (Agent)
1 Lafayette Center
1120 20th Street N.W.
Suite 530
Washington, D.C. 20036
Tel: (202) 887-1900
TWX: 248890 HORN

SINGAPORE

General Engineers Corporation Pty. Ltd.
Units 1003-1008 Block 3
10th Floor PSA Multi Storey Complex
Telok Blangahl Pasir
Pan Jang
Singapore 5
Tel: 011-65-271-3163
TELEX: RS23987 GENERCO
CABLE: GENERRCORP

SOUTH AFRICA

Electronic Building Elements, Pty. Ltd.
P.O. Box 4609
Pretoria 0001
Tel: 011-27-12-46-9221
TELEX: 3-22786 SA
TELEGRAM: ELBILEM

TAIWAN

Mitac Corporation
3rd Floor #75, Section 4
Nanking East Road
Taipei
Tel: 011-886-2-771-0940, 0941
TELEX: 11942 TAIAUTO

Mectel International, Inc. (Agent)
3385 Viso Court
Santa Clara, CA 95050
Tel: (408) 988-4513
TWX: 910-338-2201
FAX: 408-980-9742

YUGOSLAVIA

H. R. Microelectronics Enterprises
P.O. Box 5604
San Jose, California 95150
Tel: (408) 978-8000
TELEX: 278-559

*Field Application Location